FREEDOM TO ACHIEVE FREEDOM

The Irish Free State 1922–1932

FREEDOM TO ACHIEVE FREEDOM

The Irish Free State 1922–1932

DONAL P. CORCORAN

Gill & Macmillan

Gill & Macmillan
Hume Avenue, Park West, Dublin 12
with associated companies throughout the world
www.gillmacmillanbooks.ie

© Donal P. Corcoran 2013
978 07171 5775 4

Index compiled by Róisín Nic Cóil
Typography design by Make Communication
Print origination by Síofra Murphy
Printed and bound by TJ International, Cornwall

This book is typeset in Minion 12.5/15.5 pt.

The paper used in this book comes from the wood pulp
of managed forests. For every tree felled, at least one
tree is planted, thereby renewing natural resources.

A CIP catalogue record for this book is available from
the British Library.

5 4 3 2 1

CONTENTS

ACKNOWLEDGMENTS

I acknowledge the guidance, assistance and support of Donal Ó Drisceoil of University College Cork (UCC) and the advice and insights into the public service provided by Tom O'Connor. Many people generously gave information, encouragement and criticism including Peter Barry, John Borgonovo, Noel Buckley, Sarah-Anne Buckley, Kenneth Burns, Ronan Fanning, James Farrell, Richard Haslam, Paul Loftus, John Logan, Ann McCann, Andrew McCarthy, James Moran, Con Murphy, John A. Murphy, Seamus Murphy, Liam O'Callaghan, Sean O'Donoghue, James O'Donovan, Michael O'Keeffe, Tadhg Ó Murchú, James Ryan and Michael Whelan. I also thank my family, who helped in so many ways.

I am grateful for the assistance received from the staff at UCC, University College Dublin (UCD), Trinity College, and Bantry, Douglas and Louth libraries; Cork City and County Archives Institute, UCD Archive, National Archives of Ireland, Irish Military Archives, Irish Labour History Museum and Archives and the United Kingdom National Archives.

I dedicate this book to my parents, the late John and Maura Corcoran.

Chapter 1 ～

| INTRODUCTION

The First World War radically changed the political landscape of Europe. The Austro-Hungarian, German, Ottoman and Russian empires suffered defeat and collapsed, and many new nation-states emerged. The Irish seized the opportunity afforded by that conflict to gain independence from Britain, one of the victors.

Under the terms of the Anglo-Irish treaty signed on 6 December 1921, the Irish achieved political independence and in the following decade succeeded in establishing a viable independent democratic state despite the loss of a significant part of the population and national territory, and a civil war. This is the story of those who guided the state through that difficult period: their choices, decisions and actions, and the institutions they created.

Ireland's relationship with Britain was fundamentally altered in December 1920 when the Westminster parliament passed the Government of Ireland Act, which granted home rule (devolved government with limited powers within the United Kingdom). But it partitioned the country by providing for two parliaments, one for 'Southern Ireland'—the provinces of Munster, Leinster and Connacht together with three counties in Ulster—and the other for 'Northern Ireland', the remaining six counties of Ulster.

Elections for the two parliaments were held in May 1921, after which the Ulster unionists, who had a majority in the six northeastern counties and wished to remain within the United Kingdom, accepted partition and the northern parliament. Partition and both parliaments were rejected by the nationalist majority in the country as a whole. The separatist Sinn Féin (Ourselves) party and the Irish Republican Army (IRA) held out for an all-Ireland republic and continued the war of independence against the British, which had begun in January 1919, until a truce was arranged in July 1921. Negotiations between representatives of the British government and plenipotentiaries appointed by Dáil Éireann (the parliament set up in Dublin in 1919 by separatist MPs who had seceded from Westminster) resulted in the Anglo-Irish treaty. Under its terms Saorstát Éireann (the Irish Free State) was to have dominion status (political independence within the British Commonwealth) while Northern Ireland would retain home rule with an option to join the Irish Free State at a future date.

The British relinquished their hold over Ireland unwillingly. Three years after being victorious in World War I and expanding their empire in its aftermath, they lost their oldest colony and an integral part of the United Kingdom. The attempt to resolve the 'Irish question' by belatedly granting home rule failed. Armed revolt in Ireland, a war-weary population at home and a shortage of troops due to over-commitments in Chanak, Egypt and Iraq convinced British Liberal Prime Minister David Lloyd George that the Irish nationalists had to be conceded more than home rule to achieve a settlement. As the Conservatives, who dominated his coalition government, would not agree to the separatist demand for a republic, he offered a compromise—dominion status—the maximum the Tories could be persuaded to accept. Lloyd George also threatened immediate resumption of hostilities in the event of a breakdown of the negotiations which had begun in October 1921.

The treaty divided the nationalists, resulting in civil war in the Irish Free State between those who accepted it as the best deal possible, leaving outstanding matters of sovereignty to be dealt with later, and those who opposed it for a variety of reasons. Regardless of how it was presented in ideological terms, the civil war was a power struggle between two factions of the independence movement for control over the new state. Personal ambitions, vested interests and antagonisms, which had been submerged to present a united front during the war of independence, came to the fore in the aftermath of the treaty. These coupled with the frustration of some of those who had fought for an all-Ireland republic resulted in a violent outcome.

The first Irish Free State government was confronted by an internal revolt soon after it took office. Its ministers were young and inexperienced, under pressure from ruthless opponents and desperately short of money. They feared they might be unable to govern, allowing the British an opportunity to resume control over Irish affairs. Consequently they made hard and pragmatic decisions with little regard for the political, social or economic outcomes, as their objective was to restore order and create an independent democratic state.

The treaty delivered political independence on paper. Michael Collins and the provisional government immediately set about translating it into reality by seizing power before the treaty timetable prescribed and rapidly transferring governmental, judicial and administrative functions from British to Irish control. The first decade of the Irish Free State was the most crucial period in independent Ireland's history. Executive President William T. Cosgrave and his Cumann na nGaedheal (Party of the Irish) governments suppressed an internal rebellion, overcame an acute scarcity of money, enacted a constitution and defined how the state should be governed. They established an Irish civil service, army, police force, courts service and diplomatic corps; passed legislation to purchase the remaining agricultural land from the landlords; commenced exploitation of natural resources; extended the use of Irish in schools and increased the state's sovereignty. The administration of the state was changed from the British system of loosely co-ordinated boards and departments to a tightly controlled centralised Irish system.

The political and military events which took place in Ireland during and immediately after World War I have been the subject of many studies but historians have paid less attention to the creation of the Irish Free State. Yet the decisions made and actions taken by the first governments and newly formed civil service were fundamental to how Ireland has been governed and administered subsequently.

This book covers the period from the approval of the treaty by the second Dáil on 7 January 1922 to the end of Cosgrave's period in office on 9 March 1932. It seeks to explain how the new Irish state was created in the aftermath of the treaty by those who accepted it because, while it fell short of the desired republic, it gave the Irish, in the words of Michael Collins, 'the freedom to achieve freedom'. Those who accepted the treaty believed that dominion status was preferable to a continuation of a war, the outcome of which was uncertain. They were apprehensive that the British, once they had re-established themselves economically and militarily after the Great War, would more strenuously resist Irish freedom. They also feared that improved British social welfare and healthcare benefits would undermine future support for independence within Ireland.

As the treaty did not deliver the republic it was accepted reluctantly. The Dáil-appointed plenipotentiaries signed it because they believed they had achieved the maximum possible through negotiation. The second Dáil ratified the treaty and the provisional government began the task of creating a new state. Cosgrave resolutely stood by the terms of the treaty, which he considered an international agreement. He did so because he feared the British would use any deviation by the Irish to renege on its terms and regain influence over Irish affairs. However, while Cosgrave succeeded in keeping the British out of Irish internal affairs, he exposed himself to criticism, particularly from the opposition Fianna Fáil (Soldiers of Destiny) party, that he supported the treaty—while in reality he was surreptitiously unravelling it. Cumann na nGaedheal's poor party organisation, inept public relations, near-obsession with law and order, inability to reduce unemployment, and failure to understand the extent to which both Britain and Ireland changed in political terms during the decade after 1922 ultimately led to its rejection by the Irish electorate at the 1932 general election.

The Cosgrave governments faced the harsh reality that political independence alone would not provide a resolution to the problems confronting the fledgling state. They settled down to the mundane task of creating a new state after eight continuous years of world and national warfare, disruption, terror, violence and dreams of independence. They did not meet the Irish people's expectation of prosperity, nor did they perform as well as they could have. Expectations were unrealistic and based on the myth that once the British left everything would improve. But, after their departure, the economy deteriorated due to the post-World War I economic depression, an unavoidable external factor, and the civil war which destroyed life and property, squandered scarce resources, undermined civic trust and left a legacy of bitter division. The high cost of that conflict resulted in diminished public services and a lack of economic and social investment, causing further discontent.

The Irish independence movement was focused on separation from Britain. Despite its rhetoric about a Gaelic Ireland, little serious consideration had been given to future public policy, government and administration apart from some administrative reforms, tariff protection, economic self-sufficiency and the restoration of the Irish language. But these were mainly political ideals that had been neither studied in depth nor developed into coherent plans and so remained aspirations rather than policies. The revival of the Irish language was a clear objective but there was no carefully considered plan to implement this mammoth task. Given the lack of realistic policies, partition, the economic depression, the civil war, the inexperience of the first governments and the conservatism of influential interest groups, it is not surprising that the state taken over from British rule continued to be administered as a going concern with minimal alteration. Future Minister for Education John Marcus O'Sullivan commented, 'Getting rid of foreign control rather than vast social and economic changes was our aim.'[1] Cosgrave and his governments succeeded in creating a viable democracy despite violent opposition and, when Cosgrave left office in 1932, he handed over a functioning state where the military took its orders from the democratically elected government, and a system of strict financial control with low inflation and borrowings.

After 1932 Eamon de Valera and his Fianna Fáil party further undermined the British connection. In 1937 a new constitution created a *de facto* republic and changed the name of the state to Éire (Ireland). John A. Costello's first inter-party coalition government enacted the Republic of Ireland Act 1948, removing the last residual political link with the British Commonwealth, and Ireland formally became a republic on Easter Monday 18 April 1949.

Chapter 2 ⌒

IRELAND BEFORE INDEPENDENCE

IRELAND BEFORE THE TREATY

Ireland played a significant part in the development of European civilisation and Christianity between the death of St Patrick in the fifth century and the arrival of the Vikings in the ninth century. The country was a patchwork of some 150 *tuatha* (groups of families) headed by chieftains, without a clearly defined central authority, although an individual chieftain occasionally achieved dominance over large parts of the country and claimed the title 'árd rí' (high king). The Irish shared a common language, Irish; a common religion, Christianity; and a common legal system, the Brehon laws. The Vikings devastated parts of the country before being assimilated into Irish society. The Normans invaded in 1169, assisted by disaffected Irish groups, and captured large areas due to their superior military technology. They brought in settlers and extended cultivation. Unlike in England, where the Normans took over the existing society and created a centralised feudal system, their arrival in Ireland initially increased the fragmentation of society.

The Vikings had founded towns and partially modernised Irish society by beginning the process of shifting it from rural to urban. The early English kings achieved a tenuous hold over the

Hiberno-Normans, who established their central administration at Dublin Castle from 1204 onwards. This remained the seat of English government and administration until 1922. In the centuries after the Norman Conquest the Irish recovered some of the ground lost but were unable to dislodge the English, whose common law was extended to Ireland by the end of the thirteenth century. Poyning's Law (1494) brought the English-dominated parts of Ireland under the administrative control of the kingdom of England. After the Reformation, the division between the Irish and English in Ireland, which had hitherto been based on the language spoken, changed to the religion practiced. Increasing pressure was exerted by the Protestant English on the native Irish and the Catholic descendants of the Vikings and Normans. The defeat of the Irish chieftains in 1603; the depredations of Cromwell, his soldiers and financiers; and William III's military victories, ending with the treaty of Limerick (1691) completed the conquest of Ireland. The English planted settlers and put down rebellions but never achieved legitimacy by prescription (continuous occupation accepted by the majority of the population).

After 1691 Ireland was firmly under English control. From then until 1801 it was administered as a colony by the Protestant Anglo-Irish ascendancy backed by English military power. The Penal Laws impoverished Catholics and eliminated them as a political force. A period of prosperity after 1750 encouraged the Protestant ascendancy to seek more powers for their 'Irish Parliament' and they achieved parliamentary independence in 1782. However, the American and French Revolutions spread radical ideas which led to a rebellion in 1798 (despite the Catholic Relief Acts, which mitigated many of the Penal Laws in force since the 1690s). Rebel leader Theobald Wolfe Tone's separatist and republican philosophy profoundly influenced later generations of Irish nationalists. He attempted to unite the Irish of all religious persuasions and break the link with England, but the consequence of the failed rising was the Act of Union (1800) which forced the political union of Britain and Ireland.

In 1641 60 per cent of the land was still owned by Catholics; by 1703 it had declined to 14 per cent and by 1778 to five per cent.[1] After the union, Daniel O'Connell mobilised the first mass movements in support of Catholic emancipation (basic civil rights) and repeal of the union. He merged liberalism, democracy and constitutionalism, offering a way forward other than through violent revolt. The country became polarised on religious lines as Catholics sought concessions which diminished the power of the established Anglican Church of Ireland. Dissenters, many of whom had supported the 1798 rebellion, competed with Catholics for land and jobs, and moved politically closer to their fellow Protestants, the greatest concentration of whom lived in northeast Ulster.

After the union, Ireland was governed not by direct rule from London but as a crown colony. Its administration was ramshackle, poorly co-ordinated and run in the interests of Britain rather than Ireland. Appointments of British and Anglo-Irish public servants were made by the lord lieutenant (monarch's representative) and the chief secretary (political head), who governed Ireland in a semi-autonomous manner together with the under-secretary, who was in charge of the Irish civil service.

The economy was in a poor state. Ireland was a primary agricultural producer supplying Britain, which had a low-cost food policy. Much of Irish industry, apart from that in the northeast, found it increasingly difficult to compete with British manufacturers after the industrial revolution and particularly when tariffs were dismantled following the union. Between the Norman invasion and the seventeenth century the ancient Gaelic system of land tenure had been destroyed as most of the land was forcibly seized by the English and granted to colonists. Many Irish were driven into the poorer land on the western seaboard while subdivision of holdings led to overcrowding, leaving the poor vulnerable to famine if crops failed. By 1845 most of the land was held by landlords, many of whom were absentees who left its management to profit-motivated middlemen.

The tithe war of the 1830s began the process of undermining the Protestant ascendancy. The great famine of 1845–49 decimated Ireland and in time halved the population through deaths from hunger and disease, and subsequent emigration. The population fell from 8.2 million in the 1841 census to 4.4 million in 1911, while that of the rest of the United Kingdom increased from 18.5 to 41 million in the same period.

The Young Ireland and Fenian rebellions of 1848 and 1867 were military failures. However, the Fenians reorganised in 1873 under the title of the Irish Republican Brotherhood (IRB), keeping alive the spirit of the 1798, 1848 and 1867 rebellions. The Municipal Reform Act 1840 ended Protestant conservative monopoly of local government. The disestablishment of the Church of Ireland in 1869 and the Ballot Act 1872, which introduced secret ballots, further weakened Protestant and landlord control. Charles Stewart Parnell's campaign for home rule, in parallel with Michael Davitt's land league agitation for land reform, based on the passive resistance tactics adopted in the tithe war, resulted in the nationalist Irish Parliamentary Party winning the majority of Irish seats at Westminster by 1885. This paved the way for a series of land acts allowing tenants to purchase the farms they occupied and discharge the debt by annuities; local government reforms; and other concessions including grants for public works and access to civil service jobs for Catholics through competitive examinations. These concessions and later Liberal and Conservative government actions were designed to 'kill home rule with kindness'. Conciliation of the Catholic majority was accompanied by coercion to demonstrate that the British government would not tolerate rebellion or agrarian violence.

The Irish Party under Parnell became a major political force at Westminster while it kept Liberal governments in power. The price of its support was home rule or devolved government with limited powers within the United Kingdom, culturally and economically linked with the English-speaking world. Despite the support of Liberal Prime Minister William Ewart Gladstone, home rule was defeated in 1886 and 1893. Parnell influenced many future nationalists, notably Arthur Griffith, but his failure to achieve home rule by constitutional means opened the door to the advocates of physical force. The supporters of home rule were not all convinced that it was the ideal solution. Some wanted complete separation from Britain; most wanted self-government, while others, less committed, were reassured that it was worth having because the unionist ascendancy vigorously opposed it.

At the same time a cultural revival was taking place. This was a reaction to the growing Anglicisation and modernisation of Ireland. In Desmond FitzGerald's words, 'Our national identity was obliterated not only politically but also in our own minds. The Irish people had recognised themselves as part of England.'[2] There had been an awareness that Gaelic culture was being destroyed in the eighteenth century and efforts were made to preserve what remained. After 1800 interest in it grew, encouraged by some of the Anglo-Irish and by the nationalist Young Ireland movement, which sought to save the literary heritage and secure a place for Ireland in the European tradition. This was part of a wider cultural movement then in progress throughout Europe. The more separatist-minded wanted to use Gaelic culture to differentiate the Irish from the English. The interest in Irish matters widened to include the Irish language, sport, music and dancing. The Gaelic Athletic Association (GAA) was founded in 1884 and the Gaelic League in 1893. While the latter was all-inclusive and welcomed Protestants, the GAA was divisive, being influenced by the tactics of the land league. It organised a boycott to exclude policemen, soldiers and participants in 'foreign games' (soccer, rugby, hockey and cricket). By doing so it shut out most Protestants, together with many of the Catholic middle and urban working classes. The driving forces behind the Gaelic revival were cultural and political, and the organisations formed provided a training ground for the politicians and administrators of the future.

When the Irish Party failed to deliver home rule it was gradually superseded by a combination of Gaelic enthusiasts and physical force separatists: the IRB (Fenians), a militant secret society with strong links to the Irish in America. The Irish Party split following Parnell's much-publicised divorce case, and the bitter infighting which followed undermined its credibility. Many people joined the multiplicity of literary societies that engaged the population, which was better educated and had more leisure time in the Victorian era of mass participation in sports and cultural and scientific societies.[3] Separatism and cultural nationalism merged and in D. George Boyce's view 'Anglicization, far from destroying nationalist Ireland, made possible its creation.'[4] The cultural revivalists were a combination of Irish-Irelanders advocating an Irish-speaking Ireland, Celtic literature devotees such as William Butler Yeats and Lady Gregory, and believers in the ideal of Thomas Davis for an Irish literature 'racy of the soil' written in English to cater for nationalists until the majority could read Irish.

After 1881 successive land acts enabled tenants to purchase their farms. This led to radical changes in Irish society and politics as increasing numbers of farmers became owner-occupiers. They reinforced the existing conservative nationalist forces: the Catholic Church, professionals, merchants and public servants. The Gaelic League and the GAA drew in many of the nation's youth, facilitating recruitment by the IRB, which infiltrated these movements. Growing numbers of educated people with few opportunities for advancement along with a hard core of IRB activists provided the membership of the independence movement. Its aim was to take over the government and administration of Ireland, rather than to destroy it, as had been the objective of earlier rebellions. Initially, home rule by constitutional means offered the best prospect of freedom from British rule, particularly while the Liberals were in power at Westminster.

The Local Government Act 1898 had far-reaching consequences as it gave the Irish their first real taste of democracy. Anglo-Irish Protestant landlords, who had been the backbone of the British administration in Ireland, surrendered power as they sold off their land and lost control of local authorities. They were replaced by nationalist politicians who were supported by the Catholic Church, which gave strong leadership, particularly in times of religious persecution. The Church was well organised and administered and had considerable political influence but, while generally obeyed on moral matters, it was not always followed where politics were concerned as, in Daniel O'Connell's words, 'we take our religion from Rome and our politics from home'. The Irish Councils Bill 1907, an ill-considered effort at devolution, was rejected by the Irish Party as step-by-step administrative reform was perceived to be no substitute for home rule. The Catholic university established in Dublin during the 1850s by John Henry Newman was formally recognised by the Irish Universities Act 1908. Old age pensions were introduced the same year and national insurance followed in 1911. The increased levels of social welfare benefits worried Tom Kettle of the Irish Party, who, along with some separatists, feared the Irish people were becoming more dependent on the British Exchequer and, if that trend continued, popular support for home rule and independence could diminish. This was one of the factors which inspired the leaders of the 1916 Easter rising, many of whom were convinced that Britain's difficulty in World War I was Ireland's last opportunity to gain freedom.

Meanwhile, the unionists had become increasingly apprehensive about home rule, which would mean Catholic majority rule. They feared home rule would result in civil war, clerical interference in politics and state bankruptcy. Unionists were determined that Catholics would not gain equality or superiority, never considered sharing power and actively organised against home rule, which was equated with 'Rome rule'. They wished to preserve the union and differentiated themselves from nationalists by emphasising their loyalty to the British crown. The Ulster unionists, who were in a majority in the northeast, were more militant than the minority southern unionists. They defined 'Ulstermen' as Protestants, leaving Catholics as second-class citizens. The Ulster unionists were ably led by Edward Carson, a Dublin lawyer, and James Craig, a Belfast stockbroker and brilliant organiser. They mounted opposition to Home Rule in 1886 and 1893. From 1905 onwards, and particularly after the House of Lords veto was ended by the Parliament Act 1911, they realised that home rule or dominion status was inevitable and would ultimately lead to a republic. British Conservative leader Andrew Bonar Law advised them that dominions 'take control of their own destinies'.[5] The unionists received vital support from the Tories, who had been out of office for seven years in 1912 and were desperate for a way back to government. They saw Ulster as the means of regaining power in Britain.

Irish Party leader John Redmond rejected unionist claims for self-determination and was personally tolerant, but insisted Ulster was an integral part of Ireland. He foresaw a peaceful constitutional process, believing that once the 1912 Home Rule Bill was passed by the House of Commons neither the House of Lords nor the unionists could stop it. But the unionists rejected home rule regardless of the assurances offered. They believed that if the Liberals could be kept out of power long enough, the majority of the Irish people could be bought off by subsidies and benefits. If not, the unionists aided by the Tories and the House of Lords would prevent home rule. The Ulster unionists were not afraid of the British, were prepared to resort to physical force and accepted arms from the Germans, who wished to stir up trouble in Ireland.

The sale of land to tenant farmers did not end agitation because the re-united Irish Party and groups like Arthur Griffith and his Sinn Féin party worked to keep nationalism alive. Griffith believed that independence should be achieved peacefully, advocated economic self-sufficiency and tariffs to support fledgling industries, but stopped short of separatism as he wished to keep the unionists in a future Ireland. He proposed the dual monarchy concept adopted by the Hungarians, suggesting that the king of England could also be king of Ireland but in a separate capacity to that of ruler of the British Empire, being answerable to an Irish parliament. He recommended that Irish MPs absent themselves from Westminster and set up an alternative parliament in Dublin. Others had different ideas. Patrick Pearse, an idealist, sought a Gaelic state, IRB leaders Thomas Clarke and Sean MacDermott focused on breaking the link with England, while James Connolly, a socialist, called for a workers' republic. For each of them home rule was at best a half-way house.

A number of significant events brought matters to a head. In 1912 a great body of northern Protestants signed the Ulster Covenant and the Ulster unionists armed themselves to oppose home rule. In response the nationalists formed the Irish Volunteers and purchased German arms. This led to a sudden rise of militarism in Ireland as both sides acquired armies which could be used to pressurise the British or to fight each other. Poor communications between the British war minister and the army in Ireland led to a virtual mutiny when officers at the Curragh army base were forced to choose whether or not to accept orders, which no one had actually authorised, to take action against militant unionists in Ulster. Faced with the threat of civil war within the United Kingdom at the outbreak of World War I, the British government placed home rule on the statute book on 18 September 1914, with a proviso that it would not be implemented until after the war, together with amending legislation to deal with Ulster.

The Irish Volunteers divided over participation in the war. The renamed Irish National Volunteers, numbering around 170,000, followed Redmond, who sought to have them converted into an officially recognised home defence force, trained and armed by the British war office, whose role would be to defend Ireland against foreign invasion. He hoped that those who enlisted would become a distinctly Irish brigade within the British army and be the nucleus of an Irish army after home rule. Redmond had a dual policy of National Volunteers at home and Irish brigades at the front. While some National Volunteers joined the British army, the majority did not and ceased to play an active role as the British refused to employ them for home defence. Around 11,000 Irish Volunteers remained loyal to founder member Eoin MacNeill, including the militant IRB faction. The war reduced tensions in Ireland as 24,000 National and 26,000 Ulster Volunteers went to the battlefront.

The First World War had a major impact on Ireland. Over 200,000 Irish men and women served in the British forces during the war and suffered high casualties, particularly in Belgium, France and Gallipoli, resulting in over 35,000 deaths. Taking advantage of Britain's preoccupation with the war, the IRB inspired a revolt on Easter Monday 1916. The rising, which was confined almost exclusively to Dublin, lasted less than a week. The summary executions of its leaders changed the attitude of an initially hostile population to the rebels. In July the 36th (Ulster) division was decimated at Thiepval during the battle of the Somme. The war had brought nationalists and unionists together in France and briefly offered some hope of reconciliation, but the 1916 rising and Thiepval ended that prospect. The executions shocked many Irish who perceived themselves as citizens of the British Empire into the realisation that they remained a colonised people, subject to severe retribution if they failed to behave as their masters in London expected.

The final event was conscription, which the British tried to introduce in Ireland during 1918 as they were running out of troops to defend against the last major German offensive. The Irish Party, Sinn Féin and the Labour movement combined to prevent it, supported by the Catholic Church.

The Irish Party lost ground to Sinn Féin, which was reorganised from 1917 onwards, becoming a coalition of interest groups seeking popular support for independence and a standalone Gaelic republic. Sinn Féin made little effort to understand the unionists, believing them to be puppets of the British who could be cajoled or overcome by force if necessary.[6] The independence movement does not seem to have appreciated the extent to which the country was already divided politically, economically, educationally and socially. The confrontation over land ownership between Catholics and Protestants, and the association of nationalism and unionism with religion, prevented the development of political forces which could appeal across religious boundaries.

The executions following the Easter rising, along with the 'German plot' (the allegation of collusion with the Germans concocted by the British to justify the arrest of Sinn Féin activists), turned the tide in favour of Sinn Féin, which won 73 out of the 105 Irish seats in the 1918 British general election, in which the number of electors had risen from 701,000 to 1,940,000.[7] The votes were counted on the first-past-the-post basis rather than proportional representation, which was used in subsequent elections. The Irish Party did not contest all the seats, campaigned for dominion status and, while it held its previous vote, it failed to gain support from the huge number of young people voting for the first time. The Sinn Féin MPs refused to sit at Westminster and 27 of them constituted themselves as the first Dáil Éireann (Irish parliament) in Dublin on 21 January 1919. The other party MPs took their seats in London. The first Dáil was in Brian Farrell's words a 'polity within a polity, barely the embryo of a government order'.[8] It claimed the right to govern Ireland but had neither the power nor the means to do so. Sinn Féin, like the Irish Party before it, became a one-big-issue party, merging politics, sport, culture and physical force in the pursuit of a single ideal: independence from Britain.[9] Everything else could wait until independence was achieved. This meant that planning for a post-independence Ireland was neglected and economic, health, education and women's issues were left in abeyance.

After World War I, separatism was promoted throughout Europe as self-determination for small nations. The first Dáil made a declaration of independence, drew up a constitution and proclaimed a democratic programme drafted by the Labour Party, which had not participated in the 1918 general election. The Dáil unsuccessfully sought international recognition for Ireland's national status and her right to its vindication at the Paris peace conference. It was vague on how a future Ireland would be governed, indicating that the people could choose the form of government by referendum. Sinn Féin failed to think through the ramifications of independence and to understand the mindset of the British, who saw it as breaking up the United Kingdom and undermining the British Empire, and of the Ulster unionists, who were implacably opposed to home rule.

The Act of Union of 1800 united Britain and Ireland politically but not administratively. The Irish administration, based mainly at Dublin Castle, was a mixture of Irish government departments, branches of British ministries and boards—some 47 in all—which did not answer to a single authority. It was poorly co-ordinated and out of touch with the people it served. The British civil service was reformed after World War I. In 1920 its newly appointed head, Sir Warren Fisher, conducted a review of Dublin Castle and concluded it needed urgent improvement. Higher calibre civil servants were despatched from London to rapidly reorganise the administration in advance of home rule.[10]

The Government of Ireland Act 1920 met little opposition as most Irish MPs no longer sat at Westminster. It legislated for home rule but provided for elections to two parliaments which were held in May 1921. The 'Partition Act' gave the unionists the opportunity to create their own state in the six northeastern Ulster counties where they had a secure majority. It also allowed Sinn Féin to take political control over the rest of the country. The northern parliament was opened by George V on 22 June and immediately began to set up its administration. Sinn Féin won 124 seats in the southern election. Only the four Trinity College MPs attended the opening of the southern parliament and, after taking the oath, they adjourned *sine die*.[11] The first Dáil resolved that the May elections should be treated as an election to a new Dáil and in August 1921 the newly elected Sinn Féin MPs (north and south) constituted themselves as the second Dáil.

The Irish Volunteers, renamed the Irish Republican Army (IRA), asserted the claim for independence by force of arms. Little political control was exercised by the Dáil, which met infrequently in private as it was soon proscribed by the British. It considered a military dictatorship on 11 March 1921 as it had difficulty functioning.[12] The war of independence or Anglo-Irish war was mainly confined to parts of Munster and Dublin and can be divided into three stages. The first, between January 1919 and the summer of 1920, consisted largely of the killing of Royal Irish Constabulary (RIC) policemen by the IRA. In reprisal, industrial, commercial and private property was destroyed by British forces, and IRA members, Sinn Féin activists and civilians were killed. The second phase occurred between mid-1920 and early 1921 after the Black and Tans and Auxiliaries (ex-British soldiers and officers) reinforced the ineffective RIC and embarked on a reign of terror. This violence increased popular resistance to the forces of the crown in Ireland and undermined support for the government's coercion policy in Britain. The last phase culminated in the July 1921 truce. By then martial law had been declared in Dublin and Munster. This was the most violent period, during which both sides suffering rising casualties.

The British response was again a mixture of coercion and conciliation. As the level of violence increased, the new civil servants sent by Sir Warren Fisher established contacts with Sinn Féin leaders. Britain held Ireland primarily for strategic reasons: to prevent an enemy occupying the country as a base from which to invade England or to interfere with sea trade. By 1921 holding Ireland by force had become a burden, as subsequently summed up by Ulsterman Bernard Law Montgomery (later field-marshal):[13]

My own view is that to win this sort of war you must be ruthless, Oliver Cromwell, or the Germans, would have settled it in a very short time. Nowadays public opinion precludes such methods, the nation would never allow it, and the politicians would lose their jobs if they sanctioned it. That being so I consider that Lloyd George was really right in what he did, if we had gone on we could probably have squashed the rebellion as a temporary measure, but it would have broken out again like an ulcer the moment we removed the troops.

The British government, faced with a war-weary population at home and shortage of soldiers due to over-commitments abroad, decided to renounce political control over twenty-six of the thirty-two Irish counties. It sought to keep the Irish Free State within the British Commonwealth and retain some naval bases, hoping that in a future war the Irish would co-operate. A truce was agreed on 11 July 1921, ending the war of independence. The extended truce was a major contributory factor to the violence which followed. It gave the separatists an illusion of victory, hastened the breakdown of law and order as the police and British army no longer exercised restraint, and allowed the new Northern Ireland government time to become established. Significantly, it brought the secret IRA into the open, making it almost impossible for it to renew hostilities and thereby increasing the likelihood of a negotiated settlement.

THE TREATY
After the truce Dáil President Eamon de Valera responded to British proposals to talk. He wasted time on fruitless negotiations and discovered there was no prospect for a united Irish republic. Lloyd George's final proposal for a settlement was dominion status: political independence within the British Commonwealth; naval control of the seas around Ireland together with access to Irish harbours; a limit on the numbers of Irish soldiers; facilities for communications and defence of the two islands; arrangements for trade, transport and commerce; and Irish responsibility for a share of the British war debt and pensions. The British expressed a hope that Ireland would, in due course and of her own free will, contribute in proportion to her wealth to the naval, military and air forces of the empire.[14]

Lloyd George calculated that the Irish nationalists would lose international support if his offer was rejected and threatened a more intensive war which the IRA, short of men and arms, would have been unlikely to win. De Valera refused to return to the negotiations. Instead on 7 October the Dáil appointed plenipotentiaries, led by Arthur Griffith and Michael Collins, to negotiate and conclude a treaty. Articles for agreement on a treaty were signed by the British and Irish negotiators on 6 December 1921. The British government made two key decisions under duress. It concluded a treaty with the separatists and allowed the Ulster unionists to opt out of a united Ireland.[15] The majority Tories reluctantly accepted self-government in the south provided that the 'loyalist' Ulster unionists were allowed remain within the United Kingdom.

The treaty terms offered were sufficient as most Irish people were anxious for peace. It allowed the British to exit the part of Ireland they could no longer control while retaining their hold over the northeast. But it was a quick fix and a lose/lose solution. The British handed over control of twenty-six counties to the Irish Free State and attempted to give the impression at home that it remained within the British Empire. But the treaty led to a civil war in the Irish Free State, and long-term misgovernment in Northern Ireland which ultimately forced the British to resume direct rule 50 years afterwards.

The treaty delivered much more than the Government of Ireland Act offered, particularly with regard to political independence, finance, defence and foreign relations. Most importantly it kept the king out of Irish Free State internal politics, a fact which does not seem to have been understood by its opponents. The king had no role in appointing ministers, could not refuse to sign into law legislation passed by the Oireachtas (Legislature), and could neither dissolve parliament nor refuse the executive if it decided to do so. The treaty gave the Irish Free State the same constitutional status as Canada, Australia, New Zealand and South Africa. It defined the relationship with the imperial parliament and the dominions, and the role of the crown and the crown's representative. It specified the oath of allegiance to the constitution of the Irish Free State and fidelity to the king in his capacity as head of the British Commonwealth to be sworn by members of parliament. It included Irish Free State liability for a share of UK war debts and pensions, defence of coasts and ports, free trade, and pension provisions. It dealt with Northern Ireland and its boundaries and made provision for a boundary commission. The treaty provided for freedom of religion and no support for a particular religion. It made arrangements for the transfer of power, a provisional government and ratification of the treaty by members entitled to sit in the house of commons of Southern Ireland elected under the Government of Ireland Act 1920.

The treaty was Lloyd George's second attempt to solve the 'Irish question' as the Government of Ireland Act 1920 had been rejected by the nationalists. It was a compromise between what Lloyd George could offer and what Arthur Griffith, Michael Collins and the Irish plenipotentiaries would accept. Lloyd George was in a very difficult position, being a minority Liberal prime minister in a Conservative-dominated coalition government. His main objective in 1921 was to create a centre party out of the Conservative/Liberal coalition, thereby securing his own position as prime minister. To do so he needed to remove the divisive issue of Ireland from British politics. Collins, faced with the threat of renewed hostilities and aware of the IRA's shortage of reliable men and arms, sought to extract the maximum possible concessions. He achieved political and financial independence and calculated that the remaining links with the crown could be eliminated over time. Articles 11–15 of the treaty were designed to bring about 'the eventual establishment of a Parliament for the whole of Ireland'. These clauses related to other parts of the treaty which gave the Irish Free State fiscal independence but bound Northern Ireland to the restrictive financial provisions of the Government of Ireland Act 1920. 'The reason of course was obvious', a British official later explained, 'to offer as much inducement as possible for the North to come in'.[16]

The Dáil debate on the treaty was long and acrimonious. Much of the focus was on the oath of allegiance with less emphasis on the more substantive issue of partition, while a minority believed the fight should continue for a united Irish republic. Under the terms of the treaty, the Irish Free State unwillingly joined the British Commonwealth. The king's functions and those of his representative, the governor-general, which were largely symbolic, were repugnant to Irish republicans, including those who accepted the treaty. Partition was reinforced as the treaty gave Northern Ireland the right to opt out of a united Ireland. The oath of allegiance together with the retention of three naval bases and the insistence that the Irish pay part of the British war debt resulted in significant opposition to the treaty.

The treaty was approved by the Westminster parliament on 16 December 1921; and with 64 votes to 57, by the second Dáil on 7 January 1922. One week later, members of the southern parliament elected under the Government of Ireland Act 1920 (the Sinn Féin MPs who accepted the treaty and the four university MPs) met and formally ratified the treaty. The Irish Free State (Agreement) Act was passed by the second Dáil on 31 March 1922 to give the treaty legal force.[17]

The Irish Free State and Northern Ireland each fell far short of their peoples' aspirations. Nationalists and unionists had not reconciled their differences, allowing the British to dictate terms. The nationalists achieved independence for twenty-six counties but received dominion status rather than a republic. The Ulster unionists retained devolved government with limited powers (home rule) instead of their preferred option, direct rule from Britain. Northern Catholics were left to the mercy of a unionist government which had scant regard for their political or civil rights, while southern Protestants had to fend for themselves in the Irish Free State. After the Treaty, the island of Ireland was divided and politically unstable. The Irish Free State was split between those who accepted the treaty, those who rejected it and a Protestant minority. In Northern Ireland there was a wide gulf between the dominant Ulster unionist Protestants and the nationalist Catholics. Lloyd George's second attempt to resolve the 'Irish question' failed and he lost office in October 1922 and never regained it.

PRE-INDEPENDENCE THINKING ON PUBLIC POLICY
The Irish fought for political independence; economic independence to create jobs, end emigration and raise the standard of living; fiscal

and administrative independence to act without external interference; and cultural independence to revive Gaelic traditions and the Irish language.

While some writers and politicians articulated aims and objectives regarding future public policy, there was no national debate on the implications of independence. The recess committee, formed and funded by Unionist MP Sir Horace Plunkett, recommended the development of agriculture, marine resources and industries based on free trade in 1896. In response the British established the Department of Agriculture and Technical Instruction in 1900 but made no effort to develop industry. After the 1916 rising, contentious issues like partition, the form of government, public policy and the nature of the republic were not debated by the separatists as the aim was unity to maximise support for getting the British out.

Sinn Féin public policies before 1916 had been largely developed by the party's leader, Arthur Griffith, whose ideas on economic self-sufficiency, reduced dependence on British trade, and tariff protection gained widespread support. Gaelic League founder Douglas Hyde sought to de-anglicise Ireland. He was backed by D.P. Moran through his newspaper *The Leader*, which advocated a broader Irish-Ireland agenda including the promotion of Irish goods and industrial development. Hyde and Moran were more concerned with the cultural nation, seeing the conflict as a battle between two civilisations. However, by 1916, Patrick Pearse regarded the Gaelic League as a spent force whose work was done, believing it was time to move on to the next phase of resistance: physical force.[18]

Michael Tierney, who subsequently became president of University College Dublin, wrote that lonely voices and thinkers before World War I were 'bidding Ireland recover some of its lost ideals'. He saw 1916 as a 'mighty call of awakening' and argued that reviving the old ideals was no longer enough as the English had 'to be got out', after which the people could decide how to replace them and build a new state. He identified two main problems: the distribution and control of wealth, and education, which in his view was more important than politics, economics or religion. Tierney argued that pure democracy in the circumstances of the time was scarcely conceivable, and believed there were enough wealth and resources to 'make us all comfortable without any need on our part to worry ourselves with extraordinary new industries, mines, American capital, and what not, which may only knock us off our balance if we get them'. He assumed that denominational schooling would continue after independence.[19]

Aodh de Blácam, who was neither official Labour nor official Sinn Féin but might well be described as both, argued that the people's views had been altered by the deaths of the 1916 leaders and they were now seeing 'the first dim view of the Promised Land'. He called for the formation of co-operatives by 'emancipated farmers' who would be joined by the Labour movement; he also sought to merge nationalism and socialism in a worker's republic and to reconcile co-ops and trade unions with the Catholic Church. De Blácam advocated a boycott of the English language and British manufactures, and was apprehensive that capitalists might join with Sinn Féin against the Labour movement. He stated that Irish Protestants would have to recognise that they lived in a land 'where the Catholic religion colours the life of the people', as French Protestants did, and recommended that Irish be the medium of all teaching, including foreign languages.[20]

Sinn Féin public policy was, in party activist P.S. O'Hegarty's view, more a 'national philosophy'.[21] It was long on aspiration, short on detail and contained little to indicate that serious thought had been given to how change would be planned, funded and implemented. There were few ideas on public administration other than to replace Dublin Castle. The cost of running the future state was not quantified, although there was an acceptance that it would have to be reduced. While the form of government was to be decided by referendum after independence, the first Dáil was set up along Westminster lines and no significant changes were made subsequently. Financial aspirations included a separate currency, more equitable taxation and reform of the unionist-dominated banks and stock exchange. Little consideration was given to defence and policing, while justice would be administered by arbitration courts.[22] Sinn Féin focused on increasing wealth rather than distributing it. Social policy was limited for fear of divisions along class lines and was mainly confined to improving public health and closing the workhouses.

The party advocated reform of local government to end corruption and inefficiency. Educational priorities were the revival of the Irish language and equality of opportunity.

After 1919 'Saorstát Éireann' came into general use as the Irish translation of 'the Irish Republic', regardless of objections to replacing the 1916 term 'Poblacht na hÉireann'. Despite the apparent activity of the first Dáil ministers, the Royal Irish Constabulary was puzzled that the Dáil, which planned to usurp the existing government of Ireland, did not do so. The Dáil formed committees, floated loans, issued decrees which were broad in scope and vague in detail but implemented little. This is not surprising as it employed few civil servants, who had little administrative experience, and it was working in a state still under British control. While the Dáil administration created difficulties for Dublin Castle, it could not easily replace it.[23]

The Irish separatists were not doctrinaire, had no defined blueprint for change and stayed clear of social issues for fear of antagonising the Catholic Church. The Labour Party drafted a radical democratic programme focused on distribution rather than creation of wealth, which was primarily used to gain international socialist recognition. Michael Collins opposed it, fearing it would lose support for Sinn Féin. Yet the first Dáil approved it despite having, in Brian Farrell's words, 'neither the means nor the intention of implementing' it.[24] Sinn Féin was very good at publicity and its policies seem to have been used mainly for propaganda purposes. But, while the party demanded national government, it failed to articulate or develop a programme for better government.

Chapter 3 ～

| THE 1922 CONSTITUTION

TRANSITIONAL ARRANGEMENTS

The Anglo-Irish treaty provided for a three-stage transfer of power: a provisional government to manage the transition, a single-chamber constituent assembly to enact a constitution, and a general election for the first Irish Free State parliament. After it approved the treaty on 7 January 1922, the second Dáil elected Arthur Griffith as its president. The provisional government met for the first time under the chairmanship of Michael Collins on 16 January.[1] Born near Clonakilty, County Cork, Collins had participated in the 1916 Easter rising, played a prominent role in the war of independence, and at 31 years, led a team of young and inexperienced ministers. He focused on maximising sovereignty, believed the form of government could be settled later, and saw the oath of allegiance as a temporary nuisance which could be dispensed with in due course. Griffith did not join the provisional government as he wished to keep it at arm's length from the Dáil, where on 26 April 1922 he stated that

> The Act of Union is gone, the British troops are evacuating the country, and the Irish troops are entering into possession. The Irish exchequer after 105 years is re-established and the revenues

of Ireland are once more restored to Ireland. The power to develop our resources to the uppermost is again in the hands of the people of Ireland, and, but for the attempt of the minority to set up anarchic conditions, the country to-day would have full employment for all its people.

The handover to the provisional government took place on 1 April 1922, the beginning of the governmental financial year. The treaty provided that the provisional government should advise the lord lieutenant on the transfer of power. However, under the direction of Collins it acted as the *de facto* government from its inception. The British set up a committee, chaired by Winston Churchill, to manage the transfer of power. De Valera and the anti-treaty side opposed the provisional government and the constituent assembly, believing they would end the republic. They also feared they would lose votes as the majority of the people were satisfied that a settlement had been reached. Nevertheless, Collins and de Valera entered into a pact whereby Sinn Féin would present a panel of candidates reflecting the strength of the deputies who accepted and rejected the treaty. After the election for the constituent assembly the party would retain power as a coalition government, with the faction winning the majority of seats allotted five cabinet places to the loser's four. This was an undemocratic device designed to maintain the status quo and prevent the people expressing their opinion on the treaty. Parties other than Sinn Féin were grudgingly allowed put candidates forward. The pact annoyed many people including Griffith, Churchill and Northern Ireland Prime Minister James Craig.

The provisional government offered an election in June 1922 on the issue of the treaty and the constitution, asking for a guarantee against intimidation. This proposal was refused by de Valera, who also rejected an election on the single issue of the treaty.[2] However, the 16 June 1922 general election, which was effectively a referendum on the treaty, gave the government a secure majority. The attempt to rig the election failed because the newspapers published details of each candidate's stance on the treaty. Non-Sinn Féin candidates, the vast majority of whom accepted the treaty, did very well despite

IRA intimidation, while proportional representation worked against the anti-treaty side as the majority voted for peace. The government won 58 seats, those against the treaty 36, with other parties and independents, all of whom accepted the treaty, winning 34. Over 78 per cent of the electorate voted for candidates who accepted the treaty. The anti-treaty deputies continued to attend the second Dáil until its last session on 8 June 1922, constantly reiterating the points made during the treaty debates and seeking to influence the actions of the provisional government, which operated independently of the Dáil. They contested the June general election but absented themselves from the constituent assembly; most of them did not participate in parliamentary politics again until Fianna Fáil entered the Dáil in 1927. The civil war began soon after the election, ending any prospect of power-sharing by the two Sinn Féin factions.

THE ENACTMENT OF THE CONSTITUTION

The constitution was drafted by a committee chaired by Collins, who, as he was busy leading the provisional government, delegated the detailed work to independent Dáil deputy Darrell Figgis, who served as vice-chairman and secretary. The other members of the committee were Hugh Kennedy, law advisor to the provisional government; former Indian civil servant James MacNeill (a brother of Eoin MacNeill); C.J. France, who had come to Ireland in 1922 as representative of the American Committee for Relief in Ireland; James Douglas, a young Dublin Quaker businessman; law professor James Murnaghan and barrister John O'Byrne. They were subsequently joined by barrister Kevin O'Shiel and Alfred O'Rahilly, professor of mathematics at University College, Cork. Figgis, who was more a literary figure than a politician, had a major influence in shaping the constitution. He was a Protestant, ambitious, argumentative, and unpopular with the militants who saw him as a 'careerist'.[3] His career was to end in tragedy; his wife shot herself with a gun given to him by Collins for his protection, and he subsequently took his own life.

The constitution committee held its first meeting on 24 January 1922. Collins instructed it to draft a constitution for a free and democratic state having regard to the terms of the treaty and the particular position of the six northeastern counties of Ulster. He requested certain safeguards for the unionist minority in the Irish Free State and asked for a draft within 28 days. The draft was submitted on time and a further two were subsequently produced. A fourth draft was prepared using material from the first three and was shown to the British cabinet. Churchill admitted in the House of Commons on 15 June that the British cabinet had been shown the draft out of courtesy and not as a right. Collins consulted the British because he had agreed with de Valera that the constitution should be presented to the people before the general election in a form that had definitely secured the approval of the British government so that the electors would know what precisely the alternative was to a republic. The British queried some sections regarding the relations of Ireland to the crown and Great Britain. Both parties agreed that the words 'practice and constitutional usage' should be inserted in article 2 in order that Ireland might have the benefit of the great advances in constitutional status by Canada since 1867.[4]

Collins instructed Hugh Kennedy to 'bear in mind . . . not the legalities of the past but the practicalities of the future'.[5] The committee converted many of the principal conventions of the British constitution into the positive law of the Irish Free State, and 'in many instances they, like the framers of the American Constitution have improved on the British Constitution as they found it'.[6] The committee reviewed the following constitutions: the United States of America (1787); the kingdoms of Sweden (1809), Norway (1814), Belgium (1831), Denmark (1915) and Serbs, Croats and Slovenes (1921); the dominion of Canada (1867); the Swiss confederation (1874); the French Republic (1875); the commonwealth of Australia (1900); the union of South Africa (1909); the Russian Socialist Federal Soviet Republic (1918); the German Reich (1919); and the republics of Mexico (1917), Austria, Czechoslovakia and Estonia (1920) and Poland (1921).[7]

The original draft constitution was a 'republican' one as Collins tried to omit the objectionable parts of the treaty to make the Irish Free State acceptable to those who opposed it. All references to the king and commonwealth were omitted. This draft, along with three others which have never been published, was modified by agreement with the British, although Kennedy later stated that 'in no respect did the British government seek to interfere with the document or to lead the constituent assembly'.[8] Nevertheless the final draft constitution was considerably modified before being published.

The election for the constituent assembly/third Dáil took place the day following the publication of the draft constitution. The constituent assembly was summoned by the provisional government to meet on 1 July 1922 but this meeting was postponed as the civil war had begun. It met on 9 September, by which date Griffith had died and Collins had been killed in an ambush. They were replaced by William T. Cosgrave, who combined the offices of Dáil president and chairman of the provisional government.

The constitution was hotly debated in the assembly but the government quickly moved ahead with its enactment. Minister for Home Affairs Kevin O'Higgins steered the bill through all its stages. Some Dáil deputies sought a compromise like that proposed in de Valera's 'document number two', to which O'Higgins responded, 'There is no constitutional hybrid between a Republic and a Monarchy. Mr de Valera had thought he had begotten one, but nobody loved it and he abandoned it himself.'[9] O'Higgins stated that,[10]

We do not propose to mould in cast iron our country's rights ... We do not think that, in passing this Constitution, we are fixing the *ne plus ultra* of the Constitution of the country. Facing the facts as we know them to-day, I say that the Irish people have consented to accept this Treaty, and, until it is repudiated by the majority of the people, it stands.

On the status of the king, Dáil deputy William Magennis stated, 'In such documents as this, the Crown, or King or Sovereign is only another name for a rubber stamp.'[11] Figgis saw the king as a 'functionary of the Irish people' just like a 'member of the Civic Guard with a more or less ornate uniform and a greater variety of them to choose from'. Farmers Party leader D.J. Gorey did not object to the king as nominal head of state and said that provided 'he conducts himself properly according to our constitution, I see no more objection to George Windsor than I have to Erskine Childers'. He summed up the views of many deputies: 'we think that the very last ounce has been squeezed out of it (the constitution), and for that reason I support it.'[12] Patrick McCartan argued that the struggle would have to go on for a republic and a united Ireland, but the anti-treaty insurgents had chosen the wrong time to fight.[13]

The act to 'enact a constitution for the Irish Free State and for implementing the Treaty between Great Britain and Ireland, signed at London on 6 December 1921', usually referred to as the Constitution of the Irish Free State (Saorstát Éireann) Act, was passed by the constituent assembly in October 1922 and came into force on 6 December, the first anniversary of the treaty.

The constitution set out the rules by which the new state was to be governed. It contained a clause which provided that if a conflict arose between the treaty and the constitution, the treaty would prevail. The treaty had been a compromise which involved concessions by both parties. The constitution reflected these compromises. The British conceded that the union of Britain and Ireland had been severed; the Irish agreed to join the British Commonwealth. As there was no common citizenship in the proper sense and no common state, the oath to be taken by members of the Oireachtas (legislature) was an oath of allegiance to the constitution of the Irish Free State in the first place and fidelity to the crown in its capacity as head of the Commonwealth in the second place.

Despite the monarchical trappings, the constitution was at heart republican. The state's official title, Saorstát Éireann, was in the Irish language even in the British act and was the same as that designated in the 1919 declaration of independence. No titles or honours were allowed. The state was vested with all lands, waters, mines and minerals formerly vested in the crown. The national flag was the green, white and orange tricolour of the republic. *God Save the King* was replaced by a number of anthems such as *God Save Ireland* and *Let Erin Remember* before being formally replaced by *Amhrán na bhFiann* (*Soldiers' Song*) in 1926. The army bore the same official title and crest as those used by the Irish Volunteers and its command was vested in the executive government. All oaths taken by judges, soldiers and other officers of the state were to Saorstát Éireann and its constitution without mention of the king. The crown disappeared and was replaced by the harp as the symbol of Irish government. While the king formed part of the Oireachtas (along with the Dáil and Senate) and had to assent to every measure before it became law, he did so not on his own initiative but on the advice of the Irish Free State ministers.[14]

The Irish, like the other countries which emerged in Europe after the Great War, regarded democracy as the inevitable form of government. Yet the constitution was closer to pre-war than post-war constitutions in one key respect. It proclaimed the rights of citizens but assumed their duties.[15] The constitution's articles can be divided as follows: introductory provisions (1–4), fundamental rights (5–10), ownership of public assets (11), legislature (12–46), initiative and referendum (47–48), war (49), constitutional amendments (50), cabinet (51–59), the governor-general (60), state finances (61–63), courts (64–72) and transitory provisions (73–83).

The constitution defined the status of the new state: 'The Irish Free State is a co-equal member of the British Commonwealth' and 'All powers of government and all authority legislative, executive and judicial in Ireland, are derived from the people of Ireland and shall be exercised through the organisations established under the Constitution.' The Oireachtas (Legislature) had the exclusive right to raise, maintain and control armed forces, and 'Save in the case of actual invasion, the Irish Free State shall not be committed to active participation in any war without the assent of the Oireachtas.'

Fundamental rights included liberty of persons and their dwellings; freedom of conscience and free profession and practice of religion; free expression of opinion; right of peaceable assembly and the right to form associations and unions. The constitution contained a proviso that 'nothing ---- shall be invoked to prohibit, control or interfere with any act of the military forces of the Irish Free State during the existence of a state of war or armed rebellion'. This was not in the original draft and was inserted as an amendment during the civil war. It was opposed by Figgis and some members of the constituent assembly and in effect brought Irish law into line with British law, which followed the principle *salus populi suprema lex*.[16]

The slogan 'Ireland, not free merely, but Gaelic as well, not Gaelic merely but Free as well' crystallised in a phrase the two chief aims of political independence and the restoration of Ireland's intellectual freedom. The constitution declared Irish to be the national language and each child was given a fundamental right to receive at least an elementary education in it.

The Oireachtas (Legislature) and elections to the Seanad (Senate—upper house) and Dáil (Chamber of Deputies—lower house) were defined, including the controversial oath to be taken by Dáil deputies and senators:

I...........do solemnly swear true faith and allegiance to the Constitution of the Irish Free State by law established, and that I will be faithful to H. M. George v., his heirs and successors by law in virtue of the common citizenship of Ireland with Great Britain and her adherence to and membership of the group of nations forming the British Commonwealth of Nations.

The constitution, significantly, provided that the Dáil could not at any time be dissolved except on the advice of the executive council (government). The rules of the Oireachtas were outlined in general terms and subsequently drawn up by its members. Dáil deputies would be elected to represent territorial constituencies by proportional representation (except for the six university seats, three each for Trinity College and the National University of Ireland). Half of the senators would be nominated by the president and half elected by the Dáil. The constitution stated that the Senate shall be 'composed of citizens ---- proposed on the grounds that they have done honour to the nation by useful public service' or 'because of special qualifications or attainments'. After the first election the rules were altered to allow half of the senators to be elected directly in a single constituency by the people, who showed little interest, and the rules were changed again to give the Dáil and Senate the powers to nominate and elect the senators. Former unionists were given assurances of a certain level of representation in the Senate, which combined the functions of a legislative 'cooling chamber' with a means of allowing unionists an opportunity to participate in government. Procedures for bills passed by the Dáil and sent to the Senate for amendment were laid down.

Executive power was to be shared by the crown and the executive council headed by an executive president nominated by the Dáil. The crown would be represented by a governor-general appointed by the king, who had to be *persona grata* with the executive. He had no real power and his main function was to sign acts into law in the name of the crown on the advice of the executive and without reference to the king. The king's power to veto legislation was as dead in Ireland as it was in Britain. The real power resided with the executive, which would be responsible to the Dáil and consist of not more than seven and not fewer than five ministers nominated by the president. The original draft constitution had favoured a majority of ministers being appointed from the best talent available, whether elected or not. The constituent assembly changed that to executive ministers, who would be Dáil deputies nominated by the president, and 'external ministers' nominated by a Dáil committee, who would not have to be elected deputies and would not sit on the executive. The president could nominate a vice-president who would replace him in the event of death, resignation or permanent incapacitation until a new president was elected.

Financial provisions included the appointment of a comptroller and auditor general. Justice would be administered in the public courts established by the Oireachtas. The judicial articles defined the powers of the high and supreme courts, the appointment of judges, the right to trial by due course of law, and military tribunals authorised by law during periods of war or armed rebellion. The final decision of whether a state of war or armed rebellion existed would rest with the courts. All judges would be independent and subject only to the constitution and the law. No retrospective legislation would be permitted. The controversial right to seek leave to appeal judgements of the supreme court to the privy council in London constituted 'the one real diminution of National Sovereignty contained in the Constitution'.[17]

The constitution provided for subordinate legislatures and functional or vocational councils. Provision was made for referenda and for initiation by the people of proposals for laws and constitutional amendments. O'Higgins argued that 'personal actual contact between the people and the laws by which they are governed is advisable in a country which is passing out of a condition of bondage and a country where the traditional attitude of the people is to be against the law and against the Government'.[18] A second reason for the referendum was to check the Dáil in cases where it might cease to be representative of the will of the people. Amendments to the constitution would be made by the Oireachtas for eight years by way of ordinary legislation and thereafter by referendum.

The constitution provided that the Senate should be constituted immediately. After the date on which the constitution came into operation, the constituent assembly would exercise all the powers and authorities of the Dáil for a period not exceeding one year and the first general election under the constitution should be held as soon as possible. The passing and adoption of the constitution by the constituent assembly and the British parliament would be announced not later than 6 December 1922, the first anniversary of the treaty.

The treaty was annexed to the constitution together with a list of the naval facilities required by the British: Berehaven, Queenstown (Cobh), Belfast Lough and Lough Swilly.[19] Aviation facilities located near the ports and oil storage depots at Haulbowline and Rathmullen were also included. It was agreed that the two governments should sign conventions covering submarine cables, lighthouses and navigational aids, war signal stations and the regulation of civil communication by air.[20]

The constitution came into force on 6 December 1922. The Dáil passed the Adaptation of Enactments and Expiring Laws Continuance Acts 1922, which carried forward all existing legislation. Administrative functions had been already handed over under the transfer of functions order of 1 April 1922. These were vital pieces of catch-all legislation and regulation which facilitated the smooth transfer of political and administrative power. The constitution was not the desired outcome for the government but it established the rules for the new state. The anti-treaty side opposed it and the Protestant minority feared it did not give them adequate protection.

British and Irish constitutional theorists disagree as to when and how the Irish Free State was established. Ireland, in the eyes of the Irish people, has always been sovereign so the British could not grant the state independence. The Irish argued that the state derived its authority from the people, who had seized power, while the British maintained they were transferring power in an orderly and legal manner. Furthermore the Irish position was that the treaty was not made with persons representing a government constituted under the Government of Ireland Act 1920, but with representatives of the Dáil, which refused to recognise the act.[21]

In the aftermath of the treaty there was confusion about the extent of independence gained. The designation of the Irish Free State as a dominion was a problem as there was no clear definition of what it meant, other than almost complete freedom. The *Daily News* informed its readers on 4 April 1922 that British dominions were not subordinate dependencies but free nations equal in status with Britain, and that the Westminster parliament had no right to pass external legislation except at the request of a dominion, while the British had admitted the sovereignty of Ireland as a treaty could only be negotiated between sovereign peoples. The newspaper gave this account despite the fact that these conditions were not formally recognised until the Balfour declaration of 1926. Constitutional lawyer Arthur Berridale Keith wrote to *The Times* in June 1922, stating that the Irish Free State constitution recognised the sovereignty of the Irish people and the crown had no power to disallow acts passed by the Oireachtas. The constitution had an imperial form but a republican substance, as the Irish Free State government was effectively free to do as it pleased.[22] However, the treaty denied the Irish state the symbolic apparel that might have made it legitimate in the eyes of most of those who opposed it and the belief in Ireland's right to self-determination made the acceptance of dominion status a compromise impossible for many.[23]

The Cosgrave governments did not regard the constitution as a permanent document and passed seventeen constitutional amendment acts before 1932. Some were minor amendments, like those which attempted to rationalise the convoluted method of electing members of the Senate and matters relating to their age and term of office (1, 6–9, 11). Another provided that the ceann comhairle (chairman of the Dáil) would be, if willing to continue, automatically returned to the next parliament (2), while the requirement that the day of a general election be a public holiday was removed (3).

Other amendments were more fundamental. The maximum duration of each Dáil was extended from four to six years (4). The executive was increased from seven to twelve members (5) and one senator was permitted to become a member (15). Articles 47 and 48 were deleted, ending the right to petition a referendum and the power of the people to initiate proposals for laws and constitutional amendments (10). The powers of the Dáil were increased at the expense of the Senate (12–14). The Oireachtas was permitted to amend the constitution for a further eight years without submission to a referendum (16). Schedule 2a was added to the constitution, making 'better provision for safeguarding the rights of the people' and 'meeting a prevalence of disorder' (17).

The Statute of Westminster 1931 gave dominions the power to make any changes they wished without British interference and cleared the way for further amendments made by de Valera's governments after 1932. The oath of allegiance was removed, the governor-general's functions were downgraded and the right of appeal to the privy council was withdrawn. Citizenship rights were altered, the representation of the universities in the Dáil was ended, the Senate was abolished and references to the king and the governor-general were removed. The Executive Authority (External Relations) Act 1936, passed after the abdication of Edward VIII, limited future monarchs' functions to the appointment of diplomatic representatives. Cork solicitor John J. Horgan observed in 1936 that the[24]

Constitution was a peculiar document, hastily conceived, painfully delivered and constantly amputated. It represented not the agreement of their best political thinkers, but an attempt to meet the necessities of the hour. In a conservative, patriarchal, agricultural country it set up a most elaborate system of advanced democratic government, with inadequate safeguards against its abuses. The miracle was that it had worked so well. One by one the elaborate provisions for limiting the power of the Executive Government had been jettisoned or become inoperative.

The constitution served its purpose as it provided the basis for establishing a democratic state during a civil war. It was replaced by a rewritten constitution in 1937.

Chapter 4 ❧

POLITICS AND THE
POLITICAL PARTIES

The deaths of Arthur Griffith and Michael Collins within ten days of each other in August 1922 suddenly deprived the government of its most popular and charismatic leaders. Griffith had led the struggle for independence in the years before the 1916 rising, contributed most of Sinn Féin's political and economic ideas and worked tirelessly as a propagandist. After the rising he had been overshadowed by de Valera but retained a leading role in Sinn Féin and succeeded him as Dáil president in January 1922. Collins was a much greater loss as he was widely perceived to be the 'coming man'. He had been the most effective leader in the war of independence (January 1919 to July 1921), during which he ruthlessly destroyed the British military and police intelligence networks, financed the armed struggle and disrupted the Dublin Castle administration. He gave inspirational leadership and managed to evade capture despite being the most wanted man in the country. In contrast de Valera spent much of 1919 and 1920 in America and struggled to regain his previously undisputed influence over the independence movement on his return. Collins was highly respected by the IRA, even by those who opposed the treaty.

William T. Cosgrave succeeded Collins as chairman of the provisional government and Griffith as president of the Dáil. He was neither as dynamic nor as well-known as Griffith or Collins and inherited the strong-willed ministers of the provisional government, many of whom had higher public profiles. Cosgrave became the first executive president of the Irish Free State and remained in office until March 1932.

After the treaty, the independence movement divided into opposing factions. Since then competition for political power in Ireland has largely been between two parties, Fine Gael (the successors of Cumann na nGaedheal) and Fianna Fáil, which differ little ideologically but remain divided along civil war lines. The Labour Party, the Farmers Party and the independent deputies accepted the treaty. Labour assumed the role of responsible opposition in the Dáil as the anti-treaty deputies absented themselves. The Farmers Party supported the government, while the independents generally did likewise. They included ex-unionists Major Bryan Cooper and Richard Henrik Beamish, old-style nationalist William Redmond, businessman Andrew O'Shaughnessy, academic Sir James Craig and participants in the struggle for independence sidelined in the aftermath of the treaty like Darrell Figgis. Three small parties had brief existences. The National Group and Clann Éireann broke away from Cumann na nGaedheal over the army mutiny and the boundary commission respectively, and William Redmond's National League, founded in 1926, attempted unsuccessfully to supplant the government party.

The position of the parties after the three general elections held between 1923 and 1927 was as follows:[1]

Party	August 1923 Fourth Dáil	June 1927 Fifth Dáil	September 1927 Sixth Dáil
Cumann na nGaedheal	63	47	62
Sinn Féin	44	5	-
Fianna Fáil	-	44	57
Labour Party	14	22	13
Farmers Party	15	11	6
National League	-	8	2
Independents	16	14	12
Independent Republican	-	2	-
Independent Labour	1	-	1
Total	**153**	**153**	**153**

Those who accepted the treaty took some time to organise themselves as Cumann na nGaedheal and then did so ineffectively. Cosgrave was unenthusiastic about political parties and Minister for Defence Richard Mulcahy opposed the party's formation. Its objectives were a united Ireland; preservation and fostering of the Irish language and culture; development of agriculture, fisheries and natural resources; stimulation and safeguarding of manufacturing industries; completion of the land purchase; utilisation of depopulated grasslands; a national scheme for housing; encouraging physical development of the children of Ireland; and securing the fullest opportunities for educational advancement in every section of the community.[2] The party did not have a defined political philosophy, did not recruit large numbers, used paid organisers, selected notables and personalities as candidates and was perpetually short of money. It was over-influenced by interest groups that largely agreed with its cautious, cost-conscious approach. With the exception of J.J. Walsh, who was given the job of organising the party, and Joe McGrath and Richard Mulcahy, neither Cosgrave nor the other ministers became actively involved. This neglect of party organisation was to cost Cumann na nGaedheal dearly and it lost its most effective organisers when McGrath and Walsh left politics. The party was very poor at public relations and none of its leaders, particularly Cosgrave and O'Higgins, courted personal popularity.

The anti-treaty side also took time to organise a political party. One was proposed at the World Congress of the Irish Race held at Paris in January 1922. The congress minutes dated 28 January record that 'it was unanimously decided that the name of the organisation would be Fine Gaedheal (Family of the Gael)'.[3] Its president was de Valera. This seems to have been an attempt to set up an umbrella group of those who accepted and rejected the treaty with the objective of assisting 'the people of Ireland to attain to the full their National ideals, political, cultural and economic, and to secure for Ireland her rightful place among the free nations of the earth'. It achieved nothing and de Valera, who wished it to be autonomous and under his control, was against any government representation on its governing body despite seeking a loan from the Dáil to keep it afloat. De Valera subsequently formed an anti-treaty party, Cumann na Poblachta (Republican Party), on 15 March 1922. It appears to have run its course during the civil war, although disputes over the control of its finances continued until 1926.[4] However, when the anti-treaty side participated in the August 1923 election it did so under the banner of Sinn Féin, as the government party had by then been organised as Cumann na nGaedheal. After the election, the Sinn Féin deputies did not take their seats in the Dáil.

In 1925 de Valera proposed that Sinn Féin deputies should enter the Dáil if the oath was removed, but was outvoted. He left the party in March 1926 and founded Fianna Fáil in May as a 'national movement' and grassroots party. Seán Lemass is reputed to have organised it along the lines of the French communist party with a cell (*cumann*) in each parish, using anti-treaty activists as its core membership. Fianna Fáil was flexible, pragmatic and populist. It was not revolutionary, favoured private enterprise and sought working-class support.[5] It differentiated itself from Cumann na nGaedheal by emphasising 'republican' ideals and advancing a range of socioeconomic policies. In early 1927 Dan Breen severed his connections with Fianna Fáil, took the oath and entered the Dáil, where he tried but failed to have the oath removed.[6]

After the June 1927 election for the fifth Dáil left Cumann na nGaedheal vulnerable as it had lost seats, Fianna Fáil deputies attempted to gain admittance to the Dáil but were refused entry unless they took the oath. They brought a case against the government, which received legal opinion that the ban should stand. On 26 July Fianna Fáil Deputy Patrick Belton took the oath and his seat in the Dáil.[7] The Electoral Amendment No. 2 Bill 1927 (which never became an act), put forward after the murder of Kevin O'Higgins, ended Fianna Fáil abstention. It provided that candidates be obliged to swear an affidavit in advance of the election that if elected they would take the oath prescribed by the constitution and failure to do so would result in disqualification. Whereupon de Valera, who had insisted he would never sit in the Dáil while the oath was a requirement, discovered it was an 'empty formula', in effect the price of admission. Fianna Fáil deputies took the oath with 'mental reservations' and entered the Dáil on 12 August 1927. Cosgrave indicated he was pleased to see them take their seats.[8]

The government barely survived a motion of no confidence put down by the Labour Party and supported by Fianna Fáil and the National League and, after winning two by-elections, Cosgrave dissolved the Dáil on 25 August. The election in September 1927 for the sixth Dáil gave Cumann na nGaedheal, supported by the Farmers Party and independents, a majority. Under the constitution a referendum could be initiated if 75,000 people signed a petition. Fianna Fáil collected 96,000 signatures for a referendum on the oath. In response, the government passed the Constitution (No. 10) Act 1928, abolishing the referendum and the initiative.

After 1927, Cumann na nGaedheal moved to the right, leaving the centre ground to be occupied by Fianna Fáil, which gained wider public approval as it gradually accepted the legitimacy of the state and the ballot box as the sole means of changing governments. Fianna Fáil dropped its more radical ideals, kept the door open to its opponents and sought to bring the IRA along the constitutional route. Cumann na nGaedheal lost support due to its fiscal and economic policies, partition, special legislation, bad organisation, poor attendance of deputies in the Dáil and its distrust of the people. It lost the backing of many clergy over the lack of social advances, of businessmen and farmers over tariffs, and floating voters as it had no convincing answers to Fianna Fáil's catch-all policies.[9] That party set out clear aims: a united Irish republic; restoration of the Irish language; making resources subservient to the needs and welfare of the people; economic control and self-sufficiency; and decentralising essential industries to rural areas. It downplayed partition and amendments to the treaty. In contrast, Cumann na nGaedheal was a law-and-order party focused on developing agriculture, lowering taxation and balancing the budget.[10]

While Cumann na nGaedheal neglected publicity, de Valera was aware of Napoleon Bonaparte's maxim that 'four hostile newspapers are more to be feared than a thousand bayonets' and was conscious of the value of public relations, particularly to enhance his personal popularity. After his release from prison in 1924, he began to raise funds for a newspaper from the party faithful at home and the Irish in the US. He unsuccessfully tried to gain control of Dáil funds in the US, despite having agreed with Collins that they should not be used for party purposes. He later managed to persuade many Irish in America to hand over Dáil bonds which were due for repayment in exchange for shares in his newspaper. They were assured that 'Mr. de Valera will, of course, not derive personally any monetary profit from them.'[11] He formed a company in Delaware over which he exercised control despite being a minority shareholder.

The *Irish Press* was launched in September 1931 and greatly assisted the party in the 1932 election. De Valera remained controlling director of the *Irish Press* after he became executive president in 1932 and subsequently handed over his controlling shares to his family, who still retain them.

The Labour Party did not contest the 1918 and 1921 general elections and lost ground as a result. It performed the role of responsible opposition between 1922 and 1927, campaigning for social welfare benefits, lower indirect taxation, prevention of profiteering, house-building, and nationalisation of the railways and canals. Its leaders failed to recognise the need to integrate nationalist and socialist aspirations and saw the nationalists as opponents rather than potential allies. Jim Larkin divided the party after he returned from the US and it split again when some of its Dáil deputies supported public safety legislation in 1931.

The Farmers Party sought to advance farming interests but became increasingly divided over tariffs. It generally supported Cumann na nGaedheal and continued to do so after 1927 despite its former leader D.J. Gorey joining the government party. By 1932 Labour and the Farmers Party were weaker than they had been in 1923, and Labour supported a minority Fianna Fáil government after the February election to dislodge Cumann na nGaedheal from office.

Few women were elected to the Dáil after 1922. Only one, Margaret Collins-O'Driscoll, took her seat between 1923 and 1927. Before independence women had been active in the suffragist, labour and separatist movements. After 1922 gender roles reverted to pre-World War I norms and, in an era of high unemployment, males ('breadwinners') got preference, particularly as jobs for ex-soldiers were needed after the civil war. Politically minded women resisted this retreat from equality and were marginalised by both Cumann na nGaedheal and Fianna Fáil. Many opposed the treaty and lost their wider public influence. Cumann na nGaedheal and Fianna Fáil saw women in predominantly domestic terms ('*Kinder, Küche, Kirche*'). As in many other countries at the time, married women worked outside the home only out of necessity. The Catholic Church opposed women serving on juries and working except as servants, nurses or teachers. While some jobs were reserved for women, like those of writing assistants and typists in the civil service, employment was difficult to find and female emigration increased after 1926. Some women resisted the diminution of their level of political representation. When Senator Alice Stopford-Green died, Mary E. Kettle argued that 'undoubtedly the vacant seat should go to a woman'.[12] Yet the Women's International League for Peace and Freedom got Cosgrave and de Valera together in the same room in 1927 for the first time since the last session of the second Dáil on 8 June 1922, although they did not speak with each other. The absence of women in political life after independence meant that women's and children's issues were largely ignored.

By the end of the 1920s the Irish public had become disillusioned with Cosgrave's governments, which sought to prove they were capable and respectable without regard for the political consequences. These governments lost the support of many voters who had expected prosperity, of intellectuals like former Cumann na nGaedheal deputy Alfred O'Rahilly, and businessmen James and T.P. Dowdall. T.K. Hancock expressed the view in 1937 that[13]

> The Irish Free State under Mr Cosgrave was the objective, the unemotional scientific, intellectual state. Throughout Europe, and not least in Ireland, people were beginning to tire of this kind of state. They wanted more emotion and more drama. The political artists were pushing aside the political scientists. The party state was challenging the neutral state. In Ireland, people were getting weary of their Government's very virtues.

When the expectations of a higher standard of living did not materialise, the electorate became disenchanted with the government's strict financial control, focus on law and order, and neglect of social and economic development.

Cosgrave's governments gave the state a stable political life and an organised government system, impartial in justice, tolerant of the Protestant minority and with some concern for the large number of Irish who served in the Great War. The murder of O'Higgins was a major blow as he had more vision and energy than Cosgrave, who observed the treaty to the letter but not the spirit.[14] Yet Cosgrave was perhaps the wisest choice to succeed Collins as, being a practical down-to-earth businessman, he focused on building the new state and moved forward without dwelling on the past. Cumann na nGaedheal had to prove itself, so government became an end rather than a means to an end. This may explain its intransigence, insensitivity to public opinion and reluctance to court popular support.[15] The government, hard pressed by armed opponents, maintained control by centralising power to the detriment of national and local democracy. Nevertheless, in Padraic Colum's words, 'Cosgrave left an administration which had no taint of graft or inefficiency and an array of national institutions, which are practically foolproof'.[16]

Chapter 5 ~

SECURING CONTROL OVER THE STATE

INTRODUCTION

The Irish Free State was born in tumult. After centuries of English rule, there was little respect for government. Some of those who rejected the treaty took up arms against the state, leading to civil war. As the government was desperately short of money, expenditure needed to be drastically reduced. Collins and the provisional government had to quickly raise a large army to defend the state, establish a civil service to transfer power from the British, deliver public services and restore financial stability. As law and order had broken down, new systems of justice and policing were urgently needed. Unemployment was high and the economic outlook poor due to the post-World War I economic depression. Agricultural, industrial, infrastructural and social investments were required immediately but money was scarce and difficult to borrow due to the state's instability and fears that it might be unable to repay.

After the civil war, succeeding governments were confronted by a series of crises, any of which could have brought about their downfall: the extreme shortage of money (1922–26), the army mutiny (1924), the boundary commission report (1925), the murder of Kevin O'Higgins (1927), and the worldwide economic depression after the Wall Street crash in 1929.

COSGRAVE AND THE PROVISIONAL GOVERNMENT

After the 16 June 1922 election, the constituent assembly was summoned to convene on 1 July, but this event was postponed when the provisional government ordered an attack on the Four Courts in Dublin, which were occupied by insurgents. Collins and some government ministers returned to the army, leaving Minister for Local Government William T. Cosgrave as acting chairman of the provisional government and acting minister for finance. Griffith died on 12 August and Collins was killed 10 days later. The constituent assembly was summoned by proclamation and met on 9 September 1922. Labour Deputy Cathal O'Shannon warned that[1]

> The majority, the great bulk of the people, without any denial, are at the back of this Government. They were at the back of the late John E. Redmond for many longer years than they are at the back of this movement and Party, and they are just as ready and willing to change to-morrow if thwarted as they were in 1916 and 1917.

Cosgrave succeeded Collins as chairman of the provisional government and Minister for Finance. Born in Dublin in 1880, he was educated by the Christian Brothers and left school at 16 to work in the family bar and grocery business. He was a founder member of Sinn Féin and was elected to Dublin City Council in 1908, where he gained experience of public finance. He did not join the IRB but participated in the 1916 rising, after which he was sentenced to death. The sentence was commuted and he was subsequently released, was elected MP for Kilkenny in 1917 and served as Minister for Local Government in the first and second Dáil. A compromise candidate, he became leader by accident after the deaths of Griffith and Collins, and was surrounded by strong personalities whom he inherited rather than selected as his ministers.[2] Unlike the charismatic de Valera, Cosgrave was more a chairman or *primus inter pares*. He was a businessman who made up his mind quickly and stuck to it, was unpretentious and witty, and spoke briefly and to the point. Along with some of his ministers he was old-fashioned in his style of dress, favouring wing collars and formal morning suits. While many international politicians dressed in similar fashion, it unfortunately created the image of a government continuing in the British tradition.

Cosgrave was deeply religious and sought to avoid confrontation with the Catholic Church, which influenced government decisions on censorship and tax breaks for the clergy and prevented the vocational schools from competing with secondary schools.[3] He was very different from Collins, as illustrated by their attitudes to the civil war and Northern Ireland. Collins tried to end the civil war, but Cosgrave conducted it in military fashion without regard for former friendships.[4] Collins expected Northern Ireland to collapse— and actively tried to make sure it did—but Cosgrave was uncertain that would happen and, with County Antrim-born Minister Ernest Blythe, he argued for a peaceful approach. He stood tenaciously by the treaty, which he considered an international agreement. Cosgrave did not seek the limelight, leaving the imperial conferences and League of Nations to Vice-president Kevin O'Higgins and his ministers for external affairs and, apart from short visits to London, Rome and Geneva, his only major trip abroad was to the US and Canada in early 1928, where he met President Calvin Coolidge and was received by both houses of Congress. He told the *New York Times* it would be a good thing if there was a change of government to give the opposition a chance to run the Irish Free State.[5]

Diarmuid O'Hegarty was appointed secretary to the government. Born in 1892 near Skibbereen, County Cork, he worked in the Department of Agriculture and Technical Instruction, joined the IRB and Gaelic League and, after being released in error following the 1916 rising, played a prominent role in re-organising the Irish Volunteers, becoming IRA director of organisation. He left the army with the rank of lieutenant-general after the civil war and served as secretary to the government until February 1932, when he was appointed Commissioner for Public Works, a position he held until 1957.

Following a short phase of conventional warfare, the civil war became a guerrilla conflict after August 1922. Cosgrave operated on the premise that anti-treaty armed forces (referred to as irregulars to distinguish them from the regular army) could end the conflict at any time by surrendering their arms. The government warned that snipers and bombers would be shot, and no hunger strikers would to be released.[6] No reports of hunger strikers' condition were issued while they were alive, and if they died, no inquests were held and they were buried in unmarked graves in prison.[7]

Cosgrave insisted on unconditional surrender and rejected any compromise on the treaty. During the 1923 hunger strike, Dáil Deputy Dan Breen suggested a meeting to discuss the decommissioning of arms, a full political amnesty and acceptance of the treaty by the anti-treaty side, which would act in future along democratic lines, but the government refused to meet him.[8] The British were doubtful of Cosgrave's ability to win but the predominantly civilian government proved capable of defeating the militants.[9]

CENTRAL GOVERNMENT

On 6 December 1922, the first anniversary of the treaty, the Irish Free State formally came into existence. On 7 December the Northern Ireland government exercised its right not to unite with the Irish Free State under article 11 of the treaty, thus confirming the partition of the island and triggering the boundary commission to decide on the border between the Irish Free State and Northern Ireland.

The third Dáil, which the constituent assembly had become on 6 December 1922 as prescribed by the constitution, was dissolved on 9 August 1923 and a general election was held for the first parliament to be elected under the new constitution. The fourth Dáil convened on 19 September 1923. While Cosgrave did not win an overall majority, he could govern without other party support as the anti-treaty deputies remained absent from the Dáil. He was elected president of the executive council and appointed O'Higgins vice-president. The government consisted of the executive council, an inner cabinet comprising the president and six ministers nominated by him, and four 'external' ministers nominated by the Dáil who did not sit on the executive. The theory of external ministers was that people of talent inside or outside the governing party could become ministers but not form part of the decision-making executive. This concept had been originally advanced by constitution committee member James Douglas, who envisaged expert outsiders, not members of the Dáil.

However, in practice the government nominated deputies as external ministers and the Dáil approved them. After 1927 all ministers sat on the executive. The president had difficulty in dismissing ministers because to do so he had to resign and present a new cabinet for approval by the Dáil.

The small executive kept policy-making in too few hands. It is difficult to quantify the effect that exclusion from the executive had on the external ministers. Patrick Hogan in Agriculture had considerable influence over economic policy while the others, notably J.J. Walsh in Posts and Telegraphs, who openly clashed with the government over tariffs, did not. The executive paid little regard to suggestions made by its own supporters, who were concerned at the dominance of the Department of Finance, or by the opposition Labour Party. This was detrimental to good government as the executive's main sources of advice were senior civil servants and the commissions it appointed. The executive centralised authority to maintain political control over the state, it had exceptional powers at times of emergency and there was no formal safeguard or redress from intentional bureaucratic tyranny.[10]

Collective cabinet responsibility was agreed by the provisional government in 1922, when it decided that all cabinet decisions should be regarded as unanimous and should be treated as strictly confidential. This had not been the intention of some members of the first Dáil who sought more direct participation in the conduct of government by means of committees attached to ministries.

Although the government party Cumann na nGaedheal was a loose-knit organisation, the executive received consistent support from a reliable majority in the Dáil. Cabinet hegemony was established because the devices provided in the constitution for checking governments and giving the Dáil a more active role depended on it being composed of small and loosely organised groups, and free votes. The executive faced a major task as, in O'Higgins's view, the Irish people had been 'against the government' for centuries, and he believed that an efficient democracy alone could save Ireland and enable it to keep its peace.[11] However, deliberation on policies and decision-making took place not publicly in the Dáil, but privately in the upper echelons of Cumann na nGaedheal, in consultation with senior civil servants and in the executive. The government treated both its supporters and the opposition in a manner not markedly different from contemporary British practice.[12]

In theory the policy-makers were the executive, the Oireachtas and senior civil servants. They were influenced by political parties, interest groups, the churches, civil servants in central and local government, the media and public opinion within the state, and externally by the British and world economies. The executive formulated policy on the advice of senior civil servants. The Dáil's role was to make or break governments, ensure the executive behaved itself, enact legislation, exercise control over finance, and make peace or war.[13] However, the really important influencers of policy between 1922 and 1932 were the senior civil servants in the Department of Finance.

The Senate, whose functions were mainly advisory and consultative, played a minor role. It was entitled to be informed, to advise and to warn, could not block legislation but could hold up non-financial bills for 270 days and had the power to force a referendum. The first Senate was comprised of 36 Catholics, 23 Protestants and one Jew, and proved that nationalists and former unionists could work together. The ex-unionists, in Clerk of the Senate Donal O'Sullivan's view, unreservedly accepted the Irish Free State, never put English interests before Irish, believed they were Irish and were free of religious bigotry. The government and many Dáil deputies disliked the Senate, considering it an unnecessary control mechanism. Fianna Fáil was strongly against it, claimed it was too expensive and was particularly hostile to the former unionists. Yet good work was done in amending bills 'tossed' into the Senate by the Dáil, which expected them to be promptly passed, much to the annoyance of senators.[14] The volume of legislation was high, 50 acts being passed in 1923 alone, although some were temporary acts, generally replaced in the following year by permanent measures. The governments between 1922 and 1927 passed an extraordinary volume of legislation quickly and without sufficient scrutiny by the Dáil, whose members were still learning how to legislate and which lacked an opposition capable of replacing the government. Before Fianna Fáil entered the

Dáil in 1927, the most effective opposition came from independent senators.

Government policy was not well developed. After the civil war, its focus was on consolidating power, reducing expenditure, reconstruction and stability. The executive was fiscally conservative, knowing it would have to pay its way without outside help. It did not wish to be over-dependent on the British, who were the state's main trading partner, its lender of last resort and source of work for its many emigrants. The Cosgrave governments favoured agriculture as the engine of economic growth and the means of maximising the number of people on the land. Agriculture failed to deliver and as a consequence economic performance did not meet expectations.

The government did not co-ordinate its activities effectively. This was in part due to the absence of an overall strategy. Cosgrave presided rather than led and his small department acted as a secretariat instead of co-ordinating political and economic policies. Government departments operated independently with insufficient concern for the implications of their actions on other parts of the administration. Finance focused on control of expenditure regardless of the impact on development. Finance and Agriculture were allowed to dominate the economic departments to the detriment of Industry and Commerce, and Fisheries. Education failed to meet the needs of agriculture and industry. Posts and Telegraphs was starved of investment for telephones. Finance Minister Ernest Blythe allowed his civil servants to determine fiscal policy and money was not discussed in the executive in the early years except in relation to the army.

The government, which contained many lawyers, seems to have had the mistaken belief that if it legislated for something it would happen. But laws have to gain acceptance from the people, they must be capable of being enforced, and resources need to be devoted to their implementation and maintenance. All of these conditions were not met, so law enforcement remained a problem.

Muiris MacCarthaigh argues, 'For most of the state's existence, its parliament has been seen as effectively powerless to challenge the dominant government it elects.'[15] This was particularly true between

1922 and 1932 when there was no formal obligation on ministers to answer questions or account for their actions. Pre-independence Sinn Féin had envisaged a strong legislature which would elect coalition governments formed from vocational or interest groups. In the anti-British political mood after independence, there was distrust of large disciplined parties like those at Westminster, coupled with a determination not to adopt the old Irish Party model where MPs pledged to 'sit, act and vote' as directed by the party executive. This may explain the government party's reluctance to organise itself formally as Cumann na nGaedheal and Cosgrave's scepticism about political parties. However, the civil war crystallised most of those who accepted and rejected the treaty into two opposing political camps and led to adversarial rather than consensual politics: in effect the zero-sum politics of Westminster which pre-treaty Sinn Féin had sought to avoid. This reduced the ability of the Dáil to carry out parliamentary scrutiny as deputies were reluctant to break ranks and obeyed the parliamentary whips whenever party politics dictated. Under the constitution, the Senate had a purely legislative role; it could delay but not prevent legislation being passed, had no control over finance bills and could not change the government.

In a parliamentary democracy governments are responsible to the people, who can vote them out of office at the next election, but some means of holding them accountable while they are in office is essential. Between 1922 and 1932 parliamentary questions were the most effective means of scrutiny as there were no Dáil committees with powers of enquiry apart from the public accounts committee, which belatedly examined revenue and expenditure. Dáil standing orders were modelled on Westminster and favoured the executive. A large volume of legislation was hastily enacted, especially in the early years. The Dáil had long recesses. Consequently, little time was left for examining the government's performance in detail and holding it accountable. Also, during the 1920s, the level of public awareness of government actions was low as newspaper reporting was partisan and poor.[16]

Private member's bills were a means of influencing government policy but only seven were passed between 1922 and 1932. The tribunal, a mechanism of ensuring government accountability, was used four times for prices (1928), grain (1929), marketing of butter and ports and harbours (1930). Proportional representation with the single transferable vote had been implemented before independence to protect minority rights, making it difficult for parties to win by large majorities—thereby in theory rendering them more accountable as they could easily lose office. But accountability in the Irish Free State between 1922 and 1932 was focused more on apportioning blame than on seeking to learn by experience.

The government was cautious about whom it employed and trusted, and civil servants were required to make a declaration of allegiance to the Irish Free State and its constitution. After the civil war the government did not relax its vigilance, although anti-treaty activist C.S. (Todd) Andrews later stated that it was less vindictive than expected.[17] In Dermot Keogh's view, 'the government showed scant willingness either to broaden or to deepen the scope of popular democracy in the country. It was a time to centralise power and remove any possibility of a recrudescence of armed subversion.'[18] In order to consolidate their position Cosgrave and his ministers changed the government and administration of the state from the loosely controlled decentralised British system to a tightly controlled centralised Irish system and curtailed the powers of the local authorities.

The Ministers and Secretaries Act 1924

The Ministers and Secretaries Act 1924 was one of the most significant pieces of legislation enacted and remains the bedrock of the status of ministers and the distribution of government functions. It implemented the constitution by defining the future government of the state and provided for eleven government departments, which replaced the Dáil ministries.

Under the act each minister became a 'corporation sole', in essence the personification of the department, and could sue and, with the permission of the attorney general, be sued. The term 'corporation sole' is not defined in the act, but its concept was already well known in law as it was closely associated with the monarch, who had a dual capacity, being both a natural person and a body politic. All orders and instructions issued by government departments were given in the name of the minister. Ministers passed responsibility for their departments to those succeeding them once they ceased to hold office. They delegated most of the work to officials in their departments. It had long been recognised in English law that powers vested in ministers could be exercised by responsible officials on their behalf, even without any express act of delegation. This was adopted, ensuring that in law the action of a civil servant is deemed to be that of the minister.

The act provided for a council of defence, powers of the executive with respect to statutory bodies and the appointment of parliamentary secretaries. It allowed considerable ministerial discretion and permitted delegated legislation which empowered ministers to make regulations and orders, and set enforcement dates. Delegated powers included amendment of acts of the Oireachtas where there was a mass of previous legislation. There were two safeguards: changes to acts had to be laid before the Oireachtas, and all orders and regulations published in *Iris Oifigiúil (Official Gazette)*. For some acts there was provision that public notices be inserted in newspapers or a requirement for preliminary consultation with designated bodies. Ministers were given extensive powers of enquiry and judicial functions could be delegated to departments and tribunals. There was a right to redress in the courts but the trend was towards final decisions being made by the executive, civil servants and tribunals. The President's Department was assigned responsibility for the government secretariat, certain public archives, official publications and administration of public services not under any other government department.

LOCAL GOVERNMENT

The system of local government in 1922 had been established under the Local Government (Ireland) Act 1898. It included a basic public health system which was administered by the Local Government Board (LGB) and the local authorities. After 1922 the government centralised control. Local authorities lost further power when agricultural rate rebates made them more dependent on central government for funding.

The first Dáil had in 1920 set up a ministry of local government under Cosgrave, which attempted to assume the functions of a central authority in order to undermine the British administration in Ireland. The LGB lost control of nationalist-dominated local authorities and its headquarters at the Custom House in Dublin was destroyed by the IRA in 1921. It withheld grants and a Dáil commission chaired by O'Higgins examined the problem of survival without support from the LGB. By the time the treaty was signed many local authorities were short of funds and unable to deliver services.

Cosgrave was appointed the first post-independence minister for local government and was succeeded by Ernest Blythe in August 1922. Blythe was replaced in turn by lawyer James Burke in September 1923. Burke was born near Roscrea, County Tipperary in 1893 and educated by the Jesuits at Clongowes Wood, and subsequently at Trinity College and King's Inns. He was imprisoned by the British during the war of independence and was subsequently elected unopposed to the Dáil. Burke was an external minister and was demoted to parliamentary secretary with responsibility for the Board of Works in 1927 to make way for the return of Richard Mulcahy to the executive as minister for local government. E.P. McCarron, a former LGB official, was controversially appointed secretary. He served until 1936, when he was dismissed due to a difference with his minister.[19]

The principal services delivered by local authorities in 1922 were those developed in a rudimentary manner during the nineteenth century and included public roads, highways, streets and footpaths; relief of the poor; care of the sick poor and housing of the working classes; control of infectious diseases, water supply, drainage, sewage, waste collection and disposal, street cleaning and lighting; enforcement of public health regulations; registration of births, marriages, deaths, voters and jurors; technical education, scholarships and public libraries; fire brigades; regulation of markets and fairs; and gas and electricity supply. The services were funded by rates, charges and grants from central government. Local authorities were responsible for reconstruction of war-damaged cities and towns. Capital projects undertaken in the 1920s were limited to essential work due to the shortage of money.

The Ministers and Secretaries Act 1924 assigned public services in connection with local government, public health, relief of the poor, care of the mentally ill, unemployment and health insurance, maintenance of public roads, elections and vital statistics to the local authorities and a renamed Department of Local Government and Public Health (Local Government). The government opted for a highly centralised state, in the belief that local authorities were corrupt and inefficient and because it was apprehensive that the anti-treaty side might use them as a base for opposition. The constitution made only incidental reference to local government. The constitution committee favoured centralisation and only one of the three drafts submitted recommended decentralised administration and regional autonomy. The Devlin report 1969 summed up the situation: 'local administration was brought unambiguously under the control of the new government. Thus was established a highly centralised system of both central and local government.' The Local Government (Temporary Provisions) Act 1923 gave the necessary powers to dissolve the smaller local bodies and extend the same level of tight central control to all local authorities as that which had existed over Poor Law guardians since 1838. The act also transferred all local government staff to the new department. Audits were conducted by local government auditors who were empowered to surcharge individuals responsible for any payments found to be illegal or unfounded. Their findings were published in public reports. This was initially a dangerous job and some auditors carried revolvers for their protection.

The civil war exacerbated an already difficult situation as local authorities had been severely disrupted during the war of independence and many failed to hold meetings. Rates were not collected so funds were not available for services, resulting in severe cutbacks and outsourcing. Labour Deputy Timothy Murphy stated in 1926 that 'secondary roads are getting worse and will be little better than goat tracks', towns were in a filthy condition, county homes and workhouses were cheerless and bare and more suitable food for elderly people needed to be provided.[20] The government evaded a difficult decision on rates, which were based on outdated mid-nineteenth-century valuations, by passing the Valuation (Postponement of Revision) Act 1923. An annual grant of £599,011 had been provided since the Local Government Act 1898 to compensate for the de-rating of agricultural land. It was in effect a subsidy to the agricultural industry. Funding from central government was reduced after 1922 but the local authorities still had to allow the rate rebates. As a result rates were increased. The level of de-rating was subsequently doubled under the Local Government (Rates on Agricultural Land) Act 1925 and the local authorities were compensated by a matching grant from central funds. The annual grant was increased by £750,000 in 1931, when rates were further rebated at a time of falling agricultural prices.

Local government reform
In line with pre-independence Sinn Féin thinking, the government sought to clear away the multiplicity of small local bodies at sub-county level. The first to go were the boards of guardians in 1923, followed by rural district councils, which were abolished under the Local Government Act 1925. County boards of health were given responsibility for the administration of public health. New and enlarged sanitary districts were created. The functions of rural district councils, mainly related to the maintenance of roads and sanitation, were transferred to the county councils.

The government took drastic action to gain control of local authorities using its powers to dissolve councils: first Kerry and Leitrim county councils and other local authorities, followed by Cork and Dublin city councils in 1924. The public acquiesced in this deprivation of its civic rights, perhaps because it occurred at a time of civil strife but also because there was little respect for local authorities. Twenty bodies were dissolved and replaced by government-appointed commissioners in the first three years of the state.[21] Most of the commissioners appointed were competent administrators, apolitical and amenable to central direction. While the displaced councillors were furious, ratepayers welcomed the commissioners because they ran the councils economically.[22] After centralising control, Local Government gave direction to local authorities, provided a large portion of their funding, decided on accounting methods and maintained a veto over borrowings, appointments, salaries and pensions. This built on the systems of inspection and audit implemented during the nineteenth century in the quest for efficiency and uniformity.

The most significant long-term change was made in city and county management. Reform of city government was advocated by solicitor John J. Horgan in 1920.[23] He founded a civic reform body, the Cork Progressive Association, which helped bring about the dissolution of Cork City Council. The Cork City Management Act 1929 was passed despite Labour Party objections and Fianna Fáil criticisms. It reduced the number of councillors from 56 to 21 and became the prototype for Irish city and county management. The act set out precisely the reserved powers of the elected members. These included setting the rate, borrowing, legislation and elections. It specified that the city manager was to be an officer of the corporation, appointed but not selected by the members, who would prepare the city budget, attend council meetings, and take part in discussions but not vote. The Local Government (Dublin) Act 1930 was passed despite strong resistance and Dublin Borough Council was restored with its members reduced from 86 to 35.

The first two city managers had contrasting styles. Philip Monahan in Cork was autocratic and often clashed with the council, while Gerald Sherlock in Dublin left decisions to the council and its committees and operated more like a town clerk. Monahan was an ex-schoolteacher who had been imprisoned at Frongoch and Lincoln after the 1916 rising, was subsequently elected mayor of Drogheda in 1920 and was appointed commissioner in Kerry in 1923. Kerry was a turbulent county during the civil war and minister Ernest Blythe was reluctant to appoint a Dáil deputy as commissioner for fear he would be shot. Monahan was paid a salary of £130 a month and given a car and a revolver. He quickly established a reputation by making hard decisions, collecting outstanding rates and reducing wages and pensions.[24]

Minister James Burke then appointed Monahan as commissioner for Cork City in October 1924. He initiated a tough regime and described the corporation as 'not an institution for relief of unemployment, it is not a waiting room for the old age pension, it is a business concern, to be run on business lines, with a definite programme of work to be done in a definite period of time, and for a definite amount of money'.[25] Monahan promised the citizens he would communicate with them through the *Cork Examiner*, stopped the lord mayor's salary as there was no longer a council, walked around the city to see what was happening, laid off surplus staff, cut wages, introduced electric cleaning trucks, borrowed money to asphalt the main streets and considered using the compensation money for the city hall to build 150 new houses (British forces had destroyed Cork city hall by fire in December 1920).[26]

In March 1929 Monahan was appointed city manager. He was to be the model for future city and county managers. It was a lonely job as his power was deeply resented by many politicians—but he delivered results, in contrast to the former inefficient corporation. He restored solvency, enhanced services, supported industrial development, built houses, reduced the rates and introduced differential rents for local authority tenants.[27] Vice-president Ernest Blythe announced a reform of county government in 1931, under which the number of councillors would be radically reduced and managers appointed.

The Electoral Act 1923 provided for a universal franchise over 21 years (30 for Senate elections) and the Prevention of Electoral Abuses Act 1923 legislated against corrupt and illegal practices. Local elections were postponed during the civil war by the Local Government (Postponement of Elections) Act 1922, the first of a number of deferrals before elections were held in 1925. There were fewer electors in local elections as they were confined to owners or tenants of premises (1 million in 1929 compared with around 1.7 million at general elections).[28] Local authorities were obliged to adopt the Public Libraries Act 1855 and provide more comprehensive services in 1926. The Tourist Traffic (Development) Act 1932 empowered local authorities to contribute to government-approved tourism companies.

Reformatories and industrial schools were transferred from Local Government to the Department of Education in 1922. The administration of technical education remained the responsibility of the county technical instruction committees set up under the Agriculture and Technical Instruction Act 1899. After 1922 technical education was funded from the rates levy and a grant from Education.

The Local Appointments Commission

The Local Authorities (Officers and Employees) Act 1926 provided for a Local Appointments Commission with the duty of selecting and recommending to local authorities suitable persons for appointment to senior posts. This was in line with the pre-treaty Sinn Féin policy of implementing a fair employment code. The local authority was required to appoint the candidate recommended (or one of the candidates, if more than one was put forward). This mode of selection was to become an integral part of the machinery of local administration.

The Commission was a major challenge to politicians, clergy and local dignitaries who had traditionally influenced appointments. They were indignant that boards of independent assessors might evaluate candidates on their professional merits rather than on who they were or who they knew.[29] The backlash came when the Commission, after interview, nominated Letitia Dunbar Harrison, a Protestant graduate of Trinity College, for the post of Mayo county librarian in 1930. The county council refused to sanction the appointment on the grounds that her knowledge of Irish was inadequate, whereupon the government dissolved the council and appointed a commissioner. Local politicians together with the Catholic clergy, led by Dean D.A. D'Alton of Tuam, supported another candidate, Ellen Burke, on various grounds including her knowledge of Irish.[30]

The routine appointment of a county librarian soon escalated into a conflict with national consequences. It pitted church against state, Mayo County Council against Local Government and members of Cumann na nGaedheal against each other. The Local Appointments Commission was accused of corruption. Cosgrave sent Sir Joseph Glynn, head of the National Insurance Commission, to investigate, and he found that Ellen Burke had been rejected by two interview boards and had failed two Irish tests. Fianna Fáil focused on Harrison's lack of Irish in a 'Gaeltacht' county rather than her religion and university. A boycott of most of the library services, which largely depended on voluntary workers, was organised at the behest of the clergy, county councillors, Irish-language enthusiasts and opponents of the government, who demanded that appointments be made locally. Members of the Mayo Vocational Education Committee boycotted meetings, resulting in technical teachers not being paid as their salaries were not authorised.[31] In January 1932, Harrison was transferred to the Department of Defence 'in the national interest'.[32] Another librarian, a Catholic, was appointed in October on the recommendation of the Local Appointments Commission.

The centralisation of local government
Ruth Barrington states that the Cosgrave governments set out to achieve greater efficiency, economy and honesty in local government in conformity with pre-treaty Sinn Féin ideas on how local authorities ought to conduct their affairs having regard to prudent fiscal policy.[33] In its special report in 1931, Local Government pointed to its achievements in improving housing, roads and sewage services. Efforts were being made to move non-geriatric patients out of county homes to other institutions. County medical officers of health had been appointed in 15 counties and major bills had been introduced for housing, traffic, local bodies' planning powers and redistribution of Dáil seats.[34] Economies were sought and initiatives on mutual insurance and combined purchasing had been commenced. Improved fire regulations were needed. This was demonstrated forcibly when 48 people died in a cinema fire at Drumcollogher, County Limerick, in 1926.[35]

After independence there had been an opportunity to change local government from the British system to one closer to the continental model, with services delivered by smaller local authorities more responsive to the needs of the public. A national health system might have been initiated if the government had taken over the voluntary sector and used a combination of the sweepstakes, national health insurance, benefit and friendly society contributions, direct billing and private health insurance to fund it. But shortage of money and an unwillingness to antagonise the Catholic Church, which viewed government intervention in the health sector with suspicion, prevented any major reforms. Instead, a combination of political, fiscal and security imperatives led to greater centralisation of local government, insufficient investment in social housing and few radical changes in healthcare; and opportunities for reform were lost.

Pre-treaty Sinn Féin had focused on achieving independence without working out what kind of value system should follow. The Irish Party had envisaged a highly centralised administration, understanding that public spending would have to be sharply reduced and that British standards of social provision could not be funded. T.J. Barrington has argued that central government should concentrate on the great affairs of state and leave detailed administration to subordinate authorities which people have a say in electing. But, in the troubled conditions of the civil war, the government had to take a hard line against local authorities which refused to strike rates and failed to deliver services. Centralisation suited Dáil deputies who fostered the idea that constituents would not get their rights without representation. It also satisfied the civil servants in Finance who wished to maximise control over expenditure.[36] Cumann na nGaedheal and Fianna Fáil were both against local autonomy so no radical reform of the system took place. De-rating agricultural land reduced the ability of local authorities to raise money directly and made them more dependent on government block grants, although a majority of the commission of inquiry into de-rating of land found that no general breakdown in the agricultural industry would arise if relief from rates was not granted. The end result was that local authorities were funded largely from, and therefore tightly controlled by, central government.

Chapter 6 ∿

| IRELAND AND THE WORLD

INTRODUCTION

After independence, a large part of Irish foreign policy was concerned with a readjustment of relations with Britain. As the Irish Free State wished to demonstrate its sovereignty and prove its independence, it had to build relationships with other states and raise Ireland's profile on the world stage. At the same time, the British Commonwealth was evolving as the dominions sought more independence and a new relationship with Westminster. Consequently, much of the Irish Free State's readjustment of its relationship with Britain between 1922 and 1932 took place in the context of the Commonwealth rather than in a bilateral sense.[1]

THE DEPARTMENT OF EXTERNAL AFFAIRS

The objective of the Irish Free State diplomatic service was to cultivate and instruct worldwide public opinion so that the independence of the state might be safeguarded at times of international crisis. The Department of External Affairs was set up under the Ministers and Secretaries Act 1924 to advise the government on international relations, co-ordinate policies of all branches of government in international matters, manage diplomatic and consular representation, negotiate treaties and conventions, promote foreign trade, disseminate information, process passports and visas and handle issues such as protocol and state visits. The need for the department was not recognised by all and in the Dáil debate Darrell Figgis suggested that it could be 'dispensed with at the present time'.[2]

The international background against which External Affairs operated during the 1920s was a complex one. Around sixteen million people died during World War I, while the 'Spanish flu' in its aftermath resulted in over 50 million fatalities worldwide. After the war some ethnic groups freed themselves from imperial rule and turned on smaller ethnic and religious minorities. In Germany the Weimar governments lurched from crisis to crisis. Stalin was consolidating his power in Russia. The new nations which arose from the remains of the old empires found it hard to progress in difficult economic times. Britain and France struggled but remained politically stable. The US did not join the League of Nations and retreated into isolationism. After the Wall Street crash in 1929 international trade collapsed and unemployment increased, leading to social chaos. Japan invaded Manchuria in 1931 in quest of raw materials and markets, re-starting the cycle of violence.[3]

From 1922 onwards the main Irish diplomatic focus was on Britain out of necessity, on the League of Nations as a means of increasing sovereignty and international status, on the US to gain recognition from the most powerful state in the world, and on the Vatican to legitimise the state and to counter anti-treaty and British influence in Rome. Sovereignty and partition were the key foreign policy issues: sovereignty as unity had been lost, partition because it remained the greatest political challenge.[4]

Michael Collins adopted a 'stepping stone' approach, believing that further concessions on sovereignty could be won as the state became established and strengthened its bargaining position. Journalist Desmond FitzGerald was appointed Foreign Affairs Minister in August 1922. Born of Irish parents in London in 1888, he worked as a clerk before going to live in France and subsequently moved to Kerry. He joined the IRB and the Irish Volunteers, participated in the 1916 rising and served as Dáil director of publicity before and after the treaty. Joseph Walshe, who had represented the second Dáil in Paris, was appointed acting secretary of the department. Born in 1886 at Killenaule, County Tipperary, Walshe was educated by the Jesuits at Mungret and Gemert in the Netherlands. He returned to Ireland in 1910, taught languages at Clongowes Wood and qualified as a solicitor.[5] Seán Lester, a former editor of the *Freeman's Journal*, took charge of propaganda and later had a distinguished career at the League of Nations, from which he retired as secretary-general after World War II.

Diplomats not loyal to the state in the aftermath of the treaty were dismissed and the government took steps to counter the actions of anti-treaty activists in the US and Australia. Politicians and the press attacked the department for too much and too little diplomatic activity. Farmers Party leader D.J. Gorey stated, 'We are concerned with no foreign affairs', while the *Freeman's Journal* accused the government of having a colonial mentality by allowing the British to make its treaties.[6]

The small Irish Free State diplomatic service was essentially a symbol of independence and sovereignty in the international arena. The British disapproved of Commonwealth countries pursuing independent foreign policies or developing their own diplomatic services. Although state correspondence with Britain was channelled through the governor-general, the British found it easier to deal directly with Cosgrave, thus threatening the independent existence of External Affairs. However, being preoccupied with domestic matters, Cosgrave did not involve himself in foreign relations and left them to Vice-president Kevin O'Higgins and Ministers Desmond FitzGerald (1922–27) and Patrick McGilligan (1927–32). McGilligan, a native of Coleraine, County Derry, and the son of an Irish Party MP, was educated at St Columb's College, Clongowes Wood and UCD, where he became Assistant Professor of Latin in 1918. He qualified as a barrister in 1921, and served as secretary to O'Higgins and James MacNeill before being elected to the Dáil in 1923. From 1927 to 1932 he held the portfolios of both External Affairs and Industry and Commerce.

External Affairs inherited nothing from the old British administration and had to be built up using staff who did not always have the necessary linguistic, administrative or diplomatic skills. Walshe played a major role in organising and directing it, supported by FitzGerald, but External Affairs had to fight hard for resources and equality of recognition with other government departments. In late 1922 diplomats were despatched to Geneva (the League of Nations), London, Washington, Paris and Rome. Representatives were appointed in Brussels, Berlin, Rotterdam, Santiago and New York in 1923–24.

The Irish Free State quickly achieved international recognition. Walshe was promoted to secretary in August 1927, a position he held until 1945. He argued that External Affairs was cheap at £53,000 per annum and that Norway, Sweden, Finland, Denmark and Cuba spent more.[7] McGilligan, who was one of the main driving forces in the government after the death of O'Higgins, convinced it to expand the department, upgrade the quality of its staff and extend its representation. Among those recruited were Frederick Boland and John Hearne, who later played major roles in Irish diplomacy.

By 1932 External Affairs had the nucleus of a strong, independent-minded, apolitical diplomatic service committed to the state. Considerable advances had been made despite opposition from the British, the anti-treaty side, some of the Irish in America, a few bishops and the Irish College in Rome. Walshe made a significant contribution to the development of the department, although his preference for verbal communications means that the extent of his input into policy formation cannot be fully assessed, as he submitted few proposals in writing.[8]

The Eucharistic Congress, a major international religious gathering, was planned for 1932 and Cosgrave, being unwilling to politicise it, foolishly held the election earlier than necessary, thereby losing an opportunity to gain badly needed votes and presenting de Valera with an early triumph.

THE LEAGUE OF NATIONS

Cosgrave decided to seek admission to the League in 1923 and the Irish Free State's case was prepared by North-Eastern Boundary Bureau staff Kevin O'Shiel and Bolton Waller. The advantages of joining the

League, set out in a memorandum written by Waller, were to improve security, gain influence in world affairs, share in the League's co-operative activities and promote world peace.[9] Michael MacWhite was appointed Irish delegate. Born at Reenogreena, west Cork, in 1883, he first met Arthur Griffith in 1900, after which he travelled extensively in central Europe, Scandinavia and western Russia. Following a period in Denmark studying agriculture and co-operatives, he set up Sinn Féin branches in west Cork. He covered the first Balkan War as a war correspondent, joined the French Foreign Legion in 1913 and fought at Arras, Gallipoli and Macedonia, winning the Croix de Guerre on three occasions. MacWhite was also a member of a French military mission to the US seeking the fourth liberty loan. A brilliant linguist who spoke seven languages, he was instructed to make the Irish Free State's application quietly without advising the British, and the Irish were unanimously admitted to the League on 10 September 1923. The matter was largely unnoticed at home as Irish newspapers paid little attention to the League. Joining it was an important step as Irish independence was thereafter effectively guaranteed by its 53 members and as a result Ireland was no longer isolated, in the words of a French diplomat, 'an island behind an island'.[10]

The government registered the treaty as an international agreement with the League on 11 July 1924 against British wishes and subsequently registered the settlement of the boundary dispute in 1925.[11] The British strongly objected to agreements between Britain and the dominions being brought into the international domain, contending that they were internal Commonwealth matters. The registration of the treaty as an international agreement reinforced the Irish Free State's position within the League and the Commonwealth. The Irish made little impact initially at Geneva as the government was preoccupied with the army mutiny and the boundary commission. However, in 1926 Ireland stood for election to the League council, making a late application. While it was unsuccessful, it gained good, but not British, support. British Foreign Secretary Austen Chamberlain stated in 1927 that Britain would represent the Commonwealth on the League council as it had a permanent seat; the dominions could continue to represent themselves in the League assembly, where each of them had a seat. This prompted the dominions to seek a non-permanent seat on the League council and Canada, the senior dominion, was successful.

The Irish Free State offered 'critical support' for the League, backing its general aims but reserving the right to criticise aspects it did not approve. It sent representatives to conferences and ratified protocols and conventions including those on obscene publications, gas and opium. But the Irish interest in the League was predominantly as a means of demonstrating sovereignty. They participated more actively after 1928, paradoxically because McGilligan became preoccupied with domestic affairs and League representative Seán Lester was given freedom of action. The Irish gained a seat on the League council in 1930.

THE BOUNDARY COMMISSION

Partition had psychological as well as political implications. After independence, Northern Ireland came to be seen as a different, even foreign, place and that made partition appear more tolerable to some, while others saw Ulster as the main repository of the Gaelic past and an integral part of the Irish nation. Partition made the achievement of greater sovereignty more urgent and led to the focus being shifted from unity and supporting northern nationalists to maximising the freedom of the Irish Free State.

In *The Irish Free State and its Senate*, Donal O'Sullivan asked if the British tricked the Irish during the treaty negotiations or whether they subsequently changed their minds regarding the boundary commission. It is possible the British were genuine in 1921 when they were under pressure to achieve a settlement. However, there was a succession of different governments in London in the years following the treaty which were loath to re-open the Irish question by allowing a substantial transfer of territory.[12] The prime ministers who succeeded Lloyd George were less committed to Irish unity. Andrew Bonar Law, a Canadian of Ulster descent, sided with the Northern Ireland government while Stanley Baldwin and James Ramsay MacDonald had little interest in Irish affairs and each had a degree of anti-Catholic prejudice.[13]

The British tried to delay the boundary commission for as long as possible. Northern Ireland Prime Minister James Craig adopted a 'what we have, we hold' policy and blocked progress. The Irish treaty signatories had accepted the boundary commission as part of a package of measures, one of which was that the Northern Ireland government would not gain financially if it opted out of joining with the Irish Free State. But the British subsequently conceded most of the financial demands made by Craig, and the Colwyn commission gave him nearly everything he wanted. This enabled him to overcome financial pressure and began the subsidisation of Northern Ireland by Britain. The Irish protested but were ambivalent as they saw the treatment of Northern Ireland as a precedent which could be used when negotiating their own financial settlement.

While a plebiscite might have been the fairest way to resolve the boundary issue, most of the minority population in Northern Ireland was not located in easily detachable blocks of territory. Where possibilities for readjustment existed they were situated in the poorest parts of Northern Ireland and their loss would leave the rest of the northeast better off and less likely to favour unification. Moreover, the sizable nationalist minority in Belfast, which would have been outvoted in a plebiscite, was apprehensive that a loss of territory and population to the Irish Free State would copperfasten unionist dominance and make eventual unity even less possible. Craig ended proportional representation (PR) in local elections in order to weaken the northern nationalists' case prior to the boundary commission, as they lost seats under the straight vote system while the nationalists damaged their cause by boycotting an election. The loss of PR and local government gerrymandering made northern nationalists politically impotent. The control of councils and the special police were to be Craig's trump cards.

The treaty stipulated that if the boundary clause was triggered by the Northern Ireland government's refusal to unite with the Irish Free State, the border of Northern Ireland would be determined by a commission 'in accordance with the wishes of the inhabitants, in so far as may be compatible with economic and geographic conditions'. The Irish treaty negotiators appear to have envisaged one-way transfers of land, making Northern Ireland's survival impossible, disregarding the reference to economic and geographic conditions. The Northern Ireland government stated that 'not an inch' would be conceded. The British government wished to keep Ireland out of its internal politics and after 1922 did not allow questions on Northern Ireland at Westminster. But by late 1924 they reluctantly began to advance the boundary commission, fearing the Irish might involve the League of Nations. The Irish also wished to achieve closure and were concerned that an incident on the border precipitated by a fool or an *agent provocateur* could derail the process.[14] Cosgrave was under pressure to get the boundary commission under way as there was a risk that soldiers demobilised after the civil war might be encouraged to take action against Northern Ireland.

After the death of Collins, Irish Free State policy towards Northern Ireland had changed dramatically from trying to undermine it to a 'pacific and friendly disposition' in advance of the boundary commission to 'put ourselves right in the eyes of any impartial arbitrator'.[15] The North-Eastern Boundary Bureau was set up to carry out research and publicity. Its head, Kevin O'Shiel, concluded that the best case scenario would be a plebiscite and the worst a round table conference in private, which was the approach adopted by the commission.[16] In 1923 the government was concerned that the northern nationalists were 'disorganised and apathetic', that unionists were 'prejudiced against the Free State' but that economic union was 'universally desired'.[17]

Kevin O'Higgins realised that 1 million people of a different tradition, almost a quarter of the island's population, could not be forced into the Irish Free State and put forward a proposal that the two parliaments sit together; an all-Ireland authority be set up to meet alternately in Dublin and Belfast; joint customs, excise, income tax (imposition but not necessarily collection) and fisheries be controlled by the all-Ireland authority; the governor-general be appointed alternately by the two governments; the customs barrier ended; proportional representation restored; gerrymandering abandoned; the special police in Northern Ireland disbanded; the northern minority to enter the Northern Ireland parliament; and a minor alteration of the border or Northern Ireland to be the nine counties of Ulster.[18] The latter option was acceptable neither to most of the inhabitants of Cavan, Donegal and Monaghan, nor to the Ulster unionists, as the nationalist and unionist populations of a nine-county Ulster would be almost equal and the unionists risked losing their dominant position. This proposal was later amended to a federal solution with a subordinate parliament in Belfast, a new, partially elected council of Ireland and a central assembly with safeguards.[19] It got nowhere and was the last serious attempt to end partition. Attorney General John A. Costello later stated that O'Higgins, having nearly completely established the internal structure of the state and building of the rule of law, could have devoted 'his matchless talents and indomitable courage to finding a solution for the problem of partition'.[20] He was murdered before he could do so.

Craig opposed the boundary commission, while the British feared the Irish would declare a republic if the commission went against them and resolved to blockade Ireland rather than declare war as their troops were committed in Egypt and Iraq. They selected a Welshman, Richard Feetham, who was a South African supreme court judge, as chairman of the commission. He was an odd choice for a Labour government, being an imperialist with Tory links. The Irish Free State nominated Eoin MacNeill. Craig refused to nominate anyone so the British appointed J.R. Fisher, a close friend of Craig, to represent Northern Ireland. Fisher's objective was to bring Irish Free State Protestants living along the border into Northern Ireland. MacNeill accepted the job because nobody else wanted it and described it as the 'most disagreeable duty ever undertaken'.[21] He approached the task from a judicial viewpoint while Feetham and Fisher focused on the political dimension. Feetham was warned by Craig that any major transfer of territory would have disastrous consequences for the peace of the UK as unionists would fight to retain their new state. The fact that the principal negotiators of the treaty on both sides were no longer in government was a disadvantage for the Irish Free State. Collins and Griffith were dead and Lloyd George had lost office. Lord Birkenhead and Churchill were steadfastly against any concession of territory, while the Labour government had no interest in promoting Irish unity.

Northern Ireland and its border with the Irish Free State had been insoluble problems for the treaty negotiators and they had left them in abeyance in the hope that a resolution could be achieved at a later date. But as time elapsed, Northern Ireland become more permanent, making any change difficult. Northern nationalists living along the border had hopes of reunification; many people in the Irish Free State had unrealistic expectations, while the government hoped it might somehow claw back sufficient territory to render Northern Ireland nonviable.

The commissioners met for the first time in November 1924. Feetham interpreted the economic and geographic conditions as limiting the boundary changes to ones that would not interfere with the economic hinterlands of local towns. Their adjudication, which was by majority vote, transferred part of south Armagh to the Irish Free State but unexpectedly put portions of east Donegal and north Monaghan into Northern Ireland.

MacNeill naïvely adhered to the pledge to maintain secrecy, so Cosgrave was surprised when the result was leaked to the press, while Fisher had kept Craig informed. After the leak, MacNeill resigned from the commission in November 1925 and the Northern Ireland government pressed for implementation and publication of the report. Craig was willing to accept either the award or the existing boundary. Cosgrave did not want publication as his government could have fallen. He had two choices: accept the award or keep the existing border. As the former would have been political suicide, he had no option but to reluctantly accept the latter. The British wanted the issue resolved and entered into negotiations with both sides. Craig insisted on scrapping the council of Ireland but agreed not to publish the report. He got financial concessions and a subsidy towards the cost of social services but not the parity with Britain he sought, and was forced to disband the A (full-time) and C-1 (part-time) special police. However, he retained the B Specials, which were the most resented by northern nationalists.[22]

The Treaty (Confirmation of Amending Agreement) Act 1925 confirmed the existing boundaries of Northern Ireland; released the Irish Free State from its financial obligations under article 5 of the treaty; freed the British from liability for malicious damage done since 21 January 1919; increased compensation within the Irish Free State for malicious damage done between 11 July 1921 and 12 May 1923; and transferred the powers of the council of Ireland in relation to Northern Ireland to its government. It also provided that the governments of the Irish Free State and Northern Ireland 'shall meet together as and when necessary for the purpose of considering matters of common interest arising out of or connected with the exercise and administration of said powers'.

There were no further meetings between Cosgrave and Craig after the boundary commission and a hands-off approach was adopted by the Irish Free State towards Northern Ireland, army intelligence (G2) alone keeping an eye on security matters there. However, Eamonn Duggan, Parliamentary Secretary to the President, travelled to Belfast in April 1926 and had 'a very useful talk' with Minister for Finance Hugh Pollock, the only such visit by an Irish minister until the Lemass/O'Neill meeting four decades later.[23] Border issues became less contentious and, apart from smuggling, were mainly confined to police requests to cross the border to gain access to isolated places in each other's jurisdiction. Cross-border co-operation was nonetheless minimal and limited to tourism, animal diseases, electricity and the related drainage of Lough Erne.

A significant consequence of the boundary commission was the feeling of helplessness by the anti-treaty side, which had been unable to influence events because its deputies abstained from attending the Dáil. Many of them began to consider ending abstention if the oath could be removed. This was a major contributory factor to the split in Sinn Féin and the founding of Fianna Fáil in 1926. Another fall-out from the boundary commission was the formation of a new party, Clann Éireann, by William Magennis in conjunction with two other Cumann na nGaedheal Dáil deputies and a senator. The deputies lost their seats in the June 1927 election.

THE GOVERNOR-GENERAL
The governor-general was the king's representative in the Irish Free State and the official channel of communication between the Irish

and British governments. He had very limited powers, was not a viceroy and was amenable to Irish civil and criminal law. He was paid by the Irish Free State and could be removed by it at any time, while the king he represented was a constitutional monarch who reigned but did not govern.

Although the governor-general was a figurehead, his office was a political embarrassment to the government. Collins tried to downgrade it in the draft constitution but the British apparently insisted on the strict implementation of the treaty. Normally the British appointed noblemen or diplomats as dominion governors-general. The Irish executive shrewdly nominated Tim Healy for the position. Healy, who was suggested by his nephew O'Higgins, was an eminent lawyer and controversial nationalist politician who had played a major part in the downfall of Parnell, opposed the reunited Irish Party, retired from active politics in 1918 and forged links with Sinn Féin leaders. He was one of the few nationalists acceptable to the British and after some hesitation they agreed to his appointment and offered him a seat on the privy council, which he declined. This was a modest but important coup for the Irish Free State since it established a precedent: no dominion had previously nominated its own governor-general. Anti-treaty and left-wing critics objected to Healy's appointment while unionists were not convinced he was a suitable representative of the king. Lord Oranmore recalled that Parnell had described him as a 'guttersnipe', but to the general public Healy was preferable to anyone the British might have nominated. He allayed concern in London over the protraction of the civil war and used his connection with Lord Beaverbrook to write articles in the *Daily Express* supporting the government, stating in July 1923, 'The Free State is established definitely, despite the internal assaults that have been made on it.'[24]

Healy was treated courteously by Cosgrave, who nevertheless bypassed him and dealt directly with the British. The governor-general entertained at the viceregal lodge in the Phoenix Park, where he was obliged to live against his wishes for security reasons, and attended public events like the Dublin horse show and race meetings. The *Irish Times* commented on his death in 1931 that 'he, perhaps, more than any other man, helped to allay the fears of the ex-unionists'.[25] Healy signed bills passed by the Oireachtas and in theory had the power to reserve them for the king's pleasure, but this power was circumscribed as the Irish Free State was equated with Canada, where reservation was already a dead letter. Additionally, unlike in Canada, the Irish Free State government could not be refused if it wished to dissolve the Dáil. Healy reserved no bills, but questioned the Public Safety (Emergency Powers) (No. 2) Bill 1923 on the grounds that it suspended an article of the constitution and the Intoxicating Liquor Bill 1923 as the Dáil had been dissolved. Confronted by O'Higgins on the first, and by an opinion of the attorney general and a decision of the executive on the second, he relented.

By the mid-1920s Healy began to make political speeches and partisan statements, some of which embarrassed the government, leading to a decision to limit his term to five years. This angered him, as he believed he held office for life, but he went quietly on 31 January 1928.[26] He was replaced by James MacNeill, a former Indian civil servant and chairman of Dublin County Council who had been the first Irish high commissioner in London. The British made no suggestion regarding the appointment. While the governor-general was in place, the British had no diplomatic representation in Dublin. De Valera subsequently forced MacNeill out of office prematurely in 1932, replaced him with Dómhnall Ó Buachalla and downgraded the office by stripping away its functions. He seized the opportunity afforded by the abdication of Edward VIII in 1936 to abolish the office.

APPEALS TO THE PRIVY COUNCIL

Appeals to the privy council in London were a contentious issue after 1922. The judicial committee of the privy council nominally advised the crown on legal matters. But in reality it was a court selected by the lord chancellor, who was a politician and member of the British government, and consequently not an objective body. The Irish considered it to be a useless and undesirable court. The dominions disliked it due to its ignorance of their legislation. The British justified the retention of appeals to the privy council as a guarantee of minority rights. They were keen on Irish Free State participation and asked the Irish to nominate a judge. The government refused as its policy was to end appeals or render the appeal system ineffectual.[27] It negated privy council decisions by enacting legislation, negotiating with plaintiffs and refusing to implement the council's judgements.

The Irish raised the privy council at the 1926 and 1930 imperial conferences. Minister for Finance Ernest Blythe stated in late 1929 that 'an appeal to the Privy Council was really dead' and the government was not likely to be troubled with it in the future.[28] The British felt they might not be able to get a law ending appeals through Westminster but made a statement in 1930 that 'It was no part of the policy of His Majesty's Government in Great Britain that questions affecting judicial appeals should be determined otherwise than in accordance with the wishes of the part of the Empire primarily affected.'[29] A bill to abolish appeals was being prepared in 1931 before Cumann na nGaedheal lost office. Fianna Fáil enacted the necessary legislation in 1933.

THE IMPERIAL CONFERENCES

Relations between the Irish Free State and Britain were fraught with difficulty after partition and the treaty. The civil war poisoned Anglo-Irish relations as well as Irish political life, a fact that British politicians failed to understand. World War I and its aftermath fundamentally changed relations between Britain and the dominions, which were keen to be formally recognised as Britain's equals rather than her subordinates. The Irish Free State, preoccupied with the civil war, made little impact at the 1923 imperial conference, which declared that the 'views and conclusions on Foreign Policy (were) necessarily subject to the action of the Governments and Parliaments of the various portions of the Empire'. In essence this meant that the dominions had gained autonomy in external affairs, ending the common imperial foreign policy. The Irish, South Africans and Canadians sought a clearer recognition of that autonomy.[30] British Foreign Secretary Austen Chamberlain stated in 1925 that dominions 'take their actions freely and we make no pretension to bind them'.[31]

O'Higgins sought to advance the concept of the Irish Free State as a distinct entity at the 1926 imperial conference and get a clear definition of dominion autonomy. He was the only Irish minister interested in the evolution of the dominions, perhaps because he saw it as a means to achieve Irish unity. The Balfour declaration issued after the conference stated that the

> dominions were autonomous Communities within the British Empire, equal in status, in no way subordinate one to the other in any aspect of their dominion or external affairs, though united by a common allegiance to the Crown, and freely associated as members of the British Commonwealth of Nations.

British laws were to apply only if dominions consented, and dominions had power to make laws having extra-territorial operation and could repeal existing laws. The king would in future only act on the advice of the ministers of the dominion concerned. This was an attempt by Britain to keep the dominions in the Commonwealth. At O'Higgins' suggestion, the king's title was changed in the Royal and Parliamentary Titles Act 1927 to 'king of Great Britain, Ireland, the Dominions, and of other realms beyond the Seas'. The insertion of the 'O'Higgins comma' indicated that the monarch was king of Ireland in a separate capacity to being king of Great Britain, thereby facilitating his removal at a future date.[32]

Prior to the 1930 imperial conference the British decided to repeal the Colonial Laws Validity Act 1865 with regard to the dominions, the right of the governor-general to reserve assent and to remove anything inconsistent with equality.[33] At the conference, the Irish delegates took the most aggressive line. The main issues for debate were *inter se*, the privy council, defence and treaties.

The doctrine of *inter se* (between themselves) was fundamental to preserving the Commonwealth. It was designed to protect intra-Commonwealth relations which had been threatened when the dominions entered the international arena. Britain and the dominions could not engage in the full range of relationships open to sovereign states as certain matters needed to be resolved within the Commonwealth framework. *Inter se* asserted that just as the king was one person, the crown was indivisible. But after the Balfour declaration the monarch in effect had become king of each of the dominions and the Irish promoted the multiple kingships concept. *Inter se* also had ramifications for preferential tariffs, common nationality and diplomatic unity, and prevented intra-Commonwealth disputes being heard by international bodies like the League of Nations council or the permanent court of international justice.

Inter se worked while all the dominions were in agreement with Britain. The Irish took a number of actions which undermined it. They established the precedent of a dominion selecting its governor-general in 1922, registered the treaty with the League of Nations in 1924, and in 1929 independently accepted the optional clause of the permanent court of international justice without any reservation as to intra-Commonwealth disputes. The Irish agreed with South African Prime Minister J.B.M. Hertzog, who wanted the right to secede from the Commonwealth, on the need to eliminate *inter se*, allow the dominion high commissioners direct access to the king, change the status of citizenship and end the practice of the British making treaties on behalf of the dominions.

South Africa wanted a Commonwealth court to replace the privy council but the Irish were not interested.[34] With regard to the Colonial Laws Validity Act, McGilligan, speaking in the Dáil on 16 July 1931, stated that its repeal was 'absolute and unconditional' as far as the Irish Free State and other members of the Commonwealth were concerned. It remained on the statute book solely for British colonies and dependencies.[35]

The Irish did not become involved in a system of joint defence of the two islands, proposed by the British, for political and financial reasons.

Treaties were a crucial symbol of independence and the Irish began to query the signing of international treaties by the British on behalf of the dominions without consultation. The Irish had not signed the Locarno pact and had reservations about ratifying the Lausanne treaty.[36] Darrell Figgis objected to treaties signed by the British in the name of Ireland before the Dáil had any say on the matter.[37] However, treaties were an area where extreme caution was needed. The Irish had inherited most favoured nation status with regard to trade with almost every country in the world. They had to be careful as the terms negotiated under a new treaty might not be as favourable as those currently enjoyed. The Irish attended the Geneva Naval Conference in 1927, despite having no navy, asserting their right to demonstrate sovereignty. They were the last to ratify the naval treaty, which was an attempt to strengthen the Kellogg-Briand pact, doing so under pressure from the US. The government considered using the great seal of the Irish Free State on the ratification but put it off until the next treaty. It had objected to the great seal of the realm being used in treaties and had commissioned its own seal. The changeover to an Irish seal was later seen by constitutional lawyer Arthur Berridale Keith as the 'most decisive step towards the termination of the diplomatic unity of the Empire'.[38] The trade treaty with Portugal was the first occasion where the Irish made a direct approach to the king, bypassing his ministers, when McGilligan met him on 19 March 1931.

Significant changes were made at the 1930 imperial conference and the Statute of Westminster 1931 gave legal effect to them. The statute effectively marked the end of the British Empire. In future dominions were to be freely associated with Britain in the British Commonwealth and could do as they pleased without British interference. The dominions accepted the statute to the extent that they wanted freedom. The Irish and South Africans alone accepted it without reservation. Winston Churchill complained that the statute would allow the Irish Free State to abolish the oath and appeals to the privy council.[39] Cosgrave wrote to British Prime Minister Stanley Baldwin, pointing out that the treaty could be altered by consent as it was an agreement between two sovereign governments, and cautioned against drawing up legislation to safeguard it. Baldwin subsequently warned the House of Commons that it was not only the Irish they were dealing with: the other dominions were jealous of their status and any action taken could also offend them. The statute received the royal assent on 11 December 1931. While it did not give the Irish everything they wanted, it gave them the freedom to implement the actions taken subsequently when the oath, the governor-general, appeals to the privy council and the Senate were abolished: the constitution was replaced in 1937, while the state remained neutral during World War II and seceded from the Commonwealth in 1949.

DEMONSTRATING SOVEREIGNTY

After the civil war, the government wished to upgrade its representation in Washington to the level of minister. This was a significant move as until then no dominion had made a similar appointment. The British Foreign Office delayed it as long as possible. Appointments of Irish diplomats had to be cleared with the Foreign Office as they were accredited by the king on the advice of the Irish government, a practice which lasted until 1949. The British canvassed the views of the dominions. Canada and South Africa approved, New Zealand disapproved and Australia thought the matter should be left to the next imperial conference. Arguments took place over the king's title, the refusal to have the envoy attached to the British embassy and the Irish insistence that the British foreign minister should not countersign the appointment. In the end T.A. Smiddy, who had been permanent representative since 1924, was granted full diplomatic status in 1927. The US sent Frederick A. Sterling as envoy to Dublin later that year.

The Irish Free State's relationship with the Catholic Church was complex as it had local, national and international dimensions. The government and the anti-treaty side both recognised the political advantages of Church approval and sought to gain it to further their political aims. The majority of the Catholic hierarchy accepted the treaty. The Vatican, which in Cardinal Michael Logue's view had a 'very hazy notion of the state of Ireland', sent Monsignor Salvatore Luzio to Dublin at the request of the anti-treaty side during the civil war. His mission was disguised as an ecclesiastical visit. He was an incompetent delegate who did not meet Archbishop Edward Byrne of Dublin and failed to enlist Logue's help. Luzio was boycotted by the bishops, who had not been advised of his arrival, although Monsignor John Hagan of the Irish College in Rome thought they had planned it. Luzio did not present his credentials, his public offer to mediate had not been discussed with the government in advance and Cosgrave instructed External Affairs to request his recall. By the end of the civil war, the hierarchy and the government had moved closer together, although Hagan continued to support the anti-treaty side. Nevertheless, he pressurised de Valera to enter the Dáil even if meant taking the oath.[40]

The centenary of Catholic Emancipation in 1929 prompted the government to seek the appointment of a papal nuncio whose presence in Dublin would further legitimise the state. The appointment of a nuncio presented the Vatican with problems, one of which was that the primate of all Ireland was based at Armagh in Northern Ireland, so it tried to appoint a lower level apostolic delegate. The appointment was sensitive because the Catholic Church in the dominions was slightly larger than the Church of England and Presbyterians combined and the Vatican was careful not to offend anyone. It moved slowly, aware of the opposition of the Irish bishops. Charles Bewley, lawyer and Oxford-educated convert to Catholicism, was appointed Irish envoy to the Vatican in 1929. Later that year Irish Franciscan Archbishop Paschal Robinson was made papal nuncio to the Irish Free State. This was an excellent choice as he was an accomplished diplomat, was highly thought of in the Vatican and became a stabilising influence in church/state relations.

Cosgrave wrote to British Dominions Secretary Leopold Amery in February 1927, advising him that all future communications between the two governments would be through External Affairs, formally bypassing the governor-general.[41] In August 1928 he signed the Kellogg-Briand pact for the pacific settlement of international disputes, the first time a dominion had signed an international agreement in its own right. McGilligan sought to overcome the ambiguous position of Irish Free State envoys *vis-à-vis* British diplomats, and followed the precedent set by the Canadians, who had sent ambassadors to Toyko and Paris, by appointing envoys to Paris and Berlin. In 1930 the Irish were not enthusiastic about an initiative by French Foreign Minister Aristide Briand, who claimed descent from Irish high king Brian Boru, to establish a European Federal Union.[42]

The Irish education system was changed to one with an emphasis on the Irish language and a nationalist version of Irish history was taught, with British history almost entirely neglected. The Irish made changes to emphasise their independence and to differentiate themselves from the British by flying their own flag, adopting a new national anthem, removing the king's head from coins, issuing Irish stamps and currency, renaming town and street names and using Irish on official documents. They passed repressive legislation without interference and introduced tariffs without retaliation. The Cosgrave governments conducted constitutional guerrilla warfare against the British between 1922 and 1932. Whenever an opportunity presented itself they seized more sovereignty. In particular, they diminished the role of the king and made sure his authority immediately disappeared in the courts, the army and civil administration. The government gave a diplomatic refusal to a British proposal for a royal visit by George V in 1925, making it clear that it alone had control of invitations.

Honours were not allowed by the constitution. The Irish peerage died out as the government did not nominate anybody and the British limited new appointments to members of the royal family. None were appointed after 1936. The Order of St Patrick was never formally abolished and its last member died in 1974. Foreign honours, except papal awards, could only be awarded to Irish residents by permission of the government. Ernest Blythe considered setting up an Irish honours system but Cosgrave opposed it.

The British Foreign Office sought to limit Irish sovereignty, particularly in relation to the issue of passports. The Irish countered by charging US visitors with British visas who stopped off at Cobh $10 each to get an Irish visa. Despite these and other minor confrontations, the Dominions Office maintained good relations with the Irish and did not sound the alarm as the link with Britain was stealthily eroded. The British failed to appreciate how much ground had been lost and received a shock when de Valera aggressively moved to make further gains after 1932.

The department's special report 1931 suggested that relations with Britain had improved due to the 'growing spirit of liberalism and democracy in that country'. The old desire to keep Ireland in subjection had almost disappeared. Most of the inequality had been got rid of 'by negotiation and constant reiteration of our claims'. Yet, while seven trade treaties had been signed and another six were being negotiated, trade representation abroad was poor. Trade with

Northern Ireland was neglected, leading the *Irish Times* to complain in 1927 that the Irish Free State had no representative in Belfast while it had one in Shanghai.[43] The poor performance on trade promotion is surprising, considering that McGilligan held the portfolios of External Affairs and Industry and Commerce after 1927.

The Statute of Westminster gave the Irish freedom to make any political changes they wished, confirming Collins's belief that full sovereignty could be achieved by constitutional means. In Arthur Berridale Keith's words, the statute was the 'final recognition of true equality'.[44] The British were apprehensive about the impact on the empire of the changes made, particularly as the Egyptians and Indians were closely monitoring Irish progress.[45] Partition, however, remained intractable. The boundary commission made the border more permanent and thereafter the two parts of the island functioned independently of each other.

By 1932 a professional diplomatic service had been set up and international recognition had been achieved together with membership of the League of Nations, the International Labour Organisation and the permanent court of international justice. While External Affairs performed well, it did not deliver votes for the government, which did not appreciate the domestic political potential of the considerable progress made in a constitutional, non-confrontational manner despite being harassed by 'knockers and begrudgers'.[46] The government's secret and low-key diplomatic action achieved tangible results. This is the best form of action open to small states and is more effective than megaphone diplomacy, which, while appealing to the populace, fails in the long run as it antagonises other states.

The government did not communicate the significance of what had been gained so its achievements were not recognised by the public, which was not impressed with incremental quiet changes, while Cumann na nGaedheal, keen to garner votes from every quarter, did not publicise the extent to which it was surreptitiously unravelling the British connection.[47]

Chapter 7 ∽

| CIVIL WAR AND THE ARMY

INTRODUCTION

Óglaigh na hÉireann (the Irish Volunteers) were founded on 25 November 1913 in response to the formation of the Ulster Volunteers. They evolved into the Irish Republican Army in 1919 and the national army in 1922. The army was hastily recruited by the provisional government to defend the newly established state against insurgents opposed to the treaty. Its numbers were expanded rapidly and as a consequence its training, discipline and administration were not up to acceptable military standards. The army defeated the irregulars (the anti-treaty armed forces so-called to distinguish them from the regular army) in the civil war but hostilities did not cease as sporadic acts of violence continued throughout the 1920s. After the civil war, the army was drastically reduced in size, resulting in dissatisfaction among a minority of officers which led to the army mutiny in 1924. The mutiny was suppressed; subsequently the army was de-politicised and a small professional defence force was developed along conventional military lines whose loyalty would be to any future democratically elected government.

Prior to independence, Ireland's external defence had been organised by the British. Internal security had been the responsibility of the Royal Irish Constabulary (RIC), which could be supported by the large garrison of British soldiers in Ireland when a necessity arose. That garrison had three functions: to hold Ireland against the Irish, repel foreign invaders and provide a strategic reserve for the British army. It was paid for by Irish taxpayers.

The Irish Volunteers divided over participation in World War 1; the great majority (National Volunteers) followed Irish Party leader John Redmond. A minority of the remaining Irish Volunteers participated in the 1916 rising along with the left-wing Irish Citizen Army and the Hibernian Rifles. Some of the Irish Volunteers subsequently reorganised as the renamed Irish Republican Army (IRA) and fought in the war of independence 1919–21. The IRA were guerrilla fighters concentrating mainly on hit-and-run raids, were flexibly organised, not usually uniformed and generally part-time. Most of the fighting was done by flying columns and active service units organised into brigades and divisions, with minimal control being exercised by IRA general headquarters. Michael Collins's intelligence operatives infiltrated the British administration, police and military intelligence services, and killed a number of their key operatives. The IRA made it increasingly difficult for the British to govern parts of Ireland and, as casualties mounted, support for the war diminished in Britain.

THE CIVIL WAR

Between January and June 1922 there was a power struggle between those who accepted the treaty and those who rejected it. The civil war which followed was ostensibly fought over the Anglo-Irish treaty and particularly the oath of allegiance. But the treaty was the occasion rather than the cause of the conflict. The issue was whether the Irish people had the right to choose their own government. Because many of the combatants followed their leaders, Collins and de Valera, there was no clear line between constitutionalists and militants. Some constitutionalists ended up on the anti-treaty side, some militants stood by the government, while many veterans of the war of independence refused to take up arms against their fellow countrymen. Democracy won out over autocracy as the Irish people were not willing to exchange imperial rule for Irish dictatorship.[1]

By December 1921 the nominal strength of the IRA was estimated at 114,652 officers and men, organised into 16 divisions. This was a huge increase from those serving when the truce was signed. Only a small number were armed and the vast majority had seen little or no action before the truce. The organisation of the IRA had not been based on any idea of military theory but rather on the principle of survival.[2] The government recruited 4,000 selected IRA men in early 1922 for 18 months' military training in a national army modelled on the British army and armed with weapons purchased from it.[3] It was difficult to convert recruits into a trained, disciplined force, especially when there was a dearth of officers and non-commissioned officers, while equipping and accommodating them was a huge logistical problem.

Michael Collins focused on strategy while Waterford-born, 36-year-old Minister for Defence Richard Mulcahy, a 'desk man' who never fired a shot after the action at Ashbourne in 1916, organised the fighting force.[4] Mulcahy had left school at 16 years, began work at the Post Office, where he gained promotion in the engineering branch, and furthered his education by attending night classes at technical schools. He joined the Gaelic League, IRB, and the Irish Volunteers at their inaugural meeting in the Rotunda ice rink, and participated in the 1916 rising. He was elected an MP at the 1918 general election and was appointed Minister for Defence by the first Dáil, being later replaced by Cathal Brugha. He served as IRA chief of staff before the treaty but had little influence over military intelligence, which reported directly to Collins.

Few veterans of the war of independence were trained as soldiers. Even Collins was hardly a soldier in the conventional manner, although he was a strategist and great leader of men. The army recruits included Irishmen with combat experience in World War I who, unlike the IRA, were accustomed to the discipline of regular army life. While training was in progress Collins adopted delaying tactics aimed at avoiding conflict until the army was ready to fight. The government tried to reach a political compromise with its opponents but, faced with armed resistance, agrarian unrest, labour disputes and a significant rise in crime, it was unable to restore law and order by peaceful means.

As the British army vacated barracks, IRA units occupied them. Some accepted the treaty, others opposed it. In some cases government and anti-treaty supporters shared barracks. Gradually the state divided into two armed camps. 'Army convention' meetings were held in March and April 1922 at which Tom Barry and other 'fire-eaters' advocated a military dictatorship. Commandant Seán O'Hegarty, officer commanding Cork No. 1 brigade of the IRA, addressed the Dáil on the state of the IRA on 3 May 1922:

What is the condition of the army? The army two days ago was drifting but now it is driving to destruction. You have two sections of the army in Ireland and you have for many months feverish activity on both sides, recruiting on both sides, and putting arms into the hands of men that never saw a gun. Both sides have been recruiting and making an army in portions of Ireland where a shot was never fired when shots should have been fired. For the past week little conflicts have occurred here and there, and most of them in places where there was never anything done when hostilities were on. Let that progress and once the south gets into it there is nobody can stop it. What will that result in? We are told … that the Republic cannot be maintained unless this thing is allowed to go on, unless there is civil war. What does civil war mean? To my mind it means not alone that you do not maintain the Republic but that you break for ever any idea of it, that you break the country so utterly and leave it in such a way that England simply walks in and has her way as she never had it before. You will leave a print on Ireland and a print in every man's mind that can never be removed: you break the country utterly and destroy any idea of a Republic.

O'Hegarty admitted that 'Neither side is clean' and indicated that the responsibility for preventing civil war rested with the political and army leaders. They failed and the state continued to drift towards civil war. The anti-treaty side, despite preparing for war, were irresolute and lost the chance of crushing the newly formed army at its formative stage.[5] Collins also hesitated as he was reluctant to go to war against the men of the south—who later killed him in an ambush. The extreme anti-treaty IRA, commanded by Rory O'Connor, Liam Mellows and Ernie O'Malley, occupied the Four Courts and other buildings in Dublin in April 1922. O'Connor had no time for politicians. De Valera was taken aback when he heard of the occupation but retrospectively endorsed it. Collins sought common ground with O'Connor when they co-operated to arm the IRA in Northern Ireland. Such action put the treaty at risk. Collins may have been reacting to loyalist attacks on Catholics, but he may have also been trying to secure peace in the south by exporting trouble to the north. This action damaged his credibility with the British government, allowing Northern Ireland Prime Minister James Craig to introduce repressive measures and obtain subsidies from London.[6]

The provisional government ordered an attack on the Four Courts on 28 June 1922. It needed to establish its authority and was under pressure from the British to act, particularly after the murder of General Sir Henry Wilson, the Anglo-Irish former chief of the imperial defence staff, and then security adviser to the Northern Ireland Government, who was shot in London by two IRA volunteers. The army quickly recaptured the courts and drove the irregulars out of the other buildings in Dublin. As in the burning of the Custom House in 1921, important national legal, administrative and historical archives were lost when the irregulars blew up the public records office. Collins had hoped to make peace with the majority of the anti-treaty IRA, who were more moderate than O'Connor, but the escalation of fighting following the attack on the Four Courts led to Liam Lynch and many of his mainly Munster-based followers joining the conflict. The provisional government set up a war council. Collins returned to the army as commander-in-chief with the rank of general. Richard Mulcahy served as chief of staff along with regional commanders Major-Generals J.J. 'Ginger' O'Connell (Curragh), Emmet Dalton (East), J.T. Prout (South-East), Eoin O'Duffy (South) and Seán MacEoin (West). The army soon dislodged the anti-treaty forces from towns and cities and became proficient at sea landings which placed soldiers in the irregulars' rear. After the death of Collins, Mulcahy resumed command of the army while remaining Minister for Defence in the provisional government. De Valera proposed an end to the conflict but was snubbed by Liam Lynch.[7]

The early months of the civil war were chaotic. Organisation on both sides was based loosely on the war of independence order of battle of divisions and brigades. There were no set plans of campaign. Commanding officers recruited personnel as desired. The government dispatched troops around the country as the operational situation demanded. Emmet Dalton later complained that the civil war could have been ended by September 1922 if there had been proper co-ordination. The anti-treaty IRA was divided between extremists who were determined to overthrow the new state and moderates who sought a peaceful solution. While some of the moderates joined the battle after the Four Courts were attacked, many did not and remained neutral throughout the civil war. The anti-treaty leaders showed little appreciation of tactics and even poorer co-ordination. Its most effective branch was its communications network, largely staffed by Cumann na mBan. Army intelligence mounted surveillance of the irregulars and reported that they had no immediate objective; they were 'waiting for something to turn up' and 'relying on Cork'. Mulcahy observed that violence was no use, restoration of order was a 'step forwards not backwards', unnecessary destruction and loss of life were to be avoided, while avenues for peace and every constitutional way must be left open to the irregulars provided 'they accept the people's will and authority'. He stated that 'we must work hard' to build a new state and could sort out labels like 'republic and sovereignty' afterwards while not missing 'the real meaning of freedom' as the treaty, which the people approved, had got 'the substance of freedom'.[8]

British intelligence monitored events and Major-General G.M. Boyd, officer commanding Dublin district, reported for the week ending 7 October 1922 that

It is noticeable that the feeling of hate shown by the Republicans both active and passive towards the P.G. (Provisional Government) forces is growing more rapidly than that shown by the P.G. Forces for the Republicans, and there is consequently every sign of increasing bitterness and barbarity in the near future.

After losing control of urban areas, the irregulars embarked on a campaign of guerrilla warfare, causing widespread destruction to the state's infrastructure—roads, bridges, posts, telecommunications and railways—and disruption of farming, trade and commerce. Banks, post offices, and public, commercial and private properties were attacked, looted and burned; businesses failed and jobs were lost. Many civilians were murdered, among them the father of Kevin O'Higgins. Some participants and criminal elements used the opportunity to settle old scores, terrorise opponents and grab property, land and livestock. Dáil deputies, senators and civil servants' houses were set on fire, including those of Cosgrave, Sir Horace Plunkett, Gordon Campbell, and James McGarry, whose seven-year-old son Emmet died from burns; two senators were kidnapped (they both escaped).[9] The struggle became increasingly bitter, far worse than the war against the Black and Tans and Auxiliaries. Despite its successes, the army was not a model of military effectiveness. In Eunan O'Halpin's view:[10]

> Throughout the civil war the army was dogged by the inadequacies of many of its officers, by the ill-discipline, poor condition, and inexperience of its troops, by ill-feeling and disputes between senior commanders, by the weakness of central control and the disastrous performance of its supplies organization.

In the latter part of the civil war the irregulars continued to destroy the infrastructure, not for military reasons, but because they despaired of victory.

The irregulars employed the tactics that had been successful in the war of independence: ambushes and roadblocks with land mines planted to kill soldiers clearing them. Against these tactics, Mulcahy called in vain for discipline to be maintained and no reprisals carried out. Nevertheless, a mined roadblock at Knocknagoshel resulted in the death of five soldiers and led to a savage reprisal at Ballyseedy, when nine irregulars were tied to a mine which was then detonated. Similar events occurred at Countess Bridge and Cahirciveen, proving that the reaction of soldiers, even well-trained and disciplined, to this type of warfare is not guaranteed or predictable. The army made wholesale arrests, employed dubious methods of interrogation, was hard pressed and under severe stress, had poor discipline, and there were many cases of unofficial violence and executions.

Mulcahy feared discipline would break down unless the army was allowed to carry out executions and legalise its actions. The Labour Party, which adopted a neutral stance, opposed this and Cathal O'Shannon spoke of growing revulsion at both sides' behaviour.[11] The government passed special legislation ruling that people found in possession of guns would be executed. In response, irregular leader Liam Lynch ordered the execution of all government ministers and Dáil deputies who voted for special powers. Two deputies were attacked, resulting in the death of Seán Hales and the wounding of Padraic Ó Maille on 7 December 1922. The executive ordered Rory O'Connor, Liam Mellows, Joseph McKelvey and Richard Barrett to be shot in reprisal, an act publicly condemned by the Hales family. The murder of Hales and the subsequent executions were widely reported in the international press. Dáil deputy Liam de Róiste, who was buying timber in 'Sunsvall (Sweden) within one degree of the Arctic Circle', got the news of Hales's death from a local evening paper.[12] The four executed had not been tried and had been in prison for most of the civil war. Ministers Kevin O'Higgins and Joe McGrath expressed grave reservations about the executive's decision but Cosgrave defended the executions on the grounds that 'Terror must be met with terror'. Minister for Education Eoin MacNeill argued that 'every Government has the power to deal with extreme emergencies', while Labour Party leader Tom Johnson complained that there was 'no pretence of legality'.[13] The executions had the desired effect, however, as no other sitting Dáil deputy was killed during the civil war.

The army began to seriously address its organisational problems and by October 1922 a proper system had evolved for the issuing of orders and instructions to regularise recruiting, enlistments and pay. A centralised system of reporting to general headquarters (GHQ) was initiated which enabled the general staff to better plan its operations at a tactical level. The state was divided into nine commands in January 1923. The organisation, location and strengths of the battalions were laid down, the various corps established and GHQ, particularly the adjutant-general's branch, began to exercise increased authority.

The last British troops, except a small number left guarding the treaty ports, sailed for England on 15 December 1922.[14] The army, now numbering 55,000, began to exercise control. Over 12,000 irregulars were imprisoned in overcrowded accommodation. The death of Collins allowed the politicians to take control over the army. He had argued for restraint, but by November 1922, the government resolved to use draconian measures. It mounted a 'ruthless war' on 'passive irregulars' and Cosgrave stated that it would 'put down the revolt regardless of cost'.[15] As the government had difficulty functioning politically and economically, and to prevent the state from slipping into anarchy, the army was given increased powers, including the establishment of military courts which could and did enforce the death sentence.

The irregulars discovered belatedly that this was a war they could not win. Ernie O'Malley believed they lost because they fought a defensive war and did not realise that their opponents 'would go so far'.[16] But in reality they were defeated because they lacked the popular support the IRA had enjoyed during the war of independence. They came to understand that the army was as ruthless as they were and was willing to meet atrocity with atrocity. The government would not compromise with the irregulars, who feared that if the war was intensified their best people would be lost: 73 of them were executed after being tried by military courts set up under the special powers legislation. O'Higgins moved to secure civilian control over the military. Mulcahy, who was more soldier than politician, was an outsider in the executive having, for sound military reasons, operated from army headquarters at Portobello Barracks rather than Government Buildings during the civil war. He was further marginalised after he met de Valera secretly without cabinet approval in September 1922, although the meeting lasted only a few minutes. (Mulcahy met de Valera in an effort to secure peace despite being 'obsessed with de Valera's responsibility for the Civil War'.[17])

As fighting in most of the country petered out, hostilities dragged on in Cork, where irregular leader Liam Deasy was captured and sentenced to death. He agreed to appeal for peace but was rejected by Liam Lynch, who remained optimistic that the war could be won. The government offered an amnesty but fighting continued until Lynch was killed in April 1923. His successor, Frank Aiken, published peace proposals along with de Valera, who had recovered credibility with the irregulars now that the war was lost and his political skills were needed. The government insisted that all political questions were to be decided by the majority of the people's elected representatives and all arms must be under its control. While this was not acceptable to the irregulars, Aiken ordered a ceasefire and instructed that arms be dumped. The last execution took place on 24 May 1923. No agreement was reached on the cessation of hostilities and the state slipped into an uneasy peace.

There are no reliable figures for combatant and civilian casualties in the civil war. A figure of 4,000 killed seems a reasonable estimate, of which between 500 and 800 were army, with irregular deaths probably higher. (The numbers were low in comparison with the civil war in Finland around the same time, when 25,000 were killed.) The civil war resulted in deaths, injuries, widespread destruction and a waste of scarce resources. It delayed the development of the new state. Many talented people died or emigrated in its aftermath. The brutality of both sides left a bitter legacy, particularly as it had been perpetrated by the Irish upon the Irish. The civil war exacerbated the division between those who accepted and rejected the treaty, and reinforced partition as it gave the Northern Ireland government the opportunity to establish a permanent administration.

THE ARMY MUTINY
The executive sought to reduce army numbers and soldiers' pay after the civil war and was apprehensive that a large army could be detrimental to the internal and external security of the state. Its intention was to create a small, professionally trained force that would be loyal to whichever government was democratically elected in the future.

After the civil war, Major-General James Hogan was appalled at the growth of factionalism and indiscipline in the army and believed that the increasing concern with political matters by some senior officers posed a threat to the democratic institutions of the fledgling state.[18] Despite the continuing threat from the irregulars, the government needed to demilitarise and reduce the size of the army as the state was running a huge budget deficit. The demobilisation envisaged a reduction of 30,000 soldiers (including 2,200 officers) by March 1924. It did not cause much friction among the ranks, as most had signed on for six to twelve months, but a small group of officers led by Major-General Liam Tobin and former members of Collins's counter-intelligence 'squad' attempted to resist the demobilisation. They set up the Irish Republican Army Organisation (IRAO), sometimes known as the old IRA, to block perceived preferment of former British soldiers and counter the actions of the Irish Republican Brotherhood (IRB), which had been resurrected to prevent it falling under the control of the irregulars in late 1922. Tobin wanted a seat on the IRB supreme council.[19] The revival of the IRB was seen by some ministers as incipient mutiny as it weakened the allegiance of soldiers to the government.

Many officers were aggrieved at demobilisation, while fewer promotional opportunities and lower pay for those accepting a reduction in rank to remain in the army caused discontent. Mulcahy appreciated the importance of finding jobs for ex-servicemen and suggested they be employed in reforestation and public works. There was also the issue of northern men who had joined the army, some of whom had been disappointed when no invasion of the north took place. They were appeased by being allowed to hold their pre-truce ranks and so got ahead in terms of promotion. This annoyed the IRAO, who felt that the northern men had done little during the war of independence.[20] The IRAO were dangerous men, included experienced assassins and were a potential source of trouble, particularly as they believed they were being overlooked and marginalised.

Cosgrave met Tobin in an effort to defuse the situation and was conciliatory, fearing an army revolt would create political instability and damage the state's credit rating at a time when the government was very short of money. The IRAO had an aggressive idea of Collins's 'stepping stone' policy and did not rule out force against Northern Ireland. Cosgrave feared that, if left unchecked, large-scale military action could ensue at a time when he needed peace and stability. Matters came to a head in September 1923, when a small number of officers refused to accept demobilisation papers. They were charged with insubordination, convicted by court martial and dismissed. Tobin and Colonel Charles Dalton issued an ultimatum in May 1924 demanding the removal of the defence council and the immediate suspension of demobilisation. Nine hundred officers accepted demobilisation papers without trouble but a small number deserted, taking arms and transport. Minister for Industry and Commerce Joe McGrath, who had been associated with the IRAO and whose house had been raided on Mulcahy's orders, resigned, alleging 'mishandling and incompetence' by the government, which appointed police commissioner Major-General Eoin O'Duffy as inspector-general of the army. He was appointed without Mulcahy's knowledge and given direct access to the cabinet, thereby undermining the minister's position.

Cosgrave decided to hold an enquiry, and offered officers who had deserted the option of returning to duty with the arms and transport taken in exchange for a parole pending its outcome, whereupon Tobin and Dalton withdrew their ultimatum.[21] However, matters escalated after an army raid on a public house where IRAO men were meeting. The government called for the resignations of the three senior army commanders, all of whom were 1916 veterans. Major-Generals Gearóid O'Sullivan and Seán Ó Muirthile sought legal advice from Judge Advocate General Cahir Davitt, who advised them that if they did not resign they would be dismissed. They resigned but chief of staff General Seán McMahon, who was also the head of the IRB, refused and was dismissed, after which Mulcahy resigned as minister. O'Duffy, who was a high-ranking IRB member, was appointed general officer commanding forces and inspector-general. Thereafter the IRB ceased to function within the army.

The government's action appeared to condone mutiny and punish the army commanders, as the IRAO had mutinied while the IRB had held the line. Mulcahy feared a *coup d'état* and took action to prevent it. However, O'Higgins pushed the conciliatory Cosgrave aside and took control of events. He used the mutiny to undermine Mulcahy, whom he held responsible for the army not prosecuting the civil war with sufficient determination. There were also demarcation disputes between the army and police, with O'Higgins arguing that the military should do more to reduce armed crime and improve military discipline, and he singled out the soldiers of the Dublin guard in Kerry, which had lost the support of the local population because of their bad behaviour.[22] The government at that stage was extremely annoyed with both the IRB and IRAO.

The enquiry, held under the chairmanship of Justice James Creed Meredith, reported in June 1924 that a mutiny had occurred and that secret societies damaged military discipline.[23] Yet the significant outcome of the mutiny was that almost all the soldiers obeyed the government. Only 96 officers resigned and six deserted.[24] Disaffection did not spread to the vast majority of NCOs and lower ranks. However, the mutiny had the potential to destabilise the new state and there were few protests over the army changes in the Dáil. The mutiny showed the strength of the regime rather than its flaws. The soldiers obeyed the politicians. No violence occurred despite Sam Maguire's suggestion that the IRAO assassinate the executive.[25] After the mutiny, merit rather than record became the rule. The significance of the army mutiny was not what actually happened but that when it was resolved the supremacy of civilian authority was established over the military for the first time since 1913.

Joe McGrath formed the National Group with eight like-minded Cumann na nGaedheal deputies to oppose the executive over its handling of the army mutiny. They resigned their seats in 1924 and lost them in the by-elections that followed. After McGrath and Mulcahy resigned, O'Higgins dominated the executive. Mulcahy remained out of office for the next three years but worked to keep the government in power by participating actively in Cumann na nGaedheal party organisation and speaking at meetings until his supporters forced Cosgrave to restore him to the cabinet in 1927.

THE BIRTH OF THE MODERN ARMY

Peter Hughes was appointed Minister for Defence, replacing Cosgrave, who had temporarily succeeded Mulcahy between March and November 1924. When asked to accept the appointment, he protested that he knew nothing about the army. Cosgrave replied, 'That is why I want you'.[26] Hughes was a Dundalk merchant who left the Irish Party to join Sinn Féin in 1916 because of the growing influence in the local party of the Ancient Order of Hibernians, led by his rival James Coburn, who succeeded him as Dáil deputy in 1927 representing the National League. Hughes was imprisoned after the 'German Plot' and served as a judge in the Dáil courts before being elected unopposed to the Dáil in 1922 and 1923. His appointment was controversial: Deputy Margaret Collins-O'Driscoll objected to him on the grounds that he did not have sufficient education.

The appointment of a civilian was a slight to the army. The government's policy was to demilitarise the state, reduce the army's size, make it more professional and de-politicise it. As the police took over internal security duties, the army shrank in size and political influence. O'Duffy prepared an organisational plan designed to weaken the authority of the chief of staff and GHQ. The plan ensured that the chief of staff, adjutant-general and quartermaster-general were independent, with each working to the minister, while general officers commanding were placed in command of the army (regional commanders) who had direct access to the minister if the need arose. General staff appointments were made by the executive, general officers commanding by the military. As in the police, O'Duffy focused on morale and morals. He demanded better pay, longer contracts, renewal of recruitment, and urged that all officers deemed worthy be commissioned. The Defence Forces (Temporary Provisions) Act which governed the army was renewed every year from 1923 until the passing of the Defence Act 1954, despite protests from Dáil deputies who questioned why Defence was treated differently to other government departments. When Labour Party leader Tom Johnson raised the attendance of army officers at the Imperial Defence Council, Hughes responded, 'The Irish Army is the Army of the Irish people and has no connection whatever with the army in London.' External Affairs Minister Desmond FitzGerald added that 'in the event of a general attack on these islands—it is perfectly obvious—our Army must co-operate with the British Army' and 'understand that army's approach to the defence of the two islands'.[27]

The Irish Free State inherited a legacy from the British in its parliament, judiciary and civil service. The army was in a similar situation as it used Sam Browne belts, swords, breeches, leggings, riding crops, rankings, etc. Drill was similar to that in the British army except that orders were issued in Irish. One of the few significant changes was the adoption of the French title of commandant, which had been used in 1916 in place of the rank of major.

After the civil war, the military was starved of resources, pay was poor, security of tenure was uncertain and staff shortages occurred in ranks where alternative employment could be found outside the army. The engineering corps lost skilled men to the British army and air force. The medical corps also experienced difficulties in staff retention. To improve morale, participation in sport was encouraged, and the army began to organise hurling, Gaelic football, athletics and boxing matches. Objections to tennis and golf were overruled and soldiers were allowed into some, but not all, golf clubs. O'Duffy resigned from the army in February 1925 while remaining Garda commissioner and was replaced by Lieutenant-General Peadar MacMahon. A native of Ballybay, County Monaghan, MacMahon had joined the Irish Volunteers in 1913, and took part in the 1916 rising, after which he was interned at Frongoch before serving in the IRA Limerick brigade and GHQ during the war of independence.

After the civil war, army intelligence continued to gather information even though the police were responsible for internal security. Military intelligence maintained 33,000 dossiers on those engaged in activities against the state, studied the national security position and kept abreast of developments in armaments, aircraft, poison gases and new weapons of war.[28] It reported on the IRA and Sinn Féin's unsuccessful attempts to gain control of the GAA and public bodies, anticipated a split in the movement over entry into the Dáil and noted with concern efforts to reconcile the anti-treaty side with Cumann na nGaedheal by Dan Breen, Tom Crofts, Liam Deasy and J.J. Sheehy. The fallout arising from the boundary commission north and south was assessed and stronger action against subversives was suggested. Morale in the army was reported to be poor due to the demobilisation of troops, and the need for pensions was stressed.[29]

Pensions were addressed by the Army Pensions Acts 1924, 1925, 1927 and 1930. However, pensions were not conceded easily, particularly for service before 1922.

THE DEPARTMENT OF DEFENCE
The Department of Defence was set up under the Ministers and Secretaries Act 1924 with responsibility for raising, training, organising, maintaining and equipping the armed forces together with their management, discipline, regulation and control. Defence was a department of state rather than a military headquarters with a brief to defend the state against armed aggression and to aid the civil power. It did not exercise military command and, unlike other government departments, was not run solely by civil servants as senior army officers participated in policy- and decision-making.[30] A council of defence, each member of which was assigned specific responsibilities, was provided for under the act, comprising the minister (chairman), parliamentary secretary (financial oversight), chief of staff, adjutant-general, quartermaster-general and the department secretary. An inspector-general was also envisaged.[31]

Chief of staff Lieutenant-General Peadar MacMahon replaced the first secretary of the department, former British army officer Cornelius B. O'Connor, in 1927, and held that position for the next 30 years. He was succeeded by Lieutenant-General Daniel Hogan. The army continued to improve its public image at home through its bands, tattoos and parades. The army band and school of music had been established in 1922 under the direction of former German army bandmaster Colonel Fritz Brase and talented musician Captain Christian Sauerzweig. Both made significant contributions to the development of symphonic music in the state. The band was a great morale booster for the troops, and provided most of the brass and woodwind players for the early symphony orchestras. The army show-jumping and boxing teams participated in international events, raising the army's profile abroad. Officers were sent to the US for training and the slow process of replacing the army school of instruction with a military college was begun. The air corps, which had been hit hard during the army mutiny (eleven officers had resigned), recovered and gained international recognition when Commandant James Fitzmaurice was one of the crew on the *Bremen*, which made the first east/west air flight across the Atlantic in 1928, along with German airmen Günther von Hünefeld and Hermann Köhl.

Desmond FitzGerald replaced Hughes as Minister for Defence in 1927. Major-General Hugo MacNeill of the defence plans division submitted reports on military preparation but, while the government formally accepted them, it reduced the army to 6,700 all ranks by 1932. Army expenditure in the years after the civil war dropped significantly and showed a definite downward trend until 1931.[32] The Department of Finance effectively decided the size of the army and no additional weapons were purchased between 1923 and 1931.[33]

A defence policy review took place in July 1925 and a memorandum on defence prepared in advance of the 1926 imperial conference stated that the Irish Free State 'cannot in its present state of development adopt a policy of isolation'. The government formally stated its defence policy in June 1926:[34]

> We are to have an independent national force, so organised, trained, and equipped as to render it capable of assuming responsibility for the defence of the Saorstát against invasion and capable of preventing internal disturbance and disorder.

The state would have a 'small standing army', which could be expanded in time of war and would co-operate with British forces in the event of 'an attack on these islands' subject to article 49 of the Constitution, which stipulated that the Oireachtas must decide on such action. Prior to the naval conference at Geneva in 1927, the government held discussions with the British and offered to take over the treaty ports and maintain the existing defences. The British declined and failed to convince the Irish to provide a minesweeping service between Dublin and Rosslare together with anti-submarine defences. The British navy sought to resume cruises around Ireland but Cosgrave diplomatically put them off.[35] The treaty ports were subsequently handed back to the Irish in 1938 as part of British Prime Minister Neville Chamberlain's policy of appeasement. The

British unsuccessfully tried to get them back by diplomacy during World War II. Winston Churchill considered the use of force but was advised against it.

The army estimated that 100,000 soldiers would be needed to resist an invasion. It sought 25,000 regular troops with provision for a reserve. Unlike in other countries which had territorial armies or national guards, the reserve was not a paid force that could be detailed to travel abroad and undertake active military service. Nevertheless, the government steadily reduced the size of the standing army while Finance wanted the number of reservists limited to 4,500.[36]

Fianna Fáil sought to reduce army numbers and queried the army's purpose, arguing that guerrilla tactics were the only useful method of defence against an invader. Cumann na nGaedheal Deputy T.F. O'Higgins stated that the only 'real insurance against internal disorder or external aggression was a reasonably strong and thoroughly efficient army'.[37] Commandant J.C. Brennan-Whitmore pointed out that the army was one of the smallest organised armies in the world and its cost per man was very low.[38]

HEIGHTENED TENSIONS IN THE LATE 1920s

The renewed outbreak of IRA activity in the late 1920s was mainly dealt with by the police. Army morale was low and the National Defence Association was formed in 1929 to support serving and reserve officers. Its members included former chiefs of staff Major-General Joe Sweeney and Lieutenant-General Seán MacEoin. The latter had resigned to fight a by-election after disagreements with Minister FitzGerald and Secretary MacMahon.[39] The National Defence Association clashed with Defence and this led to the resignation of officers in the worst crisis since 1924. However, Major-General Michael Brennan kept order. He was to remain chief of staff until 1940.

Despite O'Duffy's fears, IRA activity did not increase following the murder of O'Higgins, but after the Public Safety Act was suspended in 1928 the security situation deteriorated as the IRA revived its campaign against the state. O'Duffy was frustrated at the difficulty of securing prosecutions as witnesses and jurors were intimidated, and he was convinced that the government was being soft on the IRA, which he believed was being tacitly encouraged by Fianna Fáil. Matters got worse when a police superintendent, a detective and two witnesses were murdered while Peadar O'Donnell and Saor Éire's campaign against payment of the land annuities threatened to increase the level of agrarian violence. The prospect of Fianna Fáil gaining power led O'Duffy to canvass for support for an army coup in 1931 among disgruntled army officers (including former IRB member and 1916 veteran Hugo MacNeill), Cumann na nGaedheal politicians and policemen. Department Secretary MacMahon reported MacNeill and other officers to Vice-president Ernest Blythe, who summoned MacNeill to account for his actions in Chief-of-Staff Brennan's presence but did not dismiss him. Brennan is reported to have transferred several senior officers from sensitive commands and warned O'Duffy that he would be arrested in the event of any impropriety. David Neligan, head of the Garda special branch, was summoned by Cosgrave, who demanded to know what O'Duffy was up to, but without denying the rumours, he assured the president that everything was under control. Neligan summoned retired Major-General James Hogan, who had returned to academic life, and he travelled from Cork and strongly advised O'Duffy to desist from violent action, arguing that one civil war was enough. After the election in 1932, MacNeill and Michael Hogan approached an 'appalled' Mulcahy for support in overthrowing the government. He told MacNeill 'not to be an ass'.[40]

The government rushed the Constitution (Amendment No. 17) Bill (the Public Safety Bill) through the Dáil in October 1931, providing for military tribunals to try alleged members of the IRA, Saor Éire, Cumann na mBan, Friends of Soviet Russia and seven other banned organisations.[41] Once the bill was passed the IRA went underground. There were no problems during or after the 1932 election, as government control over the army had been clearly established, but also perhaps because many soldiers had grown disenchanted with Cumann na nGaedheal over the army cutbacks.

The *Freeman's Journal* commented that the national army 'had been born and reared on the battlefield'.[42] Its first priority had been to win the civil war. Training, discipline and administration were neglected in the interests of military expediency. After the civil war the army was considerably reduced in size, de-politicised and professionalised. By 1932 it accepted without question that its function was to defend the state from external aggression and internal unrest while taking its orders from any government democratically elected by the people.

Civilian control over the military is vital in a democracy and establishing a standing army after a rebellion is a difficult political process. There is always the risk of a coup until it is clearly decided that the army is under the control of the politicians rather than its own commanders. Demobilisation is risky as there are too many generals and senior officers, and men lose rank, privilege and status. The new army contained a potentially explosive mix of former IRB, IRA, Collins's 'squad' and ex-British soldiers. Democratic control had to be established as soon as possible. O'Higgins's instinct was correct when he insisted that the government must have control. His success can be judged by the attitude of the army to the first Fianna Fáil government in 1932—'Do we shoot or salute?' The soldiers saluted and there was no crisis.

Ireland, because of its location and Britain's need to defend its seas and air space in its own interests, has never had to confront the difficulties that isolated, neutral and uncommitted states have to face, as its defence has long been effectively carried out by the British. The state does not have a real military ethos or tradition of soldiering and continues to operate with an army too small to resist an invasion and an air corps and navy incapable of protecting Irish air and sea space.

Chapter 8 ～

| RESTORING LAW AND ORDER

INTRODUCTION

The British handed over a state in which law and order had almost completely collapsed as there was no longer an effective police force or a fully functioning legal system. The provisional government's priorities were to defeat those who opposed it by force of arms and restore the rule of law.

Ireland had an independent legal system before 1922, with its own lord chancellor and attorney general. It had two police forces, the armed *gendarmerie*-style Royal Irish Constabulary (RIC) and the small, usually unarmed, Dublin Metropolitan Police (DMP). Gaols were run by a prison board. The courts and police did not command the respect of the majority of the population as they enforced British rule. In 1922 the laws then in force, together with English common law, were adopted by the Irish Free State with minor exceptions and amended where necessary. The existing law courts were retained. A national police force was established despite opposition from the anti-treaty side. Law and order was restored and crime decreased— but an undercurrent of politically inspired violence persisted which threatened to destabilise the state. Social legislation was enacted to contain rather than resolve issues.

THE DEPARTMENT OF JUSTICE

The provisional government assumed responsibility for law and order after the treaty but had no immediate means of enforcing it. Lawyer Eamonn Duggan was appointed Minister for Home Affairs in January 1922 and was replaced by Kevin O'Higgins in August that year. O'Higgins, who was born at Stradbally, County Laois, in 1892, was educated at Clongowes Wood and Knockbeg before taking a law degree at UCD. He served under Cosgrave in the pre-treaty Dáil Ministry of Local Government and subsequently became Minister of Economic Affairs.

The Ministers and Secretaries Act 1924 changed the name of the department from Home Affairs to Justice, and government law officer Hugh Kennedy's title to attorney general.[1] The Department of Justice was given responsibility for the administration of law, justice, public order and police, aliens, immigration, sale of liquor, betting, lotteries, censorship, regulation of vivisection, importation of firearms, storage of explosives, and dangerous drugs. It took over gaols from the prison board in 1928. Henry O'Friel, a native of Donegal, was appointed secretary of the department. He had graduated from UCD with an honours degree in mathematics before joining the civil service as a customs officer in 1911 and was later dismissed for refusing to take an oath of allegiance to the crown. He subsequently became a tax consultant, chairman of Dublin County Council, Dáil court judge and secretary of the pre-treaty Ministry of Home Affairs. O'Friel was seconded to the tariff commission in 1931 and succeeded on a temporary basis by Stephen A. Roche. He was formally replaced by the Fianna Fáil government in 1933 and later appointed chairman of a reconstituted tariff commission.

O'Higgins was murdered on his way to Mass on Sunday 10 July 1927 by IRA members Archie Doyle, Bill Gannon and Timothy Coughlan, who were never brought to justice.[2] Before he died he said, 'I have been shot. I do not know for what ... I have always done the best for Ireland and I forgive those who have done this.'[3] W.B. Yeats wrote to his widow, 'What can one say but that the country has lost the man it needed, its great builder of a nation.'[4] The government lost its strongman and his death led to an increase in police activity, arrests, interrogations, allegations and counter-allegations. However, it also led to the Electoral Amendment (No. 2) Bill 1927, which copper-fastened democracy in the Irish Free State by forcing Fianna Fáil to take the oath and enter the Dáil. After 1927 that party maintained its links with the IRA as de Valera valued their support and hoped to draw them into constitutional politics. Fianna Fáil remained, in the words of Seán Lemass, 'a slightly constitutional party'. O'Higgins was replaced as minister on a temporary basis by Cosgrave and after the September 1927 election by Mayo-born 49-year-old lawyer James Fitzgerald-Kenney KC. Educated at Downside and UCD, he was a supporter of the Irish-language movement.

THE LAW AND THE COURTS
Under article 12 of the constitution, the Oireachtas had the 'sole and exclusive power of making laws for the peace, order and good government of the Irish Free State'. The laws in force were carried forward under the Adaptation of Enactments and Expiring Laws Continuance Acts 1922. A judicial committee appointed by the government reported in May 1923 and the new courts structure was largely drawn up by O'Higgins and Hugh Kennedy. They sought to create a 'new machine' and the courts established under the Courts of Justice Act 1924 continued to operate with some minor adjustments until 1937.[5]

The pre-treaty Dáil set up arbitration courts to undermine British authority and provide justice in parts of the country where the RIC had lost control. During the war of independence many magistrates resigned. After the arrival of the Black and Tans and Auxiliaries the Dáil courts were put under pressure but continued to sit, however tenuously, until the truce in July 1921.[6] Between the truce and the treaty the Dáil courts' activity increased considerably. The government abolished the Dáil courts as it needed a new legal system implemented quickly and knew that most of the judges and court officers of the existing Irish legal system would be loyal provided their pay and conditions remained unchanged.[7] A secondary reason was to prevent the anti-treaty side from using the Dáil courts to subvert its rule. The courts were wound up under the Dáil Éireann (Winding-up) Act 1923, which provided for the appointment of commissioners with wide powers to settle questions arising out of the courts' judgements. From 1924 decrees of the land settlement court (established by the Dáil in 1920) were treated as arbitration awards subject to confirmation by the Land Commission. The government stressed that the Dáil courts had been established as an alternative to those operating under British rule but as the courts had passed to Irish control there was no longer a need for two legal systems. As a temporary measure 27 solicitors and barristers were appointed district justices to replace the magistrates. They quickly gained public acceptance and were made permanent. Most of the other judges were retained in office without formal re-appointment pending legislation. The supreme and high courts were slimmed down to three and six judges respectively. Most of their serving judges retired and only two remained in office: Charles O'Connor for one year and W.E. Wylie for 12 years.

Cosgrave rushed the Courts of Justice Bill 1924 through the Dáil. It did not follow the recommendations of the judicial committee on all points. Lawyers, academics, the Labour Party and independent deputy William Redmond attacked it, particularly the sections relating to the appointment and independence of judges, the influence of the executive on the rules of court and the prerogatives of the bar and bench.[8] Kennedy, who was a Dáil deputy, faced the onslaught in the Dáil rather than O'Higgins. The extended debate had the effect of informing the public that changes were being made, it showed the government that it could not introduce complex legislation without serious examination, and it demonstrated that non-lawyers could have a say in passing laws which regulated the courts and legal profession.

Kennedy was appointed chief justice in May 1924 and was replaced as attorney general by John O'Byrne, who was succeeded by John A. Costello in 1926. Costello, who was to become Taoiseach in 1948, had been hired as a legal assistant by Kennedy in 1922 along with Kevin O'Shiel to carry out research and provide legal opinions on matters related to the transfer of power and the establishment of the new state.

The government took over the existing legal system and modified it. The law remained as it was, subject to amendment where necessary or desirable. The approach to the legal system was pragmatic; it had worked under British rule so it could be made to work under Irish rule. The Four Courts, which had been destroyed during the civil war, were rebuilt by 1931.

THE CIVIC GUARD/GARDA SÍOCHÁNA

After the treaty the RIC was disbanded, leaving no organised police outside of Dublin, where the DMP remained in place. The first Dáil had established a police force to restore order as the RIC lost control. Immediately after the treaty, Michael Collins set up an armed police force (generally referred to as the CID or Oriel House) which dealt ruthlessly with serious crime. From early 1922, a similar body known as the 'plain clothes squad' operated in Cork.[9]

Home Affairs Minister Eamonn Duggan requested IRA personnel assigned to police duties to rejoin their units in January 1922 and Collins set up a committee to consider policing in the following month. The government may have considered using the Dáil police force but it was small, poorly organised, untrained and did not exist in all areas; the allegiance of some of its members was also questionable in the aftermath of the treaty.[10] 'Protection corps', privately set up to prevent subversives robbing businesses or extracting protection money, offered their services but CID chief David Neligan did not want them armed.[11] The police organising committee chaired by Minister for Defence Richard Mulcahy recommended a new police force. It would be a constabulary (people's police) rather than a *gendarmerie* (state police), with policemen personally responsible for their actions, policing by consent rather than by force. There was little time to prepare, as 20 February 1922 was fixed as the date of disbandment of the RIC.

Opponents of the treaty had a vested interest in disorder, making it difficult for the government to build a consensus on the restoration of civil order between January and June 1922. Protestants, unionists and British ex-servicemen in the Irish Free State continued to be targeted; some were killed and many forced to emigrate. Collins wished to get a new police force recruited, trained and in place as soon as possible and relied on Deputy Michael Staines, then acting head of the Dáil police, and O'Higgins to recruit suitable IRA candidates, including Dáil police, together with former RIC and DMP personnel willing to train the new force. Collins envisaged an unarmed police force to differentiate it from the armed RIC. He also understood the need for armed detectives to combat violent crime, fight subversives, and defend civil servants, ministers, politicians and public buildings. The government kept quiet about the formation of the force and recruitment was neither announced nor advertised.

The police committee recommended a unified Civic Guard of 4,300 led by a commissioner responsible to the Minister for Home Affairs rather than to a police authority. This was a reduction from the RIC strength in the 26 counties, which had stood at 7,000.[12] While only 180 members of the RIC and DMP joined the Civic Guard (Guards) they made a significant contribution to the reconstruction of the police service. They included David Neligan and Eamonn Broy, a future Garda commissioner, both of whom had worked as spies for Collins against the British.[13] Ninety-three per cent of the original 1,500 recruits were ex-IRA and of these 30 per cent had served in flying columns with some experience of guerrilla fighting. The selection process was efficient as very few policemen would go over to the anti-treaty side, which intimidated recruits and their families and kidnapped recruiting officers in an effort to strangle the Guards at birth.[14] Training was rudimentary and focused mainly on drill and physical exercise, so the Guards learned little about the law, police procedures or investigation of crime.

Staines was appointed commissioner on 10 March 1922 and Patrick Walsh, a former RIC officer, deputy commissioner. A number of the most senior officers appointed were ex-RIC and this lead to dissention in the ranks. On 15 May 1922 a committee of Guards delivered an ultimatum demanding the dismissal of five of the senior former RIC officers. While this was an incipient mutiny, the police were almost entirely loyal to the state as their complaint was grounded on the promotion of ex-RIC men. Rory O'Connor and a party of irregulars seized arms and ammunition at the Guards' Kildare training depot, aided by a few policemen who opposed the treaty.[15]

Collins held talks with the Guards and appointed a commission of enquiry. It was chaired by Kevin O'Shiel, assisted by Michael McAuliffe.

Their report stopped short of recommending the dismissal of the force, proposing instead that the Guards be technically disbanded but not dispersed, and be selectively re-enrolled with every member put on probation. Staines and Walsh resigned. The police commission recommended that the Guards be unarmed and carry out administrative functions in order to bring them into a close relationship with the people. After the Guards had been reconciled with the government, recruitment recommenced.

During the truce the IRA nominal roll had increased significantly as 'trucileers' climbed on the bandwagon. Many joined in counties which had seen little or no fighting before the truce. Minister for Agriculture Patrick Hogan referred in the Dáil to the '20 out of the 26 counties in the Free State where there was not a shot heard until 1922'. The rapid increase in numbers had adverse consequences for the cohesion of the IRA, which split over the treaty, leading to an even greater breakdown of law and order. After the treaty, rebellion against the state was funded by robbing banks, post offices, shops and homes. Criminals also took advantage of the situation. O'Higgins spoke of houses crammed with loot and 'hens roosting on valuable oil paintings and silver articles scattered over the floors'.[16] Although the army quickly defeated the irregulars (except in parts of Munster) and took many prisoners, it did not attempt to restore normal policing. That task was left to the unarmed Guards.

O'Higgins appointed Major-General Eoin O'Duffy as commissioner of the Guards. He was a Monaghan-born civil engineer who had served in the IRA northern command during the war of independence and was a senior army officer during the civil war. O'Duffy was a superb organiser but he was also, in Conor Brady's words, 'vain, domineering, constantly in search of publicity, intolerant of the shortcomings of others and slow to credit their virtues'.[17] However, at the time of his appointment these deficiencies were less apparent than they later became. O'Duffy had an understanding with O'Higgins that he would have complete autonomy over the force. Eamonn Coogan, a 28-year-old former Irish Volunteer, teacher and local government administrator, was appointed deputy commissioner by Cosgrave, who instructed him to 'keep an eye' on O'Duffy.[18] Patrick Walsh, reinstated with the rank of assistant commissioner, drew up a strict disciplinary code. Coogan was given responsibility for supervising the distribution of the force and criminal investigation. O'Duffy quickly weeded out those responsible for the 'Kildare mutiny', enforced discipline, dismissed or forced out superintendents he considered inadequate, and halted recruitment of Clare men after discovering that Dáil Deputy Patrick Brennan, a former IRA commander and senior police officer, had recruited a third of the initial trainees from that county. O'Duffy appointed ex-RIC men as chief superintendents and employed experienced former policemen to fill civilian positions at headquarters without a repetition of the earlier objections.

O'Duffy insisted that strict obedience and discipline be inculcated in recruits, realising that many of them would work in remote areas with little supervision. He encouraged the Guards to become teetotallers, sought to impart a moral and national outlook among them and emphasised the necessity of being apolitical.[19] Defence Minister Richard Mulcahy insisted that the Guards take over immediately from the army in areas cleared of irregulars and they were deployed by September 1922, except where fighting continued. By the end of the year about two thousand Guards occupied 190 stations, still far short of the target of over eight hundred. O'Duffy recommended a strategy for passive resistance by the Guards against their armed opponents.[20]

Throughout the winter of 1922–23 the irregulars destroyed 485 police stations. The unarmed Guards could not always resist their armed attackers. Some 400 were physically beaten, stripped of their uniforms and robbed of their personal possessions. One Guard, Harry Phelan, was murdered. Police morale deteriorated and suggestions were made that they should be armed but O'Higgins and O'Duffy resisted the pressure. However, the Guards were unaware that irregular leader Liam Lynch had issued instructions that while they should be intimidated, their stations destroyed, uniforms removed and property seized, they should not be harmed.[21] The Guards were a vital building block of the new state. The irregulars could easily have killed them but were deterred for fear the government might resort to executions in reprisal. Instead they attempted to terrorise the police.

This backfired because the unarmed Guards resolutely stood their ground in most situations, such as at Granard, where five Guards were attacked by 20 armed men who seized their personal possessions and ordered them to clear out of the district. They refused despite an earlier attempt being made to bomb the station. However, there were exceptions where the unarmed Guards came under intolerable pressure. In one case an entire station force disappeared, leaving books and station records behind, neatly balanced with a final entry noting their departure to the US. O'Higgins and O'Duffy maximised publicity to give the force a public image of courage, determination and purpose.[22] The Guards in rural Ireland were careful and discreet in their policing and often steered clear of policing activities that might be regarded as political crime.[23]

Police processes and procedures needed to be implemented as most Guards were poorly trained, had no knowledge of crime investigation, no expertise in writing reports or preparing cases for prosecution. As telephones were few, a communications gap existed between isolated stations and headquarters; there were insufficient inspectors and superintendents to give leadership and direction at local level. O'Duffy arranged that instructions, legal notes and basic guidelines on crime investigation be circulated to each station. *Iris an Gharda* (*Police Gazette*) was used to communicate orders from 1923 and also contained lessons in the Irish language. While there was no shortage of suitable recruits, it was difficult to get sufficient qualified personnel to fill the middle and upper ranks, so an open examination was held for cadets. O'Duffy welcomed representations from Defence Minister Mulcahy on behalf of army officers facing demobilisation after the civil war. The temporary adoption of the cadet system was accepted because it was open to all members of the force.

The Civic Guard Bill was introduced in July 1923 to give legal effect to the police and at the Labour Party's suggestion its name was changed to An Garda Síochána (Guardians of the Peace). The Garda Síochána and DMP Acts amalgamated the two forces in 1924. O'Higgins began to depoliticise the Garda, stating 'The internal politics and political controversies of the country are not your concern. You will serve, with the same imperturbable discipline and with increasing efficiency, any Executive which has the support of the majority of the people's elected representatives.'[24]

Irregular leader Frank Aiken ordered his followers to cease fire in April 1923. Over twelve thousand had been imprisoned by the military and were gradually released until all were set free by December 1926.[25] The government quickly reduced the size of the army and made efforts to secure employment for ex-soldiers. However, while the majority remained law abiding, a minority engaged in criminal activities, thereby increasing the police workload.

By September 1925 Garda detectives had been divided into 'crime ordinary' for non-political crime and 'crime special' for political offences. The latter, known as the special branch, quickly and effectively moved against armed dissidents. It was widely seen as the saviour of democracy and order, a terror to evildoers, consisting of good men performing a thankless and dirty task, while conversely it was hated by the dissident minority.[26] Its commander, David Neligan, was subsequently removed by de Valera in 1932 and transferred to the Land Commission for political reasons 'in the public interest'.

The environment in which the Garda had to start policing was very difficult as the laws were relics of British rule, a minority did not accept the legitimacy of the state, there was discontent with government economic and social policies, farm prices had fallen, and unemployment and emigration remained high. After political violence, drink-related offences were the major problem following years of lawlessness and inadequate policing. Poteen (illicit whiskey) distilling had expanded nationwide between 1919 and 1923, in part because drink prices had risen sharply during the Great War. Poteen stills were even found in city locations like Blackpool in Cork, where one was cleverly located near a distillery. Poteen was cheap and highly addictive and threatened the welfare of many communities. Some people were perpetually drunk, leading to violence, poverty, and mental deterioration due to poor methods of distilling that left dangerous impurities such as fusel oil in the spirit. Gardaí reported that illicit distilling was carried out in 'broad daylight' and that 42 'shebeen houses' were located in the vicinity of Malin Head. Finance

Minister Ernest Blythe condemned clergy who kept poteen in their houses and judges who gave lenient sentences. The Guards' station at Gweedore was attacked and burned in December 1922 by poteen makers and rate defaulters.[27] By 1925 illicit distilling had been driven back into the more remote districts in the west after the Garda established a network of stations and acquired sufficient numbers to mount large-scale swoops.

O'Duffy sought to differentiate the Garda from the RIC and encouraged policemen to become involved in sport, the Irish language, music and dancing. Many were accomplished sportsmen who brought their skills to the youth of towns and villages, training hundreds of new teams. The DMP regained the tug-of-war world championship in 1924, having previously won it in 1893. O'Duffy urged Gardaí to spread the use of Irish by organising local tuition.[28] These activities helped them integrate with local communities and improved the quality of their social lives. Their policing bore fruit as crime levels dropped. However, once the army withdrew, they became the first line of defence against the enemies of the state. This damaged their non-political and impartial status in the eyes of many and they became more closely identified with the government.

An IRA offensive in Waterford and Tipperary in 1925 resulted in police harassment in Waterford. O'Duffy ordered the suspension of those responsible and initiated a sworn enquiry but was not in favour of strong action. O'Higgins disagreed and argued that deliberate brutality was not acceptable and those involved should be dismissed. Ultimately the Gardaí involved kept their jobs but were obliged to pay part of the compensation.

Garda morale deteriorated as the police came under increasing pressure from armed subversives and received little support from the public. After the economic situation worsened in 1929, pay and allowances were cut. The Garda representative body was unable to fight the reductions and was seen as a means of preventing Gardaí from joining trade unions. O'Duffy, while supportive of the Gardaí's claims, reiterated that membership of trade unions was forbidden. Recruiting was stopped and stations were closed. While the police were still relatively well paid, they were outraged at the cuts.

O'Duffy's volatile character gave the government cause for concern. He travelled extensively in Europe and the US, and led Gardaí on pilgrimages to Rome and Lourdes, using the occasions to meet Benito Mussolini and publicise himself.[29] He began to criticise the government, urging it to promote fisheries, cut taxes, reduce unemployment and discriminate in favour of ex-army men in public employment. O'Duffy was dissatisfied with the outcome of the boundary commission and feared a revival of IRA and left-wing unrest. By the end of 1931 several ministers were resolved that he would have to go after the 1932 election. De Valera dispensed with his services in March 1933.[30]

SPECIAL LEGISLATION

The government enacted temporary security legislation during the civil war which provided for trial by military tribunal and death sentences. The legislation generally worked while it was in place but on the expiry of the laws, crime and violence increased, witnesses and judges were intimidated and new measures were introduced to tighten security. The laws included the Public Safety Act 1923, the Punishment of Offenders Act 1924, the Firearms Act 1924 and continuance act 1925, the Treasonable and Seditious Offences Act 1925 (which provided for death sentences for waging war against the state and prison sentences for intimidation of judges and ministers), the Public Safety (Emergency Powers) Act 1926, the Public Safety Act 1927 and the Juries Protection Bill 1929 (secret empanelling of juries, majority verdicts, imprisonment for refusing to recognise the court and punishment for intimidation), which continued the special legislation in face of threats to the state. While the constitution provided that personal liberty was inviolable, it contained a qualification that the military had control during the existence of a state of war or armed rebellion.[31]

O'Higgins wanted permanent legislation to deal with politically motivated crime. Offences included conspiracy to overthrow the government, treason, intimidation, incitement, falsely purporting to be the government, seditious libel and unauthorised military exercises. The justifications for the security legislation were given in the debate on the 1923 bill. O'Higgins stated that it was necessary as the government had to deal with the 'aftermath of two revolutions … Men's minds are highly strung and hysterical' and it would take time for the country to settle down. Labour Party leader Tom Johnson argued that the legislation was not justified, whereupon O'Higgins asked if 'we have been living in the moon for the past twelve months'. Labour Deputy Cathal O'Shannon stated that there was enough legislation already in place but O'Higgins insisted, 'We must realise that if there is to be commercial security, if there is to be financial credit or credit in the other senses, national honour or national prestige, the country must pull itself out of that situation.'[32] O'Higgins and his successor Fitzgerald-Kenney were opposed by the Labour Party, the Farmers Party, independents Darrell Figgis, Bryan Cooper and Senator James Douglas, and, after 1926, by Fianna Fáil. The 'Treason Bill' met opposition within Cumann na nGaedheal as it was considered too drastic, and from trade unionists concerned about its implications for strikes. The response from Justice was that the special legislation was temporary, would soon expire, and would have to be replaced.

After the murder of O'Higgins, military courts were permitted by law but not set up, and the law was repealed by the end of 1928. In the late 1920s the world trade depression swelled the ranks of the IRA and a new, more left-wing organisation, Comhairle na Poblachta, was set up to co-ordinate activities. The IRA was supported by the *Irish Press*, the Fianna Fáil national newspaper, in an attempt to make it impossible for the government to try cases of alleged political crime. De Valera was ambivalent; he did not condemn the actions of the IRA and, while he accepted *de facto* rule by the government, he still questioned its *de jure* right to rule. The Catholic hierarchy pointed out that the country had a democratic government and no-one had the right to seek to overthrow it by force of arms.[33] Fianna Fáil called for a reduction in police numbers in 1928 and in response Farmers Party leader Michael Heffernan stated that if they were really anxious 'they could play their part in creating a civic spirit' and realise that the police did not belong to a party but to the country as a whole. Defence Minister Desmond FitzGerald added that a 'small murder gang' had Fianna Fáil as 'their official whiners' in the Dáil. Seán Lemass responded that the party was not hostile to the Garda.[34]

In 1931 Saor Éire began to agitate against paying the land annuities to Britain. Garda Superintendent Seán Curtin was murdered by the IRA in Tipperary. O'Duffy submitted a report in June stating that the IRA was on the verge of open insurrection, and suggested certain organisations be declared illegal and that the Garda be allowed wider powers of search, arrest and detention. Many members of the government were reluctant to introduce such draconian legislation but Cosgrave, Fitzgerald-Kenney and O'Duffy agreed that political crime was becoming more vicious and more violent. The Constitution (Amendment No. 17) Act 1931 proclaimed a state of emergency and gave wide-ranging powers including the right to suspend trial by jury and replace it with military tribunals to deal with political crime. There was no right of appeal. The bill was opposed by Fianna Fáil. Ironically, that party was later to use military tribunals to deal with the same extremists they were protecting before they formed a government in 1932.

Organisations including the IRA and Saor Éire were proscribed, but Sinn Féin was not, as it was easily penetrated by police agents.[35] The government neglected to promote the bill and convince the people of its necessity. Its main support came from the Catholic hierarchy. The act was remarkably successful in the narrow, operational police sense but the adverse impact on public relations was enormous and the Garda knew it. In the early months of 1932 relations between them and the people of rural Ireland reached its lowest point. The IRA went underground and armed crime virtually ceased.

SOCIAL LEGISLATION
Between 1922 and 1932 the government and the Catholic Church acted as self-appointed guardians of the state's morality. Many issues that should have been confronted and resolved in a transparent manner were contained under a veil of secrecy, including the treatment of children in industrial schools and reformatories, sexual crime, alcohol abuse, gambling, indecent and obscene films and publications, venereal disease, prostitution, contraceptives, abortion,

infanticide, divorce, and violence and discrimination against women. Contraceptives remained on sale albeit surreptitiously, many women resorted to backstreet abortionists, infanticide numbers increased and prostitution remained unregulated.

Unmarried mothers were singled out for particularly harsh treatment. The Catholic Church, state, community and families connived to keep secrets, and many unmarried mothers were discarded by society, made dependent on religious orders for their daily existence, traumatised by incarceration, unable to escape the societal stigma attached to their past and buried in unmarked graves.[36] Unmarried mothers were made pay for their 'sin' and were actively encouraged or forced to go to mother-and-baby homes by their families and a disapproving society. Generally women remained in the homes until their children were ready to be placed elsewhere. While in the institutions, the mothers 'earned their keep'. Many unmarried mothers migrated to Britain rather than enter the homes. There were limited choices for rearing the children. Mothers could keep them but received no state support so they were generally sent to orphanages, industrial schools or foster homes and some were illegally adopted.[37]

Women lost social and political influence in the 1920s, in part because many high-profile females opposed the treaty, advocated a continuance of physical force and were consequently sidelined. Women suffered violence with little redress in a male-dominated society despite countless reports in the newspapers.[38] Many of the beatings may have been alcohol related but could also have been a byproduct of the years of violence. Discrimination occurred against females in the civil service and the workplace, where they had few means of redress. They suffered restrictions in other areas, like the Juries Bill 1927, which was introduced to end intimidation of jurors. Under it women were no longer automatically qualified as jurors, leading to an almost total exclusion of women from jury service for the next half century.[39]

O'Higgins saw excessive drinking as a major social problem causing instability, disorderly behaviour, indebtedness, petty crime and family abuse. He introduced the Intoxicating Liquor Bill 1923, which was criticised by the temperance movement as 'mild' and by vintners who felt that 'For generations the public house has been the pivot of Irish politics, and it is not prepared to surrender its influence merely because the country has achieved self-government'.[40] The bill was held up by the Senate and O'Higgins set up the Intoxicating Liquor Commission in February 1925 under the chairmanship of solicitor John J. Horgan. It recommended halving the number of public houses to one for every 400 people, reducing the classes of licence, abolishing compensation for licences withdrawn and curtailing opening hours. Following the commission's report a second Intoxicating Liquor Bill met fierce opposition and divided Cumann na nGaedheal. O'Higgins faced substantial objections from the drink manufacturers and the licensed trade and put through the legislation at a big political cost to his party.

Gambling was disapproved of by the government. The Gaming Act 1923 and another act and regulations made in 1926 provided for the licensing of bookmakers, minimum bets, an age limit and recovery of betting duty. A Totaliser Act was passed in 1929 and a further Betting Act in 1931. However, the state derived less revenue than expected. Complaints were made that children were gambling and Church of Ireland Archbishop of Dublin John Gregg argued it was more important to focus on gambling than on other evils.[41]

Throughout the 1920s the British updated the Criminal Law Amendment (Sexual Crimes) and Censorship Acts. In the Irish Free State, changes in sexual legislation were complicated by the desire of the Catholic Church to impose its middle-class socio-moral values. The committee on the criminal law amendment acts (1880–85) and juvenile prostitution, under the chairmanship of retired barrister William Carrigan KC, was set up in June 1930 by Fitzgerald-Kenney to recommend legislation to regulate sexual offences. Many politicians, civil servants, cultural nationalists, Catholic clergy and O'Duffy believed Ireland was in danger of social and moral collapse. This was attributed to World War I, the troubles which followed it and the remorseless infiltration of foreign influences. Dance-halls, the cinema and motor cars were blamed by the bishops for the decline in morality. O'Duffy, in his submission to the Carrigan committee, detailed the widespread existence of rape, incest and child abuse. He recommended that sexual crimes be tackled by the Garda, which should play a role in shaping a new moral order. He also claimed that only 15 per cent of sexual crime cases were prosecuted and called for the recruitment of female police.[42]

The Carrigan report recommended social reforms, punitive legislative proposals, hearing of cases *in camera*, flogging of perpetrators of sexual crimes and blacklisting of persons convicted of indecency. Carrigan painted a picture of moral decline, rising illegitimacy, increasing levels of prostitution and widespread use of contraception, but recommended that doctors should be able to prescribe contraceptives for mothers at risk.[43] The commission's report was finalised in 1931 and was briefly considered by Cumann na nGaedheal before it left office. Fianna Fáil subsequently prevented its publication because neither the government nor the Catholic Church was willing to confront the implication that an independent Ireland was less virtuous than it had been under British rule.

The Catholic clergy, the Catholic Truth Society of Ireland, the Knights of St Columbanus and the Irish Vigilance Association actively opposed 'indecent' films and literature. They were supported by nationalists who wished to insulate Ireland from English influence.[44] Self-government enabled the Irish to take action and uniform censorship was introduced under the Censorship of Films Act 1923, which gave an official censor power to ban films considered 'indecent, obscene or blasphemous'. Films were censored by a single censor, James Montgomery, from 1923 to 1954, subject to appeal. Montgomery was inflexible and rejected or cut films which offended for reasons including anti-Catholic teaching on family and society, blasphemy, sex, divorce, extra-marital affairs, illegitimacy, birth control, abortion, prostitution, homosexuality, suicide, nudity, eroticism, pornography, and some 'stage Irish' and political films.[45] The newspapers backed film censorship and it is likely that O'Higgins would have introduced stronger legislation. However, after his death, his successor Fitzgerald-Kenney was less keen to do so.[46]

Obscene publications had been covered by British statutes. During and after World War I, republican and left-wing newspapers and 'seditious' articles were censored. The post was also censored by the British and by both sides during the civil war, while the government imposed a ban on the publication of statements by 'unlawful organisations' after the murder of O'Higgins. Consequently a culture of print media censorship already existed.[47] Whereas the English courts had control over publishers, the Irish courts had to penalise distributors, booksellers or newsagents as most of the objectionable publications were published outside their jurisdiction. Catholic pressure groups campaigned for increased protection from 'infidel and immoral' publications, notably English Sunday newspapers like the *News of the World* and *Reynolds News.* Lenten pastorals in 1924 stirred up public opinion. The Committee on Evil Literature was set up by the government in 1925 and, together with proponents of censorship, it called for a wider legal definition of indecent and obscene literature; restrictions on reporting of judicial proceedings; bans on birth control information, contraceptives, and indecent advertisements; blacklisting of newspapers, licensing of newsvendors and booksellers; and easier access to search warrants by the Garda. Independent deputy Sir James Craig stated he did not want to be dictated to by a 'board of cranks'.[48]

The Censorship of Publications Act was passed in 1929. It was poorly drafted, substantially amended and not draconian enough for many advocates of censorship. Unlike the censorship of films, which was done by a single censor, censorship of publications was carried out by a censorship board. De Valera proposed that women should be appointed to an enlarged board. While the main target was birth control literature, the censors adopted a very hard line on books and were not obliged to state why they banned them. Fitzgerald-Kenney later admitted that the government lost Protestant support over the 'Immoral Literature Bill' and as a result he refused to press ahead with a ban on the importation of contraceptives. The Catholic Truth Society encouraged its members to submit books to the censors with 'offensive' passages marked for attention. The government censored on the cheap by borrowing books from *The Times* book club, returning them after they were banned.[49] The *Manchester Guardian* stated that censorship 'would ban half the classics', while playwright

Lennox Robinson argued that the 'Irish will be the laughing stock of intelligent Europe'.[50] In the first year 70 books and 20 newspapers were banned as indecent or obscene, for advocating birth control or containing references to 'unnatural vices'. English newspapers were intercepted and burned. Fitzgerald-Kenney argued that they were dealing with cheap editions of objectionable books and not foreign classics, and stated that Balzac was not read in the Irish Free State. Hanna Sheehy-Skeffington commented that 'we shall probably read in the end exactly what we want'.[51] Fiction of the 'lower type' was barred from free public libraries.

Prostitution and the wartime spread of venereal disease (VD) were causes of anxiety before 1922. Feminists, clergy and the Legion of Mary campaigned against the Dublin 'Monto' brothels, which were finally closed down by 1925 through a combination of pressure, and where that failed, by police raids. VD had become a major concern when a royal commission reported in 1916 that as much as 10 per cent of the UK population might be infected. While the commission led to free and easily accessible treatment being provided in Britain from 1917, in Ireland treatment was limited to three centres. An interdepartmental committee concluded in 1926 that VD was widespread throughout the country and disseminated largely by women who were not prostitutes. Women rather than men were blamed for its spread. DMP Commissioner W.R.E. Murphy called for a single act to cover prostitution and brothel-keeping offences, but no action was taken pending the outcome of the Carrigan committee.[52]

Contraceptives became a major issue in 1930 when the British Ministry of Health recognised their health value, the Lambeth Conference decided not to ban them in all cases and Pope Pius XI published the encyclical *Casti Conubii* on Christian marriage. The appointment of Trinity College graduates (Protestant or Catholic) as dispensary doctors was opposed on the grounds that they might prescribe contraceptives, but Cosgrave advised the Catholic hierarchy that it would be unconstitutional to impose a religious test. Throughout the 1920s the import and sale of contraceptives was legal as the Censorship Act related to dissemination of information only. They were subsequently banned by Fianna Fáil under the Criminal

Law Amendment Act 1935. Pressure by the Catholic hierarchy won
out, regardless of women's health, economic necessity and sexual
well-being.[53]

Abortion came under the Offences against the Person Act 1861.
Its incidence was hard to quantify as not all deaths were certified
and where certified the data were not always accurate. There were
very few prosecutions and no new legislation was passed. Crimes of
infanticide and concealment of births were growing. Judge Kenny
stated that 'infanticide has become a national industry in parts of
this country … The numbers of newly born illegitimate children is
very great' and 'their bodies are disposed of with a great deal of skill,
so much so that the people guilty are not often brought to justice'.[54]
The Catholic bishops complained that the law was too lenient.
Between 1927 and 1932, 63 cases of infanticide became known to the
Garda: 43 were prosecuted and, of those charged, 38 were females.
In the same period 51 other murders were proceeded with by the
state.[55] Eight death sentences for infanticide were commuted to life
imprisonment between 1922 and 1932. Those convicted served short
terms of imprisonment (six months to four years). There was no law
before 1930 compelling fathers to pay towards children's maintenance
and education. Illegitimate children had no rights although the
Illegitimate Children (Affiliation Orders) Act 1930 provided that
they could be legitimised if the parents married later.[56] While this act
may have been considered progressive, its objective was to encourage
marriage and support the Catholic concept of family life. A note on
its file stated that 'a safer model would have been the very similar
Northern Ireland Act 1928 but (the) Irish Free State government did
not know of its existence'.[57] Adoption was legalised in Britain in 1926
but not until 1952 in Ireland. Even then it was for illegitimate children
only. However, children were illegally adopted with the connivance of
industrial schools and orphanages.

Divorce in Ireland before 1922 was governed by the Matrimonial
Causes Marriage Law (Ireland) Amendment Act 1870, under which
divorce could be granted on statutory grounds of adultery, cruelty
or unnatural practices, or declarations of nullity granted for causes
existing at the date of marriage. This allowed divorce but did not

permit the parties to remarry. Full divorce had never resided with the Irish courts. After independence private divorce bills had to go through the Dáil and Senate. This made divorce almost impossible. As a result, in Senate chairman Lord Glenavy's words, 'divorce died a natural death'.[58]

Chapter 9 ~

CREATING AN IRISH PUBLIC SERVICE

After the treaty an Irish public service was urgently needed to take over the administration of the state. The truce delayed the transfer of administrative authority to the south and the Northern Ireland government recruited most of its public servants before the treaty. Irish civil servants were surprised when the treaty transferred all of them to the Irish Free State, with the exception of Post Office staff in Northern Ireland, who remained in the British Post Office. Collins wished to reform the public service and make it a 'Gaelic' one but understood that immediate control over the state's administration and finances was vital for the government to secure political power. The ministers were young, inexperienced and under pressure from those seeking to destroy the state by force of arms, from lack of money and fear of failure. They were not radical thinkers and were supported by the more conservative sections of society. The pre-treaty Dáil civil service was too small, it did not have the necessary skills and its loyalty to the state was uncertain, while the Dublin Castle civil servants were willing to work for the government provided their pay and conditions remained unchanged. They knew they could be easily replaced as the government had plenty of job applications and could recruit trained administrative staff from the local authorities.[1] As the government's credibility was at stake and a breakdown of the state's administrative apparatus would fatally injure its legitimacy, Collins pragmatically decided to retain the Dublin Castle civil servants as the nucleus of the new public service.

The government had two immediate priorities: to defend the state from internal rebellion and establish a civil service. Ministers became preoccupied with the first and left the second to the senior civil servants in the Department of Finance. Dublin Castle was handed over to the provisional government on 16 January 1922, ending centuries of English rule. Collins appointed tax inspector William O'Brien as secretary of Finance and senior Dublin Castle civil servant Joseph Brennan as acting comptroller and auditor general. A native of Bandon, County Cork, Brennan was educated at Clongowes Wood, UCD and Cambridge before becoming a first division civil servant in London. He was transferred to Dublin Castle in 1912 and favourably impressed Sir Warren Fisher during his 1920 review. Despite being a senior civil servant, Brennan confidentially advised Collins on financial matters during the treaty negotiations.

The executive was inundated with job applications and canvassing was widespread. Yet, while there must have been a temptation to provide jobs for its supporters, the executive resisted it in the interest of fairness and efficiency. It set up the Civil Service Commission to end political patronage during the civil war. The Commission provided for competitive examinations in the civil service, police and army, ensuring that the public service did not become an institution of the ruling party. A public notice issued on 1 May 1924 stated that any influence used would automatically disqualify candidates. Although the government missed the opportunity to create new public service structures, the establishment of a professional civil service with entry based on merit, promotion on ability and an apolitical culture were major achievements. The existing Dáil ministries were replaced under the Ministers and Secretaries Act 1924 and were incorporated together with the Dublin Castle administration into a single civil service. That act was, in Cosgrave's view, second in importance after the constitution.

The Irish Free State took on 21,035 civil servants in April 1922, of whom 131 had been pre-treaty Dáil civil servants and 88 were ex-public servants forced to resign by the British. The largest number of civil servants, 13,500, was in the Post Office. Apart from the Post Office, the Dublin Castle civil servants were dispersed throughout the Dáil ministries. The provisional government imposed control over civil servants, ordering them to give an account of their movements after 27 June 1922, and quickly assimilated them into the new public service without trade union opposition. The public service, which had administered the country while it was part of the British Empire, was rapidly adapted to manage a newly independent state without fundamental reform. The senior civil servants in Finance, who were mainly ex-Dublin Castle, were delegated the task of creating a new administration. They seized the opportunity to impose their will on the rest of the public service.

The organisation of the civil service proceeded rapidly during the civil war. J.J. McElligott was appointed assistant secretary of Finance in February 1923. William O'Brien was made chairman of the Revenue Commissioners, a position he held for the next 16 years, and was replaced by Brennan, who had effectively been doing the job of secretary. George McGrath, a former colleague of Collins at chartered accountants Craig Gardner, was appointed comptroller and auditor general. Kilkenny-born Cornelius J. Gregg, who was seconded temporarily from the British civil service, played a major role in organising the new civil service.

The composition of civil service personnel changed after 1922 as the division between first (university graduates) and second division civil servants was scrapped. The Irish higher civil service before 1914 had been staffed mainly by the middle and upper classes, many of whom had been Anglo-Irish. In contrast, the Irish Free State was a bourgeois and republican society. Its bureaucracy was not elitist and jobs were mainly filled by secondary school output, although after 1924, on Gregg's recommendation, small numbers of graduates were recruited as administrative officers. Some civil servants completed university degrees by night. Few acquired professional qualifications.[2] Many were educated by the Christian Brothers, who were over-academic, instilled discipline and nationalism and produced intellectually able and hardworking men with narrow horizons who accepted the existing system with few questions.[3] There was little generational leadership as young people ran the country. The end result was a civil service that focused on preservation rather than development. It was not subject to external influences from the universities, professions, business or the trade unions.[4] Where external groups contributed to the national debate they did so through commissions, the members of which were mainly conservatives who sustained rather than questioned the status quo. The few radical thinkers appointed to commissions produced minority reports which were largely ignored.

Political independence did not result in independence of mind. Dublin Castle had been a clerical-style executive which did not devise policy and was poor in its execution, while few members of the government had any ideas about policy formation. They had to learn on the job and had no blueprint to guide them other than pre-treaty Sinn Féin aspirations. The government did not provide leadership in financial and economic matters and the civil service filled the vacuum. Finance was obsessed with control, and wished to preserve the reformed British Treasury system, believing it was effective while having little or no experience of alternatives. The government did not appreciate the need for economic or financial information and misunderstood or ignored political realities. Finance had some of the best brains in the state but they were conditioned by Treasury thinking and contributed few creative ideas.[5] The government lacked a vision of how to solve the deep-rooted social and economic problems facing the state. Policies were needed and people were required who could think constructively about what had to be done and how to do it. Much of this work was left to commissions.

The government made up its policies piecemeal without co-ordinating them in a coherent programme. Admittedly it inherited very little and had to start from the beginning, but it did not do so in a systematic way. However, it should be noted that developments in policymaking and planning took place mainly after 1932, arising from the economic theories of John Maynard Keynes and the application of planning to harmonise the economic and social resources of the state in a capitalist democratic context (pioneered by Jean Monnet in France after World War II).[6] Policy formation and implementation were carried out simultaneously by civil servants and no effort was made to separate these functions until the 1969 Devlin report.

The public service helped the government gain legitimacy. It began the process of a return to normality before the civil war ended and was the first state institution to gain the people's acceptance. During the civil war the state was run by the executive, the army and the civil service. Each took key decisions and none was fully accountable to the Dáil. While that was expedient in wartime, it was not the way to run a democratic state. The military's political influence waned after the army mutiny in 1924. This left Cosgrave and the by then strongman in the government, O'Higgins, in charge—together with the civil service.

After taking control of the multiplicity of boards and departments that had bedevilled the British administration in Ireland, the government created semi-state companies because it was unwilling to get involved in business or any activity which could not easily be catered for within an existing government department. The new bodies began the process of recapturing powers from the civil service. Some of the commercial companies, such as the Electricity Supply Board, were essential for the development of the state's resources, but many were not.

Personnel relations in the civil service were poor. Civil servants were paid salaries plus a cost-of-living bonus after World War I. As the cost of living fell, bonuses were reduced. Disputes arose over pay, staff numbers, working hours, productivity and exclusion of women from some civil service examinations. There was no satisfactory means of resolving disputes. The government was often hostile towards public servants, particularly those who were ex-Dublin Castle, while Finance Minister Ernest Blythe would only meet civil servants, not their representatives. The basic pay scale and annual leave of new entrants were reduced in 1924. Differential pay rates for married and unmarried men were introduced. Female civil servants could not reach the maximum of their salary scales until retirement age, suffered a ban on promotions and were forced to retire on marriage.

(The latter rule was subsequently extended to female primary teachers by Fianna Fáil in 1934.) The entry standard was kept low to allow older men and ex-national army men to qualify for jobs; after 1926 admission of university graduates was confined to men. De Valera subsequently resisted IRA pressure to 'purge' the civil service following the 1932 election, although he reinstated some dismissed civil servants.

There was much talk about economy, efficiency and effectiveness in a narrow sense which led to a smaller and less expensive civil service by 1932. Fianna Fáil supported cutbacks while simultaneously courting civil servants. However, personnel development, training, accounting, information, organisation, systems, creativity and the need for professional expertise were neglected in the interests of controlling and reducing costs.

Chapter 10 ～

EXTREME SHORTAGE OF MONEY

INTRODUCTION

During the Great War farmers and merchants made large fortunes, which they invested or deposited with the banks. Many of them were to live off this 'old money' in the lean years after the 1929 Wall Street crash, de Valera's disastrous economic war with Britain in the 1930s, the Second World War and its aftermath, and the depressed 1950s.

The Irish Free State replaced a beleaguered British administration which had been unable to collect all its taxes. As Ireland was no longer subsidised by Britain, severe cutbacks were needed to bring expenditure into line with revenue. During the civil war scarce resources were diverted to the army. Compensation was paid for damage done in the war of independence and civil war. The purchase of the remaining land from landlords had to be funded. These factors combined with the post-World War I economic depression meant that money was not available for economic, infrastructural and social development.

The Department of Finance took a lead role in the smooth transfer of power from the British, and the establishment of an Irish public service. The state lived within its means at a time when few countries did so. Budgets were balanced, expenditure strictly controlled and borrowing kept to a minimum. Parity with sterling was maintained and new notes and coins were issued. The government believed that agriculture would grow the economy and focused on keeping it cost-competitive. It favoured free trade and introduced tariffs reluctantly. Substantial investment was made in electricity generation and sugar manufacture was subsidised, but funding for industrial development, the state's infrastructure, healthcare and social welfare was insufficient as fiscal rectitude took priority. The government bequeathed a sound financial position to its successors in 1932.

THE DEPARTMENT OF FINANCE

Michael Collins was appointed Minister for Finance in January 1922. From a farming background, he joined the Post Office in London at the age of 15 and was subsequently employed by a stockbroker (1910), the Board of Trade (1914) and the Guaranty Trust Company (1915). During that time he was active in the GAA, Gaelic League and IRB before returning to Ireland, where he briefly worked for chartered accountants Craig Gardner. He was interned after the Easter 1916 rising and subsequently rebuilt the IRB organisation, served on the Sinn Féin executive and was elected an MP in 1918. He played a leading role in the war of independence, particularly in counter-intelligence, cleverly avoided imprisonment, and masterminded the Dáil loan. Collins was an administrator and organiser rather than a fighter. His death had severe consequences for the government as he was by far its most popular leader.

Collins was replaced by William T. Cosgrave, who retained the finance portfolio when he became executive president. He was succeeded as Minister for Finance by Ernest Blythe in September 1923. Blythe, a native of Magheragall, County Antrim, was the only Protestant to serve as an Irish Free State minister and remained in that post until 1932. Like Collins he came from a farming background and worked in the Department of Agriculture and Technical Instruction before becoming a journalist. A member of the Gaelic League and IRB, Blythe joined the Irish Volunteers, was imprisoned in 1915 and was one of three Protestants elected to the Sinn Féin executive (along with Dr Kathleen Lynn and Darrell Figgis). He served as director of trade and commerce in the first Dáil and opposed the Belfast boycott, fearing it would destroy north–south unity and suggesting instead a selective ban on firms discriminating against Catholics. Blythe advocated conciliating rather than coercing northern Protestants. He strongly believed agriculture would grow the economy. Aged 34 on his appointment, he had a strong personality but a narrow perspective and little interest in administrative innovation.[1] He succeeded O'Higgins as vice-president in 1927.

The Ministers and Secretaries Act 1924 assigned Finance the tasks of administering the state's public finances, supervising and controlling all purchases by government departments and responsibility for the 'business, powers, duties and functions of the branches and officers of the public service' specified in the act. The minister was also given responsibility for the Revenue Commissioners, the Stationery Office, and the Office of Public Works, which remained largely unchanged under Sir Philip Hanson.

The role of the comptroller and auditor general (c & ag) and public accountability closely followed the Whitehall model. The office of c & ag had been established by the Exchequer and Audit Department Act 1866. The c & ag was made responsible to the Dáil and provided it with an independent, apolitical and objective assessment of how the government spent money. Joseph Brennan, the then acting c & ag, wrote to all ministries on 16 February 1922 stating that Finance was in charge of the public service. He advised them that the legislature would decide on the provision and funding of public services, and proposals for expenditure would be introduced only by the government of the day. Finance would determine financial regulations and manage the financial vote process. The c & ag would supervise exchequer receipts and issues, and audit the public accounts. Each ministry would have an accounting officer responsible for financial transactions that could be called upon by the c & ag and the public accounts committee to explain expenditure made without proper authority.[2] From the beginning, Finance communicated directly with other ministries, bypassing their ministers, and exercised as tight a control over the state's finances as Treasury (Ireland) had prior to independence.

Brennan indicated that the C & AG would carry out an accountancy audit, an appropriation audit to ensure parliamentary control over expenditure, and an administrative audit to verify that expenditure was properly authorised. Appropriation and finance accounts would be prepared annually to inform the Dáil how its directions had been carried out. The C & AG would publish them, reporting where money was spent on unauthorised services, in excess of authority or where no service was provided. The public accounts committee would then examine the report.[3] In the early years of the Irish Free State it took three years to review expenditure and even by 1931 over a year to do so. Consequently it was not an effective control mechanism. The system was criticised as the published government accounts were difficult to comprehend. Independent Senator Sir John Keane called for the reform of public accountancy and the Incorporated Accountants suggested that double entry book-keeping principles be introduced with 'appropriate modifications'.[4]

The Revenue Commissioners

Inland Revenue and Customs and Excise were merged to form the Revenue Commissioners in February 1923. Most British tax legislation was carried forward. The Provisional Collection of Taxes Bill 1926 was introduced to put beyond doubt the legal validity of the procedure used to collect taxes and head off potential challenges in the courts. Taxes included income tax, super tax, estate duties, stamp duties, customs tariffs on imported goods and excise duties levied on beer, spirits, tobacco, wine and hydrocarbon oils, while licences were payable by publicans, brewers and distillers. Customs and Excise accounted for over half of the state's revenue.

The government's priority was to collect outstanding taxes and it agreed with the British that it could retain all sums recovered regardless of when they were assessed or fell due. Before the treaty, the Dáil had tried unsuccessfully to collect taxes while the irregulars also attempted to do so during the civil war. Arrears were collected with difficulty as many taxpayers had not made payments for years and a number of tax offices had been burned down after 1919. Approximately £5.7 million was due in income tax alone. Aggressive tax collection was resisted. Cumann na nGaedheal Deputy Alfred O'Rahilly complained in 1924 that court judgements were widely enforced for non-payment of taxes.[5] Fianna Fáil Deputy Seán MacEntee suggested that the Revenue Commissioners 'call off the dogs' in 1927. An investigation branch was set up in that year with the assistance of tax inspectors seconded from Britain.[6] Customs and Excise lost key staff after the treaty and acquired extra work, including tariffs and pension investigations.

Taxation policy

The 'People's' budget of 1909 had increased income tax, super tax and indirect taxes to fund the construction of battleships and new social welfare payments. This was the beginning of the welfare state in Britain and the benefits introduced included old age pensions, national health insurance and other measures, which were of great benefit to the Irish but were difficult to fund after independence. The Great War led to further increases in taxation and left the UK with huge war debts and military pension liabilities. After 1922, the Irish Free State government reduced income tax and agricultural rates, imposed additional taxes on drink, betting and entertainment, and raised customs duties on some imports. Blythe cut income tax rates from 25 per cent to 20 per cent in 1925 and further reduced them to 15 per cent in 1927. He provided an annual agricultural rate rebate of £599,011 per annum in 1925 and a further £750,000 in 1931.

A movement in Cork called for the abolition of income tax in 1925.[7] Cosgrave queried where the alternative revenue would be raised. Hugo Flinn, one of the leading campaigners, suggested reductions in the army and public services, and argued that the abolition of income tax would repatriate capital and reduce the cost of living.[8] However, the taxation system was not subjected to major review until the 1950s and 1960s.

Increased drink and tobacco duties were resisted by merchants and the licensed trade supported by independent deputies William Redmond and John Daly. Betting tax was opposed for fear it would destroy the racing and horse-breeding industry but independent deputy Bryan Cooper argued that a five per cent levy would not kill racing.[9] The government hoped that low income taxes would encourage people to keep funds at home but bank deposits of £100 million in 1927 represented a drop of 20 per cent since 1922. Nevertheless in 1926–27, Irish people had £195 million invested abroad while foreigners had £75 million invested in Ireland.[10] The old problem of plenty of Irish capital and inability to utilise it continued in the 1920s.

Even after the ultimate financial settlement with the British in 1926, Blythe remained cautious and was reluctant to increase taxes to provide funds for economic and social expenditure which could have stimulated the economy and gained the government badly needed popularity. His policies made sense according to the then prevailing conventional wisdom, but the tax regime was regressive as taxes fell disproportionately on the poor.

Balanced budgets

After World War I financial stability and balanced budgets were the order of the day as nations began the process of reconstruction and aggressively competed to regain trade and get access to raw materials, oil and investment opportunities. The British government pursued a deflationary policy and steadily reduced the amount of currency in circulation. (It had risen sharply during the war, which left Britain with a large national debt, leading to calls for economy, elimination of waste, a return to balanced budgets and a firm currency after the rapid inflation of 1918–19.)

The war and its immediate aftermath had been boom years for agriculture but in the early 1920s agricultural prices fell significantly; borrowers were unable to make repayments and unemployment increased. The Irish Free State absorbed some of the shock from the downturn in the economy as it had substantial income from external investments, pensions and emigrants' remittances.

Strict financial controls were implemented immediately after independence. The book of estimates informed the Dáil how much money was needed and the Dáil voted the amount that could be spent. Finance exercised control before money was expended and the C & AG afterwards. Government spending consisted mainly of salaries, wages and pensions for civil servants, teachers, police and soldiers, together with old age pensions. Other significant items of expenditure included home assistance, agricultural rate rebates and interest on loans, while health, social and economic expenditures were minimal. Capital expenditure was confined mainly to hydroelectricity, roads, housing and telephones. Audits began in June 1922, particularly of the army, which had been hurriedly set up, had no effective supply system and had poor accounting procedures for purchases and issues.

William O'Brien served briefly as secretary of the department before being replaced by Joseph Brennan, who was a strong proponent of fiscal rectitude. Under him Finance determined how much money could be spent, having regard to the state's revenue and credit rating. The cost of the civil war and the potential liability for bonds issued under the Land Act 1923 reduced the state's capacity to borrow.

Cosgrave presented the budget for 1923–24. Expenditure exceeded revenue by 50 per cent due to the civil war. The banks were unwilling to bridge the funding gap because of political instability, so a national loan was considered—despite the risk that it might not be fully subscribed, thereby damaging the government's credibility. Cuts were needed and, as Sir John Keane subsequently argued, government expenditure needed to be reduced by about a third through decentralising control, imposing strict financial rationing and stopping civil service recruitment.[11] Yet the Irish Free State's expenditure was less than that of Norway, a country with a similar sized population which had higher debt charges and spent more on economic and social development but had far lower pension costs.[12]

Retrenchment was advocated because the cost of living, which had increased during World War I, fell sharply after 1921 without corresponding cuts in public service wages and state pensions. The government reduced the pay of public servants by 10 per cent in 1924 and, more controversially, old age pensions, then payable to people over 70 years. Pensions were reduced by one shilling per week but were subsequently restored in 1928. The reduction was a major blunder as old age pension cuts should have been a last resort. Civil servant Bulmer Hobson suggested borrowing, but Finance was too influenced by Treasury thinking to budge.[13] Revised means testing and stricter examination of claimants by pension officers caused resentment, while some elderly people had difficulty proving their ages due to poor records (state registration of births had only begun in 1863). Labour Deputy Timothy Murphy stated that the Old Age Pensions Act 1924 was one of the most reactionary measures ever placed on the statute book and cited cases of small farmers who had their pension reduced from ten shillings to six shillings because they had a few cattle.[14] At the same time tradesmen and labourers in Cork suffered wage cuts of 12.5 and 15 per cent respectively.[15] The rapid reduction in army size eased fiscal pressure, but led to the army mutiny in 1924, which resulted in the national loan falling from 99 to 92 at a time when gilts were appreciating, and investments in savings certificates plummeted. Brennan observed, 'Credit is a very delicate fabric which is much easier to damage than repair.'[16] Yet the government, in a period of cutbacks, made its initial investment in radio.

Brennan grew increasingly annoyed at his inability to curb expenditure and became disenchanted with Blythe, whom he considered a 'dead-loss' more concerned with the Irish language than finance, and he resigned in January 1927.[17] Still only 39 years old, he was appointed chairman of the Currency Commission. He had been a hard taskmaster but popular in Finance as he ensured its primacy over other government departments. The state's credit was by then firmly established, a financial settlement with Britain had been made and the internal organisation of Finance had been set up in a form which was to endure for over 30 years. Good order and organisation prevailed where there had been uncertainty and instability in 1922. But fiscal stringency had won out over common sense.

Brennan was succeeded by Assistant Secretary James John (J.J.) McElligott. Born at Tralee in 1893 and educated at UCD, he became a first division clerk at Dublin Castle, but was dismissed for participating in the 1916 rising and imprisoned. McElligott subsequently worked as a journalist and managing editor of the *Statist*, a London financial weekly, before returning to Ireland in 1923. He did not initiate any major changes, and remained secretary until 1953.

An economy committee was set up in 1927 with objectives similar to those of the cost-cutting Geddes committee in Britain. After a few sessions, Farmers Party leader Michael Heffernan, parliamentary secretary to Blythe, was appointed chairman. The committee made preliminary findings in November 1931, recommending further reductions in teachers' and police salaries, and old age pensions. However, Heffernan was against reducing the old age pensions again, stating they 'were little more than barely sufficient to maintain the pensioners at the scantiest level of existence'.[18]

The executive devoted more time to discussing the annual estimates after 1927. Cuts in expenditure were opposed by the Labour Party but were supported by Fianna Fáil, which sought reductions in the army, police and civil service. Labour Deputy Richard Anthony challenged de Valera to explain how the army and police could be reduced to the advantage of the state as the army was needed while there was an armed threat, but he got no response.[19] After the Wall Street crash in 1929 the government set up an all-party economic committee to seek ways of stimulating the economy. It contained no experts, no professional assistance was sought and it became deadlocked along party lines on the issue of free trade.

The governments between 1922 and 1932 were acutely aware that not only could they be defeated militarily and politically, they could also be defeated financially. The state had to pay the costs of the civil war, which have been estimated as high as £50 million, twice the state's annual expenditure at the time. It also needed to provide up to £30 million for land purchased under the Land Act 1923 together with compensation for damage during the war of independence and civil war. Its financial position was very exposed and if it ran out of money, Britain was its lender of last resort. The government did not want to exchange hard-won political independence for financial dependence on Britain and the political instability that would inevitably follow.

This was a real risk, as proved by Newfoundland, the oldest British dominion, which had achieved 'responsible government' in 1855. That state suffered financial meltdown after it was devastated by the post-1929 economic depression. The prime minister was ousted and the colonial buildings (houses of parliament) were set on fire.

The new prime minister failed to arrest the economic decline and by 1933 Newfoundland was unable even to pay interest on its debt. Nobody would lend the state money. Britain assumed responsibility for Newfoundland's finances until it became self-financing again, as a default would have damaged the dominions' creditworthiness. Newfoundland was reduced to the status of a crown colony in 1934, governed by a commission. Its people voted for confederation with Canada in 1949.

The Irish governments between 1922 and 1932 operated as far as possible within balanced budgets, as the following tables demonstrate:

Receipts into and payments from the Exchequer, 1922–32

Financial Year	Receipts £m	Payments £m
1922/23	27.86	29.60
1923/24	31.41	38.64
1924/25	26.95	27.48
1925/26	25.44	26.22
1926/27	25.06	27.02
1927/28	24.12	26.08
1928/29	24.22	25.39
1929/30	24.17	25.05
1930/31	24.37	25.27
1931/32	25.50	26.14
Total	**259.10**	**276.89**

Source and use of government funds, 1922–32

		£m	£m
Source of funds:	Receipts	259	
	National Loans (net)	22	
	Savings certificates	7	
	Temporary advances	2	290
Use of funds:	Payments	277	
	Capital expenditure/repayments	11	
	Balance in exchequer	2	290

Notes:

1. Receipts in 1922–24 were high due to arrears of tax collected.
2. Payments in 1922–24 were high due to the civil war.
3. Funds for land purchase and damage compensation were raised by issuing bonds and are not included in the above tables.
4. The principal capital expenditures were the Shannon electricity scheme and telephones.

Source: Finance Accounts, 1922–32.

The government, which was accused of being parsimonious, lived within its means, disappointing politicians and the public, which expected independence to bring prosperity. There were few creative revenue-generating ideas such as Dublin's potential as a financial services centre, raised by financier Sir James Dunn in a letter to Governor-general Tim Healy in 1924.[20]

The economic situation worsened after the Wall Street crash in 1929 and fiscal policies began to be challenged as politicians looked for quick solutions to a complex problem. A more just financial settlement of the land annuities needed to be negotiated as the Irish Free State was stronger than it had been in 1923 and 1926. But the government stuck with its policy of avoidance of disputes with Britain, where there was a growing movement for protection which could seriously damage Irish exports. McElligott reviewed the financial situation in 1931 at a time of severe worldwide depression. Trade and industry were stagnant, the harvest had been poor, import duties were falling, current expenditure was rising, capital expenditure was minimal and there were no windfall taxes. The national teachers' pension fund needed an injection of £5 million and £500,000 of the first Dáil loan was due for repayment. Emigrants' remittances and returns on foreign investments were declining. McElligott speculated that if public sector costs could be cut, the private sector might follow, thereby causing deflation. He did not wish to raise tax or borrow at a time of depression so he proposed no new expenditure and reductions in police, teachers' and army pay, old age pensions, national health insurance, unemployment benefits and grants-in-aid. Local authorities' standard of service would be examined to seek economies. Small amounts of extra tax could be raised.[21] The government introduced a supplementary budget in late 1931 to address the worsening financial position rather than borrow money. Petrol was increased by four pence a gallon and income tax by six pence in the pound. Garda and teachers' salaries were reduced. It was against that background that Cumann na nGaedheal went into the general election in early 1932.

The national loans

The City of London considered the Irish Free State to be a bad risk during the civil war, while investors wanted to be sure that loans would be repaid on par with sterling, fearing that the Irish pound might be devalued. While American banks offered finance, Brennan preferred to borrow at home but was against borrowing to cover budget deficits. McElligott saw a national loan as both a means of raising money and getting the public financially interested in the state. He argued that long-term borrowing for capital projects would be acceptable.[22]

The 1923 funding requirement of £25 million was very high, the equivalent of one year's government expenditure. This led to fears of inflation. The option of issuing more banknotes was rejected by Finance as bad practice (which was borne out by the experience of Germany, where banknotes were issued to fund expenditure, leading to hyper-inflation). Cosgrave was reluctant to seek British backing for a national loan for fear it could lose him the 1923 election, so he postponed the loan and Finance managed to raise sufficient cash by short-term bank loans, deferring compensation claims and payments to creditors, securing control of government funds in Ireland and abroad, ending building schemes, stopping the recruitment of civil servants, making economies in the army and police and collecting tax arrears.[23] The government remained concerned about its international credit rating. Yet after the civil war, the credit of the Irish Free State stood next to Britain and Canada on Wall Street as it was one of the few creditor nations in Europe, it balanced its budgets, and in 1926 had external income from foreign investments of £11 million plus emigrants' remittances of US$3 million from America alone and £3 million in British military, police and judicial pensions.[24]

After the election of the fourth Dáil in 1923, a national loan of £10 million redeemable stock at 5 per cent interest was issued at a discount of 95. The loan was floated in Dublin rather than London, where it would have had to conform to the Colonial Loan Stock Act. The banks were not helpful but the stock was oversubscribed by £200,000, proving that the Irish public was more confident than the bankers. When dealing in the stock opened, it rose four points to 99. This was a 'valuable moral victory' and a major vote of confidence in the government and Finance.[25] Thereafter government fiscal policies were dictated by the senior civil servants in Finance, as Blythe had less interest in the details of state finance than his predecessors Collins and Cosgrave. Two further national loans were raised for £7 million in 1928 and £6 million in 1931.

The financial settlements

Under article 5 of the treaty the Irish Free State was required to pay a 'fair and equitable' share of the UK public debt and war pensions. The Irish sought compensation for past over-taxation, drained capital, destroyed industries and banished millions of emigrants estimated at £700 million in 1920.[26] This figure was based on the Childers commission on Irish over-taxation (1895), but when the Primrose commission reported 17 years later the situation had changed radically, as British expenditure in Ireland was by then considerably higher as a result of the Old Age Pensions Act 1908 and the National Insurance Act 1911. The British, although anxious to settle, did not press the Irish during the civil war, but the Conservative governments under Bonar Law and Baldwin were less sympathetic than Lloyd George had been.

An interim arrangement, the 'Hills/Cosgrave pact', was reached in February 1923 whereby the Irish Free State would pay the land annuities (about £3 million per annum) to the British, who waived some claims, agreed to fund the remaining land payments before the 1923 Land Act and guaranteed future land loan stock. Cosgrave was in a very poor bargaining position as he desperately needed to finance land purchase to end agrarian agitation. The deal was done in secret at the request of the Irish and was never ratified by the Dáil.

The British guarantee was not taken up as the ending of the civil war obviated its need. Liability for compensation arising from the war of independence was agreed and a commission chaired first by Lord Shaw and subsequently by Sir Alexander Wood-Renton was set up to adjudicate on claims made by both sides.[27] It heard 37,000 claims, of which 17,000 were found to be outside its terms of reference. White Cross and British government advances and insurance were deducted from claims. Compensation before and after the truce under the Damage to Property Compensation Act 1923 and Indemnity Act 1924 (which covered billeting of troops) amounted to £12.5 million. Personal injuries claims, which are difficult to quantify with any degree of accuracy, may have amounted to a further £11 million.

The 'ultimate financial settlement', relating to the dissolution of the fiscal unity of the United Kingdom, was made in 1926 following the boundary commission report. The Irish rejected the British claims but believed they had to make some settlement to maintain international financial credibility. Cosgrave may have been in a better bargaining position than he realised, as the British wanted a settlement and might have been willing to do a deal on the land annuities. The British waived their claim for war debts, pensions and interest amounting to £162 million provided the Irish Free State paid a total sum of £16 million by instalments over 65 years. This was communicated to the Dáil, and was always paid, even by Fianna Fáil governments during the economic war, until it was waived by Harold Wilson's Labour government in 1969. In return for the debt write-off the Irish agreed to pay over land annuities collected under the Land Acts 1891 to 1909 without deduction of tax. A double taxation agreement was subsequently finalised. The Irish also agreed to repay the local loans fund (£12 million) over 20 years and would recoup this money by collecting annuities from farmers who purchased land before 1891. Other items resolved or waived included war damage claims, railway compensation, properties, munitions purchases, the unemployment insurance fund deficit, and police and judicial pensions. The Irish waived any claims against the British consolidated fund assets and share of war repatriations.[28]

The land annuities

The land annuities question remained to be resolved. The landlords had been bought out mainly with loan stock repayable over a long period of time. The scheme was administered by the Land Commission, which collected annuities from the farmers, and the British Public Debt Commissioners, which managed the sinking fund into which the annuities were paid and out of which disbursements of interest and capital were made. If insufficient funds were collected the British Exchequer was liable for the deficiency. Land purchasers agreed to repay the debt by annuities (usually 66½ or 68½ years) which would fund the repayment of the loan stock and interest. But many people argued that the debt should have been written off as the land had been expropriated from the Irish. The government considered the legal position and decided to continue remitting the annuities. There was confusion as the Government of Ireland Act 1920 cancelled Ireland's liability for land annuities but it required payment of an imperial contribution of £10 million per annum. Under the treaty, the Irish Free State was not obliged to make the imperial contribution, but the British expected it to pay over the annuities, which they considered a legal debt. The annuities were not specifically referred to in the treaty, and there was disagreement regarding whether or not they were included in the British public debt under article 5. The British finance accounts indicated they were not, and annuity payments were also excluded from the Irish finance accounts.

Socialist republican and IRA member Peadar O'Donnell began to agitate against paying the annuities in 1926. In 1928 he joined forces with Senator Maurice Moore to launch the Anti-Tribute League and, encouraged by British communists in 1930, tried to separate small farmers from larger farming interests and forge them into a revolutionary alliance with agricultural labourers and the urban working class in line with the thinking of Kresintern (Peasants International, a branch of the Comintern). He subsequently began to build a new organisation, Saor Éire (Free Ireland), on the foundations of IRA units and working farmer committees which would more aggressively oppose the annuities. However, Fianna Fáil, which by then had recruited the majority of the IRA, argued that farmers would still have to pay the annuities but the government should retain the money rather than remitting it to Britain.[29] Legal proceedings were issued against defaulting annuitants and the Department of Local Government reduced local authority grants where annuities were not paid, resulting in poorer roads and services. Minister for External Affairs Desmond FitzGerald stated that the annuities were a legal obligation and the nation's honour was involved.[30]

When de Valera refused to pay over the land annuities in 1932, the British Treasury reviewed the position. It conceded that Ireland had been 'unfairly treated' but the 1916 rising had been a 'dig in the back'. In its view the treaty had been based on the premise that Northern Ireland would join the Irish Free State, at which stage the British would have wiped out the financial debts provided there was 'free recognition' of the king. When that did not happen it decided to resolve the outstanding financial arrangements and look for a wider settlement later. In the late 1930s the British sought to pacify potential enemies and make friends as war with Germany was becoming increasingly likely and, as part of Neville Chamberlain's appeasement policy, sought to end the economic war and resolve the annuities issue. De Valera also needed to end the economic war, which had been disastrous for Irish farmers. The Treasury felt it was sensible to conclude a settlement even if it cost £4.6 million per annum (police pensions, land and local loan annuities, and other smaller payments). It attempted to quantify how much the Irish Free State could afford, accepting that the full amount of £100 million due could not be collected as de Valera had by then reduced his capacity to pay by halving the land annuities owing from the farmers. The Treasury had concerns about how Northern Ireland farmers, who were still paying annuities, might react. It considered seeking a sum of £25 million but rejected it as the British would have to guarantee an Irish loan, resulting in difficult legislation and extra cost, and finally settled on a sum of £10 million, which it calculated the Irish could raise.[31] The British decided not to make an offer but to agree if the Irish suggested that sum, which was eventually paid by the Irish Free State as part of the settlement ending the economic war in 1938. De Valera, who had promised never to remit the annuities, argued that the £10 million paid did not relate to them but represented half of the capital value of the other items in dispute.[32]

CURRENCY

Currency needed to be addressed as British banknotes issued after December 1922 were no longer legal tender and the banknotes of the six note-issuing banks applied to Ireland as a whole. Finance was primarily concerned with balancing the budget and maintaining the Irish pound on par with sterling, so a cautious approach was adopted, with interventionist and expansionist policies avoided.[33]

Collins appointed the Bank of Ireland as the government's agent, giving it a monopoly of government banking similar to that held by it under the British. But the Irish joint stock banks were unprepared for the creation of the Irish Free State, were generally unhelpful, and after 1922 maintained comparable lending policies to British banks.[34] They continued to operate as they had before independence and maintained their main reserves in sterling rather than Irish currency. The Bank of Ireland acted as a *de facto* central bank until the establishment of the Irish Currency Commission in 1927, while the Bank of England remained in effect the Irish banks' lender of last resort. During the 1920s the Bank of England adopted a positive approach to the Irish Free State, providing advice on international finance and other central banking related matters. Its governor, Montagu Norman, was particularly supportive.

The government set up a banking commission in 1926. The setting up of commissions was a favourite method of Cumann na nGaedheal governments to get advice or delay decisions. The commission considered currency and note issue; agricultural, industrial and commercial credit; banking regulation and legislation; public borrowing, money market and discount conditions but did not recommend a central bank. McElligott wrote a minority report which suggested that 'after a period of, say, five years of smooth working of the proposed currency arrangements, further enquiry should be made into the question of setting up a central bank'.[35] T.J. Barrington of the Department of Industry and Commerce questioned the advisability of maintaining the link with sterling as the interests of the two states were not compatible. Richard Mulcahy suggested decimal currency.[36] The commission recommended that the Irish pound should be maintained on par with sterling. It adopted a cautious approach to currency reform; to have attempted more in 1926 could have caused public unrest and loss of confidence and might have had serious economic and political consequences.[37] The banking commission recommended the establishment of a Currency Commission which would manage the Irish currency and regulate the commercial banks but would not fulfil all of the responsibilities of a central bank. In particular, it would not be a lender of last resort to the Irish joint stock banks.

In his capacity as chairman of the Currency Commission, Brennan oversaw the banks' financial position, particularly after the Wall Street crash in 1929. In a letter to the Munster and Leinster Bank dated 24 September 1931 he emphasised the importance of keeping the currency commission promptly informed of any abnormal developments in the relations between the banks and their customers and the undesirability of 'undue creations of credit', particularly for speculative purposes.[38]

The banking commission was lenient with the banks, which retained their cartel, and left the problem of long-term funding for industry to the state, which set up the trade loans guarantee scheme in 1924. The scheme failed because the banks would not advance long-term capital. The state also part-funded the Industrial Trust Company, another mechanism for raising long-term finance for industry, but it went into liquidation. Benefiting from the experience of these failures, the third attempt to provide state funding for industry was successful when the Industrial Credit Company, a state-sponsored body, was established in 1933.

Irish coins and banknotes were visible symbols of sovereignty but not everybody wanted them. The Institute of Bankers' journal stated that 'It may be doubted if any real demand for a distinctive coinage can be said to exist'.[39] The Currency Commission oversaw the introduction of coins and notes. The Coinage Act was passed in 1926 and a competition was held for suitable designs, judged by a committee of art chaired by W.B. Yeats, who had won the Nobel Prize for literature in 1923. The result was a magnificent set of coins which won international approval and remained unaltered for 40 years. The new coins were issued in December 1928 with notes following in May 1929, at which stage banks in the Irish Free State lost their note-issuing rights and their banknotes were gradually withdrawn and replaced with consolidated bank notes issued by the Currency Commission. These banknotes remained in use until they were replaced by notes issued by the newly formed Irish Central Bank in 1943. The Currency Act 1927 made Irish currency the legal tender of the Irish Free State and the Irish pound was fixed on par with sterling and freely convertible into British currency.

The position of the Bank of England *vis-à-vis* the Irish banks from the establishment of the Currency Commission in 1927 and the creation of the Irish Central Bank in 1943 is unclear. It is unlikely that the Bank of England would have rescued any Irish bank unable to meet its commitments during that period, and it would have been even more reluctant to do so after de Valera's refusal to pay the land annuities and other debts from 1932 onwards.

Britain returned to the gold standard in 1925 against the advice of economist John Maynard Keynes, who favoured a managed currency. The conversion rate decided on was too high; a lower one would have stimulated growth. Britain left the gold standard in 1931 and devalued the pound. The government kept the Irish pound on par with sterling. It did not withdraw its gold from London as that would have damaged the pound. It was difficult to do otherwise considering the level of trade with Britain, and the Currency Commission expressed satisfaction that 'the Saorstát pound was as secure as could be reasonably expected'.[40] Fianna Fáil Deputy Seán MacEntee supported the government's decision. During the currency crisis Brennan consulted the Bank for International Settlements about the establishment of an Irish central bank. In the Irish Bank Standing Committee's view the direct effect of the suspension of the gold standard on the Irish Free State was almost negligible and there was little evidence of inflationary tendencies.[41]

THE LEGACY OF THE 1920s

Before his death, Collins ensured that Finance would have a key role in the future government of the state. This was reinforced by the Ministers and Secretaries Act 1924 and by the willingness of ministers to allow Finance officials to make the key financial and monetary decisions. Ministers did so because they had confidence in the civil servants who demonstrated that they could administer the state's finances and minimise risk during a decade of political and economic instability at home and abroad.

Many pre-treaty Sinn Féin financial aspirations were not implemented, mainly for pragmatic reasons. A separate currency was not introduced due to the preponderance of trade with Britain, the risk of a flight of capital and the fact that most of the government's supporters and advisors favoured the status quo. Finance was heavily influenced by Treasury and Bank of England thinking while the banking commission recommended no change. A break with sterling would have given the government more flexibility in economic policy but, in retrospect, the decision to remain on par with sterling during the 1920s was probably a prudent one, and parity was not ended until 1979. The banks and stock exchange remained unreformed. Taxation was shifted from direct to indirect largely at the behest of the government's business and farming supporters, while tariffs added further indirect taxes, making the system more inequitable.

Finance consolidated the new state by managing the transition from British to Irish administration, established a professional civil service and ensured it did not become an institution of the ruling party. The government's administrative and fiscal legacies included an established public service, a low-cost administration, good credit rating, minimal borrowings and significant external assets.

Chapter 11 ∿

| AGRICULTURE AND LAND

INTRODUCTION

Agriculture was the most important sector of the economy in 1922, when two-thirds of the population lived in rural areas.[1] The Great War created an agricultural boom but, in the economic downturn which followed, agricultural output declined from a peak of £108 million in 1918/19 to £69 million in 1924/25, while the farm price index fell from 288 in 1920 to 160 in 1922 and 110 in 1931.[2] Agriculture became less profitable due to falling prices, rising costs and low productivity as soil had been depleted during the war, when tillage had been increased without sufficient fertilisers. In the decade after 1922 farmers suffered from limited markets, disruption during the civil war, animal and crop disease, bad weather, poor harvests and the Wall Street crash in 1929. Land remained a contentious issue as its acquisition and redistribution was yet to be completed.

The treaty provided for a continuance of free trade between Britain and Ireland. This was at variance with Arthur Griffith's proposals on tariff protection and self-sufficiency. But his aspirations were a denial of economic reality as the Irish Free State was an open economy with a small domestic market and almost no natural resources. It was overly dependent on agriculture for its exports. However, while free

trade was essential to maximise exports, selective tariff protection
was also needed to support industrial development.

After 1918 a tariff movement gained ground in Britain. Prime
Minister Stanley Baldwin called a general election to get an
endorsement for selective tariffs to reduce chronic unemployment in
1923, but lost to the Labour Party. The 'empire free trade' campaign,
led by press baron Lord Beaverbrook, proposed the abolition of free
trade with the rest of the world, the introduction of food taxes and a
common market of Britain and her dominions, a precursor to a more
politically united empire. This gave the Irish cause for concern as
the other dominions were major competitors on the UK market and
any change favouring them, and leading to increased dependence
on or closer political union with Britain, threatened economic and
political independence. Faced with unprecedented difficulties during
the worldwide economic depression, the British introduced tariffs in
1931.

Agriculture needed free trade, intensification, mechanisation,
more fertilisers, increased productivity, greater land utilisation,
lower unit costs, better quality products and significantly improved
marketing. The government sought to increase agricultural exports,
reduce farm costs and balance the budget. It opposed import
duties, fearing higher farm input prices, increased cost of living and
retaliatory tariffs. Government policy partially succeeded as exports
reached £48 million in 1929, a figure not exceeded in value until 1948
and in volume until 1960. But agriculture failed to grow the economy,
and despite employing 51 per cent of the population in 1926, it only
contributed 32 per cent of gross domestic product.[3]

THE DEPARTMENT OF AGRICULTURE

The Department of Agriculture and Lands took over the functions
of the existing Department of Agriculture and Technical Instruction
(DATI). Under the Ministers and Secretaries Act 1924, Agriculture
received additional responsibility for the Land Commission and
forestry. The National Library, National Museum, National Art Gallery,
Botanic Gardens, Geological Survey and Metropolitan School of Art
were transferred to the Department of Education, and the Ordnance

Survey to Finance. Most functions of the Congested Districts Board (a development agency for the poorer rural areas) were incorporated into the Land Commission, whose prime responsibility under the Land Act 1881 was the acquisition and distribution of land purchased from landlords. Technical schools continued to be administered by the local authorities but after 1922 received their grants from Education.

Patrick Hogan, a 31-year-old solicitor and farmer from Loughrea, County Galway, was appointed Minister for Agriculture in January 1922 and dominated Irish agriculture until 1932. Educated at St. Joseph's College, Garbally, and UCD, he became vice-president of the Irish Farmers' Union and was interned at Ballykinlar for assisting Conor Maguire in organising a land settlement commission in 1920. While there he studied agriculture and became acquainted with Joe McGrath, who recommended him to Michael Collins. Hogan fought a rearguard action against partition when he tried to retain DATI as an all-Ireland body answerable to the Council of Ireland, but the British handed over administration of the Diseases of Animals Act to the Northern Ireland government in 1922.[4] He also attempted to withhold files from the Northern Ireland government and have Agriculture continue to inspect cattle in the northeast. Francis J. Meyrick, an ex-pupil of Blackrock College, graduate of the Royal University and senior civil servant in DATI, was appointed department secretary, a post he held until he retired in 1934.

AGRICULTURAL POLICY
Government policy was to complete land reform and develop agriculture as Ireland had a comparative advantage in that sector. Hogan was an external minister who was convinced agriculture had the potential to grow the economy. He opposed tariffs and compulsory tillage and summed up his policy as 'One more sow, one more cow, and one more acre under the plough.' Hogan wished to 'Help the man who wants to help himself and let the devil take the hindmost'.[5] He set up the Commission on Agriculture, whose report in 1924 covered tillage, conacre, marketing, transport, off-farm employment, education and credit. It quoted Edmund Burke: 'To provide for us in our necessities is not in the power of government.'

The commission recommended individual and collective voluntary effort rather than grants, subsidies and guaranteed prices. Hogan dismissed the argument that money would solve farmers' problems and insisted they had to find their own salvation. A minority report by Labour Party members of the commission advocated state intervention, professionalising co-op managers, increasing tillage for stock feeding and food security, raising home consumption, developing meat processing, controlling grain imports and co-operative marketing. Labour Deputy Thomas Nagle advocated compulsory tillage to provide jobs for 10,000 unemployed farm labourers.[6] Hogan did not accept their recommendations but was concerned about the differential between farm and retail prices and urged farmers to organise in co-operatives, arguing that agriculture needed development rather than change. The commission report provided a blueprint for 1920s agricultural policy.

Hogan was careful not to offend the larger native Irish farmers who believed the treaty was in their best interests as they supported law and order, stable government, guarantees of political freedom, completion of land purchase and security of tenure and ownership.[7] Their greatest fear was large-scale land seizures as the anti-treaty side supported landless labourers and farmers with uneconomical holdings. Unrest among agricultural labourers frightened farmers despite the Labour movement being mainly moderate. Farmers' organisations were influential in the early 1920s but their power waned as differences between large and small farmers, and between pasture and tillage interests, which had opposing attitudes to tariffs and subsidies, led to fragmentation, with local interests replacing national ones. The Farmers Party, formed in 1922, supported the government because it had policies akin to its own. In 1927 it entered a formal coalition with Cumann na nGaedheal brokered by Hogan, preferring that party's policies to those of Fianna Fáil.

Hogan saw agriculture as a business rather than a reliever of poverty and emigration, and had a low opinion of the county committees of agriculture, where he believed bad farmers dominated as they had spare time to attend meetings. He was convinced that the future of agriculture in Ireland was linked inextricably to education, with university education and research being more important than instruction at primary level.[8] Hogan regretted the government's decision to merge the College of Science and Albert Agricultural College with UCD as Agriculture lost its researchers. He supported the agricultural colleges, but numbers attending them remained disappointingly low. Agricultural education was opposed by many farmers because they perceived it as depriving them of family labour and because it was largely funded from the rates.

Land purchase and distribution

Around seventy per cent of agricultural land was already in farmer-owners' hands by 1922. Pre-treaty Sinn Féin had advocated land distribution to smallholders and landless labourers to prevent them becoming a burden on the state. Considerable land hunger existed as evicted tenants, smallholders and farm labourers realised the final major land distribution was their last chance to get land. In the breakdown of law and order during the truce and civil war there was widespread agrarian violence, cattle seizures and house-burnings. Cosgrave stated that the Land Bill 1923 'is necessary for the immediate preservation of public peace'.[9]

Hogan promoted a bill which confirmed the existing pattern of land settlement and exploited divisions between farmers, smallholders, tenants and labourers. Relief of congestion was not given preference and the act was criticised for benefiting a minority. It was a practical approach as his objective was to set up viable farmers and not to address the grievances of the many claimants for land. Untenanted land was divided by the Land Commission between uneconomic smallholders, migrants, evicted tenants and unemployed labourers. Some 50 co-operatives formed by landless men purchased 17,211 acres of land at a cost of £365,066, financed by the National Land Bank.[10] Anti-treaty Deputy David Kent suggested that land be given to IRA veterans, but Hogan evaded what could have been a contentious issue, particularly where the recipients might have had no farming experience. Objections to the price paid and the failure to divide 'ranches' (large farms) between landless men were ignored.[11]

The Land Act 1923 ended the relationship between landlord and tenant farmer as the Land Commission, which was also a court of record, took over the management of the estates. Tenants paid rents which were 35 per cent lower until title was vested in purchasers and bonds allocated to vendors or encumbrancers. Labour Deputy Sean Lyons argued that the land was the property of the state.[12] Some deputies alleged that landlords' property was being confiscated, while others pointed out that the landlords, despite complaining, were 'quietly happy' as they had feared worse treatment from a native government. Labour Party leader Tom Johnson complained that landlords were being paid too much, queried their title to the land, demanded 'rigid justice' and stated that the people would never admit a statute of limitations. In response to Johnson and those who suggested it was necessary to go back and enquire 'most searchingly' into how landlords' titles arose, Kevin O'Higgins asked if they should 'Bring O'Donnell back from Spain and plant him over three or four counties in the North of Ireland'. He cited a letter received from Simon P. O'Rorke, a New York estate agent, who asked 'when it would be convenient for us to entertain his claim to Leitrim, Cavan and certain areas around there, as he was quite sure that he was the lineal descendent of O'Rorke of Breffni'.[13] Since a large proportion of the properties had been held by landlords before 1800, sitting tenants rather than those who claimed dispossession in past centuries got the land.

The Land Act 1923 provided for the purchase of the remaining tenanted and untenanted land from landlords and ended co-op ownership of land which had been advocated by Michael Davitt. Congested District Board and co-op lands were distributed by the Land Commission. The cost of the remaining land purchase and distribution, estimated at £25–30 million, constrained the government's ability to invest in economic and social policies—particularly when combined with the almost £50 million estimated cost of the civil war given in the Dáil on 28 May 1923. Land agitation faded out as the government adopted a firm line, clearly signalling there would be no further distribution of land.[14] Compulsory purchase was used more extensively after 1923 to acquire land and to transfer tenanted land from landlords.

The final resolution of the land question during the civil war and its aftermath was a testament to Hogan's ability as a minister. Its significance was perhaps not fully appreciated at the time, leading Cumann na nGaedheal Deputy Vincent White to ask, 'Do we here in this Dáil, not to say the man in the street realise what is taking place?'[15] But once land was distributed, uneconomic smallholders and labourers had no long-term prospects in agriculture. Many left the country, in Peadar O'Donnell's words, blaming 'nobody for their lot'.[16]

Agricultural labour unrest continued after independence. Labourers achieved wage increases in a period of high inflation during World War I but in the early 1920s, farmers reduced wages when the cost of living fell. An agricultural labourers' strike took place in County Waterford in 1923, during which farmers unloaded ships and operated plants at Shandon creamery and Dungarvan Co-op, 'standing shoulder to shoulder in the fight against Bolshevism'. Cattle were killed and driven off farms, the residence of a cattle dealer was destroyed by fire, as were hayricks, and baton charges took place in Waterford before the strike fizzled out.[17]

Many smallholders needed off-farm jobs. They survived on relief and casual farm work, competing with landless labourers. Both groups migrated seasonally to get employment. To maintain agricultural competitiveness, Hogan sought to keep farm wages down, opposed increases in social welfare payments and supported low pay rates at the Shannon hydroelectricity building site. During the 1920s the demand for farm labourers fell due to increasing mechanisation, adding further downward pressure on wages.

Under the land acts passed before and after independence, a total of 450,000 holdings were transferred, consisting of 15.5 million acres, at a cost of over £130 million.[18] Responsibility for lands was moved from the Department of Agriculture and Lands to a renamed Department of Lands and Fisheries in 1928 and Martin Roddy was appointed parliamentary secretary with responsibility for the Land Commission. The main issue relating to land in the late 1920s was the slowness with which the Land Commission was acquiring and distributing it. Land Acts were passed in 1926, 1927 and 1929 to extend land purchase and in 1931 to provide for early vesting.[19]

Legislating for quality

Hogan initiated legislation to improve quality and prevent animal and crop disease. Regulations had been relaxed since 1919 and their re-imposition was opposed by farmers, merchants and politicians. The benefits of regulation were wanted but the pain of conforming was not. Not everybody was convinced of the need for a national brand for butter of a high standard, the grading of eggs or the improvement in breeds of cattle. Cumann na nGaedheal Deputy Seán Mac Giobúin considered these issues as 'trifles' when large farmers were surviving by drawing on their savings while small farmers had none to draw upon.[20]

Hogan sought to improve quality and add value to raise farm incomes and retain optimum numbers on the land. Cattle were bred for meat rather than milk as surplus calves were sold to graziers, who fattened them mainly for the live export trade. Throughout the winter herds were kept on subsistence rations, so animals had to regain weight in the spring before progressing. Ireland lost out on the British butter market every winter as it was unable to supply butter all the year round, and had to sell at lower prices in the spring to recover market share. Most cattle were exported live. Beef and lamb processors competed with the live trade for supplies and faced competition on the British market from Australian, New Zealand and Argentinean frozen meat. Bacon was the best-developed meat processing business, but while Ireland exported premium bacon, it also imported low grade bacon, much of it from the US.[21] The live trade was the main outlet for cattle and sheep throughout the 1920s. A number of attempts were made to develop meat processing by commercial firms and farmers' unions. The government did not support them as it was reluctant to interfere with the market and unwilling to spend money. Nonetheless, plants were reopened at Drogheda and Waterford. Meat processing, with the exception of bacon curing, was a precarious business but became more necessary as live cattle and sheep prices fell in 1931 to levels lower than those of 1914.

Irish butter was seldom pasteurised before 1922, was of variable quality and had no uniform packaging. It had accounted for 14 per cent of British butter imports in 1909 but sold at significantly lower prices than Danish butter. Hogan sought to rectify the situation by improving milk quality, increasing pasteurisation, prosecuting suppliers of dirty milk, and raising the standard of packaging and advertising. The Dairy Produce Act 1924 set minimum standards, despite resistance from co-ops and farmers who were against regulation and surprise inspections. Farm associations controlled butter, egg and bacon quality in Denmark, and had close links with the state technical officers. This was a cheap and effective method of quality control but the government had to legislate to get similar results in Ireland. Farmers Party Deputy Michael Heffernan warned that 'unless we have the active co-operation of the farmers, creamery managers, and all who are interested in this trade, no Bill passed by the Government can be effective'. His party leader, D.J. Gorey, welcomed the bill as 'if left to ourselves we would never reach the required standard'. Independent Deputy William Hewat complained that the act was 'practically nationalisation'.[22] Further legislation on dairy produce was enacted in 1927 and 1931.

It was imperative to upgrade the quality and yields of milk and beef. This required improved breeding and cattle testing, as advocated by independent deputy, brewer and cattle breeder Richard Henrik Beamish. The Livestock and Breeding Act 1925 raised the standard of cattle by promoting pedigree bulls. It met strong opposition and Heffernan complained that 'the country is being converted into a large stock farm with the Minister as manager'.[23] Dairy farmers needed to automate milking and improve milk quality and yield. Annual milk yields averaged 450 gallons/cow against a target of 600 while butterfat pounds per acre were 40 compared with 117 in New Zealand.[24] Consultative councils were set up under the Dairy Produce and Livestock Acts. However, Irish farmers wanted multi-purpose cattle capable of high milk yields combined with a good return when slaughtered. It was difficult to compete simultaneously against Danish cattle bred for milk and butterfat and Aberdeen Angus cattle bred for meat. An Australian delegate at the world dairy congress commented in 1928 that 'as long as you go on breeding dual purpose cattle, so much the better for us ... You cannot get cattle to be good for beef and milk'.[25]

Outbreaks of foot and mouth disease occurred in Britain throughout the 1920s, while the Irish Free State had fewer cases. Liver fluke was a major problem in 1924–25 and interest-free loans were provided to help farmers. Northern Ireland Agriculture Minister E.M. Archdale met Hogan in Dublin in 1926 to discuss agriculture and animal disease in a rare example of cross-border co-operation. In response to the severity of inspection for bovine tuberculosis in animals arriving at British ports, the Agricultural Produce (Fresh Meats) Act 1930 provided for uniform inspection of livestock prior to export.

The Agricultural Produce (Eggs) Act 1924 ensured that eggs were tested for freshness before export to ensure they had sufficient shelf life. This did much to improve sales in Britain. Ireland had had high exports of eggs during World War I, when Denmark and Russia were absent from the British market. Subsequently Denmark recovered market share at Ireland's expense. The act regulated the trade and seemed 'like forcing people to make money'. It was a 'sort of voluntary compulsion' and in Hogan's view there would have been no need for it if producers and exporters were organised for the purposes of their own business. Hogan indicated there was scope for egg production to be doubled in 1928. However, returns were less than they might have been as the bulk of Irish eggs were produced in late spring and early summer, at the time egg prices were lowest.[26] Further legislation on eggs was passed in 1930.

The Agricultural Produce (Potatoes) Act 1932 provided for registration of packing premises, grading, inspection and certification of seed potatoes, in part as a response to black scab potato blight in County Louth in 1923 and the following years. The Destructive Insects and Pests Bill 1928 legislated for protection of crops, trees and bushes and the control of Colorado beetle infestation.

The Dairy Disposal Company

The dairy sector suffered from creamery burnings before 1922 and disruption during the civil war, particularly in Munster, where some creamery managers kept revolvers for their protection. The sector was badly equipped, indifferently managed and poorly financed. There was a belief that if the state took over privately owned creameries it would reduce competition and pave the way for national co-operative marketing. The largest was the Condensed Milk Company of Ireland, and the Irish Agricultural Organisation Society (IAOS) persuaded the government to purchase it. The Dairy Disposal Company, a semi-state body, was formed in 1927 under the chairmanship of department secretary Meyrick and granted the necessary funds under the Creamery Act 1928. It subsequently acquired 170 private creameries, sold 44 of them to co-ops, closed 79 which were adjacent to other creameries and retained 47 as nobody wanted them.[27] It also took over 17 co-ops and set up creameries in parts of the country which were poorly served. The act was a lifesaver for the co-ops as it restricted the formation of new co-operatives, a fact not appreciated by all at the time.[28] However, co-op creameries were not rationalised. These were mostly small and inefficient, and aggressively competed with each other for the available milk pool and the sale of dairy products, to the detriment of farmers, the industry and the state.

Co-operatives

The failure of farmers to co-operate with each other and collectively with the government before and after independence was one of the main reasons why agriculture was not developed to its full potential. The co-ops were not a commercial success due to their fragmented nature, poor direction and management, and unwillingness to co-operate with each other in rationalising production and combined marketing. By the end of the 1920s the Irish co-op movement was in a state of stagnation and even decay in some areas. E.J. Cussen of the Cork Farmers Union expressed the view that 'co-operation was virtually unknown' in the Irish Free State. Sir Horace Plunkett pointed out that farmers were buying at retail prices, selling at wholesale prices and borrowing money at terms unsuited to the industry.[29] The Irish Agricultural Wholesale Society was crippled with debts and had to be reorganised by R.A. Anderson of the IAOS with considerable assistance from the English Co-operative Wholesale Society. Co-ops were not well managed. Committee members tended to be popular rather than business oriented. Managers needed technical qualifications and assistant managers needed to be trained in case of emergencies. The farmers' desire to have locally controlled co-ops held back the dairy and grain sectors.

Dairy marketing

Disorganised marketing was a major problem. A national brand for butter was advocated in 1927 and 1931 but action was delayed until standards were raised. The IAOS set up Irish Associated Creameries (IAC) in 1928 to market dairy produce on behalf of the co-ops. (An earlier attempt had been made to do so by the Irish Co-operative Agency Society in 1893.[30]) Eighty per cent of the co-ops joined IAC, but some of the largest stayed out, while a number of those participating delivered less than promised. Creamery managers liked trading, felt they lost status if they did not control sales, and were prepared to allow IAC to sell while it got good returns—but if better prices could be achieved on the open market they took them, thereby depriving IAC of continuity of supply. It must be said in the co-ops' favour that IAC did not always secure the best prices. The consequence was that it was wound up in 1931 at a time of unstable markets and rapidly falling prices.

Competition from Irish and foreign margarine manufacturers increased during the 1920s. The Empire Marketing Board recommended that Northern Ireland consumers buy Australian rather than Irish Free State butter in 1929. The government set up a butter tribunal in 1930 when there was a world surplus, the worst in living memory. It recommended that dairy co-ops establish a national co-operative marketing operation along the lines of the present Irish Dairy Board. The co-ops rejected it by a small majority, individualism winning out over co-operation. In 1931 the government was forced to impose tariffs on butter and bacon to prevent other countries selling into the Irish market at deflated prices.

Cheese was more profitable than butter in the 1920s but there was a very small home market. Poor quality cheese had been sold during World War I and it was hard to convince sceptical British buyers that good Irish cheese could be produced. The Danes and Dutch began to export fresh milk to Britain in 1928, followed by the Irish in 1931. A joint venture between Tipperary Co-op and a German firm to produce casein was announced in 1928.

Grain and other crops

Tillage crops included cereals: barley, malting barley, wheat and oats; and root crops such as potatoes, turnips, beet, as well as other vegetables, flax and tobacco. Barley and wheat were mainly used as animal feed, malting barley by brewers and distillers, and oats for human consumption and to feed horses (which were still important working farm animals). The quality of Irish wheat was not suitable for milling into baker's flour, so wheat and flour were imported together with low cost animal feed, used mainly for pigs, while 'Indian meal' (maize) was considered better for finishing cattle than oats or barley. Government policy was to use free trade to maximise exports of grain and minimise the cost of farm inputs. Hogan stated, 'I am of the opinion the cost of protection will fall largely on the agricultural community.'[31] The government set up the grain tribunal in 1929, which considered increasing output of homegrown cereals by compelling flour millers and animal feed compounders to use a percentage of native grains. Professor J.P. Drew, chairman of the tribunal, argued that the use of cereals to feed animals gave a better return than grain sold for milling or malting. This approach had been adopted in a number of European countries as there were few markets for surplus grain in the 1920s. Hogan supported it as an alternative to putting tariffs on grain imports, which would raise the cost of farm inputs and bread.

Grain exports did not yield maximum returns due to poor marketing and high freight costs. Farmers complained about railway charges and the fact that shipping lines were controlled by British companies. Farmers Party Deputy John Dineen stated in October 1923 that 'barley was not a paying proposition', due to 'high wages, wet seasons, and bad markets'.[32] Grain growers sought tariffs to block imports while livestock producers, pig farmers, brewers and bakers wished to import duty free. The Department of Finance set up a part-time tariff commission in 1926, but only oatmeal was subjected to duty in that year's budget. The Irish Grain Growers Association organised a conference in 1930 which demanded a ban on oat imports, a tribunal to ascertain brewers' need to import barley and malt, duties on the import of bacon followed by a ban in 18 months, and prohibition of the import of butter, dairy products and eggs. In response Hogan proposed a full-time tariff commission.[33] He had not changed his opinion on protection but realised that the existing arrangement could not continue and wished to retain a statutory body to examine tariff applications and protect farmers. The new commission made speedier decisions and showed a greater willingness to grant tariffs.

While beet had long been grown for animal feed, the extraction of sugar from beet on a large scale was mainly due to Napoleon Bonaparte fast-tracking its development in order to break Britain's monopoly in cane sugar. In 1925 Lippens, a Belgian firm, was granted a subsidy and established the Irish Sugar Manufacturing Company at Carlow the following year. Beet gave tillage farmers higher returns and this generated pressure for other factories. But there was little optimism that the sugar industry would be a success and Farmers Party deputies remained sceptical. Hogan waited to see how the first factory progressed before promoting another. Disputes over the price of beet may have contributed to the delay, and an opportunity to expand the sugar industry was lost until the Irish Sugar Company was formed in 1933 to acquire the Carlow business, extend production to meet the state's sugar requirements and encourage the cultivation of beet in arable crop rotation. Beet pulp, a byproduct, was not fully exploited.

Efforts were made to revive the linen industry in the interests of flax growers. However, it was in decline due to falling prices and rising American tariffs, and little could be done to restore it.[34] Tobacco, which had been actively promoted by Senator Sir Nugent Everard, was written off as an unsuitable crop. Distilling industrial alcohol from potatoes and reclaiming bogs were considered but not developed until the 1930s and 1940s. Horticulture remained largely neglected, although the potential for jam and cider industries was examined by the government in 1930.

Forestry had been the responsibility of the British forestry commission prior to independence and little had been done to develop it. Beech and oak were in short supply and there had been no replanting since World War I, during which many mature trees were felled. The first Dáil staged a 'national arbour day' in 1919 to raise awareness. By 1926 the total acreage planted before and after independence was 240,000 acres or 1.2 per cent of land, the lowest in Europe.[35] The target was to plant a further 600,000 acres and conserve existing forests. Twenty-seven million trees were planted between 1923 and 1928, when a Forestry Act was passed and made operative from 1930 onwards.[36]

Agricultural credit

The joint stock banks did not provide sufficient farm credit. Foreign banking models were evaluated before the semi-state Agricultural Credit Corporation (ACC) was established in 1927. The theory was that it would work through local co-op banks similar to those established by Friederich Raiffeisen in Westphalia in 1849, which had spread rapidly throughout Europe. The first credit bank in Ireland was founded at Doneraile, County Cork, in 1895 with IAOS support but few others were established at that time, although they were recommended by Sir Horace Plunkett's recess committee. A total of 106 co-op credit societies existed by 1928, of which 50 were newly formed.[37] The ACC's capital was £500,000, of which only £200,000 was provided by the banks. Due to the small number of co-op banks, ACC only managed to advance loans of £7.9 million in the first 30 years of its existence.[38]

AGRICULTURE AFTER INDEPENDENCE

During Cumann na nGaedheal's term of office, sheep numbers increased by 24 per cent, poultry by 30 per cent and pigs by 24 per cent, while tillage declined by 17 per cent and cattle by eight per cent.[39] The government's agricultural policy was producer rather than consumer oriented. Legislation and regulations did not achieve the desired results. Strong leadership and a willingness to make and enforce radical changes were needed, backed by investment and a systematic programme of work. But the government was loath to use compulsion as it adopted a hard line on security and did not wish to do likewise with the economy.

Agricultural policy was not effectively implemented, as neither the department nor the county committees of agriculture were capable of delivering the desired results. Hogan admitted, 'The most serious defect in Irish agriculture is its lack of organisation.'[40] The co-ops, which were closer to the farmers, were needed to complete the link between policy and execution. The government spent very little money on agriculture. Yet the state was not constrained by balance of payments, as it was cushioned by substantial external assets accumulated during World War I. Many large farmers used profits to raise family consumption or to provide dowries and put the rest on deposit, rather than investing it in their farms. But most Irish farmers were small or marginal, 58 per cent had less than 30 acres in 1931 and were unlikely to be able to develop their holdings unaided, and the larger commercial farmers were satisfied so long as they had free access to the British market and a government willing to reduce their costs by minimising duties and lowering taxes and rates.

Ireland's main asset was grass, but it needed more fertilisers, better seeds, less over-grazing of pastures in winter, division of pastures into smaller lots, grazing by rotation and conservation for winter feeding. Cattle breeding needed to be improved to get better meat and milk yields. Tillage land was not utilised to best effect. More homegrown grain should have been produced for pigs and as winter feed for cattle. In short, Ireland needed to produce more food units per acre.[41] The choices facing the government were to continue with the same low level of output with its consequent high unit costs, or to raise production, improve quality, reduce costs and effectively market farm produce.

Cumann na nGaedheal looked outwards for economic development as Ireland was an open economy with a small home market. Fianna Fáil looked inwards to achieve self-sufficiency and reduce the country's economic dependence on Britain. Yet Britain was the easiest market to access, it provided good returns and would have yielded more if a greater volume of higher quality products had been marketed effectively. Fianna Fáil's attachment to protection was one of principle, while Cumann na nGaedheal saw it as a temporary expedient until the conditions of trade changed.

The government expected agriculture to drive the economy forward but it failed to deliver. Ireland was too dependent on Britain for exports. The opening up of continental European and world markets would ultimately solve that problem, but the 1920s were not favourable to such a development, even if the Irish had aggressively tried to seek new markets. Agriculture as a percentage of national income continued to decline from 50 per cent in 1912 to 33 per cent in 1926 and 25 per cent in 1938. There was little change in volume between 1922 and 1932, although productivity increased.[42] Yet the Irish Free State did increase its agricultural exports, one of only nine states worldwide to do so in the 1920s. Economist George O'Brien defended Hogan's record, stating that he maximised the use of resources, maintained continuity and ensured sufficient food was produced. But much more could have been achieved if the co-ops had been given incentives to encourage greater intensification at farm level and develop national co-operative marketing. Agricultural output was to be a problem for all governments post-independence, as it only increased by 12 per cent between 1912 and 1960 and was subject to considerable short-term fluctuations.[43]

Chapter 12

FISHERIES AND THE GAELTACHT

INTRODUCTION

Ireland had a long history of fishing but prior to independence had never developed its marine resources. Many of those engaged in fishing were part-time fishermen who went to sea when fish were available and farmed when they were not. As their livelihood was not solely derived from the sea, they made minimum investments in fishing and, because of their small boats, were unable to venture too far from land. Some, such as British ex-servicemen in east Cork, became subsistence fishermen as they had no other means of employment. Since the fifteenth century English and European commercial interests had fished the shores around Ireland, and once steam replaced sail in the 1880s, foreign fishermen caught most of the fish in Irish waters. Ireland lacked entrepreneurs to develop a commercial fishery when there was a growing international demand for fish and a means of getting them to market using ice, railways and steamers. Fishermen were hampered by a lack of suitable landing and storage facilities, properly maintained harbours and efficient means of marketing and distributing fish.

Under the Ministers and Secretaries Act 1924, the Department of Fisheries was given responsibility for deep-sea, coastal, tidal and inland fisheries and their associated industries, and was charged with the administration of rural industries formerly under the Congested Districts Board. The Land Commission was transferred from Agriculture to the renamed Department of Lands and Fisheries in 1928. Thereafter much of the focus of the department seems to have been on land due to farmer pressure.

Fisheries got a separate department because of Arthur Griffith's strong commitment to develop the marine resources which he believed had the potential to employ 100,000 people.[1] Farmers Party leader D.J. Gorey argued against leaving inland fisheries in the control of boards of conservators and landowners with riparian rights.[2] Fionán Lynch was appointed Minister for Fisheries in December 1922. Born at Caherciveen, County Kerry, in 1889, he was a former school teacher, IRB activist and founder member of the Irish Volunteers. The department's first secretary, Lawrence Moriarty, was replaced by Aodh Ó Brolcháin when Lands was transferred in 1928 and he held the post until 1935. Lynch, who was an external minister, stated,

> It appears to me to be of the utmost importance that at the present juncture, when our fisheries have touched the lowest point reached by them during the past twenty-five years, government policy with respect of them should not be one of blowing hot and cold.

A plan was being prepared and in six months Fisheries would show 'excellent reasons' for its existence.[3] Lynch toured the fisheries and concluded that, after four bad years and a high level of debt, fishermen 'would do nothing without state aid'.[4]

THE SEA FISHERIES

The years after World War I were a depressed period for catches of herring and mackerel, which represented the bulk of fish caught in the offshore fisheries. The German and Russian markets had been lost during the war, the US market was saturated with fish when Scottish trawlers resumed fishing after 1918, and prices fell. Later in the 1920s overfishing in the North Sea led to increasing numbers of foreign trawlers off the Irish coast. During the civil war landings of fish decreased and many fishermen lost heart and ceased fishing.[5]

Fisheries restored branding of cured (salted) herring, which had been discontinued, with the *Harp* replacing the *Crown* brand, and specified how barrels should be constructed, fish packed and brine manufactured. The department maintained stocks of salt, barrels, nets and lines for emergencies at 30 stations in remote areas. However, demand for mackerel was declining, in part because of competition from cheaper frozen meat, and that fishery did not recover until the mid-1970s.[6]

British and other foreign fishermen were not entitled to fish in Irish waters after 1922 but continued to do so. The government updated the law on fishing rights but fisheries protection was virtually non-existent. Cumann na nGaedheal Deputy Michael Hennessy complained that poachers were destroying the fisheries, trawlers from France and other countries were fishing inside the limit and smuggling was widespread.[7] Foreign trawlers outnumbered Irish by eight to one in Irish waters.[8] The lack of sufficient trawlers, ignorance of the whereabouts of fish, the absence of canning facilities and poor marketing and distribution resulted in suboptimal returns being made by Irish fishermen, who operated as individuals and needed to be organised.

The National Fishermen's Association was set up in 1924 and sought government assistance without success; its last meeting was held in October 1925. Lynch convened a sea fisheries conference in March 1927, which was attended by fishermen, curers, fish merchants, transport providers, civil servants and politicians. Its recommendations included granting future loans to fishery co-op societies rather than directly to fishermen, powers to repossess boats, credit for curers to be provided by the Agricultural Credit Corporation, more fishery schools and fishery advisors, promotion of fish as a healthy food, support for the Irish Fishermen's Association (which had succeeded the National Fishermen's Association), powers to regulate the fish supply chain, publication of price information, branding cured herring 'Scadáin Saillte, Saorstát Éireann' and compulsory branding of mackerel cured for export.[9] Posts and Telegraphs Minister J.J. Walsh argued the case for capital investment in a deep-sea fleet.

The Labour Party issued a pamphlet entitled *Labour and Ireland's Sea Fisheries* in 1927, which concluded that the fishing industry was a social service operating in a situation of permanent uncertainty in the national interest. It proposed a national fishing fleet owned by local co-operatives, represented on a national fishery council which would advise the minister. The industry would be self-supporting through the catching and marketing activities of the co-ops, while the state would pay for research and fishery protection. Fianna Fáil urged the development of marine resources without offering any specific remedy, while Peadar O'Donnell and Saor Éire advocated the freeing of river fisheries for working fishermen.[10]

Disaster struck on 28 October 1927 when a very severe storm resulted in the deaths of 25 fishermen in Cleggan Bay (Rossadilisk and Inishbofin), 19 off the north Mayo coast (the Iniskea islands and Lacken) and two off Aran. Afterwards Fisheries sent five motorboats to Cleggan and organised crews composed of Donegal offshore fishermen and locals in an attempt to start a deep-sea fishery, but the attempt failed because the herring shoals moved away.[11]

The herring and mackerel fisheries had virtually collapsed by the early 1930s due to the world trade depression, increased US duties, foreign competition, poor distribution within Ireland and the fishermen's inability to chart the erratic behaviour of herring shoals. The late 1920s was a time of declining fish consumption in Europe and Ireland had the lowest fish consumption per head. Catches in tons between 1927 and 1932 illustrate the dramatic fall:[12]

Year	Herring	Mackerel
1927	17,598	9,446
1928	14,195	4,292
1929	6,985	4,799
1930	5,419	2,812
1931	3,665	3,770
1932	2,008	516

Irish fishing research declined after 1922 until 1960, although some British research was available on the Celtic Sea. French scientists made

important discoveries of fish behaviour off the coasts of Ireland—
but Irish fishermen remained unaware of them. The vocational
classes which had been run by the Congested Districts Board were
discontinued in 1929 and subsidies paid to industrial schools for
instruction in boat building were ended. In September 1928 Cosgrave
stated that when private enterprise came forward to support fisheries,
the state might be relied upon to facilitate and encourage the venture
in every possible way, but the government did not intervene to make
it happen.[13]

By the end of the 1920s the loan schemes that had been provided
over the previous 50 years were ceased as many fishermen were
unable to make repayments and boats were repossessed. Fisheries'
records contain details of the outstanding loans and the difficulty of
collecting them. Many had been soft loans granted by the Congested
Districts Board, which was a development agency rather than a
bank.[14] But the official files obscure the fact that most debtors were
subsistence farmers-cum-fishermen who needed continuing support
rather than once-off loans.

Lynch responded to the 1927 sea fisheries conference and the
greater attention fisheries had received since the west coast disaster
when the Sea Fisheries Association, a co-operative, was set up under
the Sea Fisheries Act 1931 with financial assistance from the state.
The act empowered the minister to hand over assets including boats,
outstanding loans, land and buildings to the Association. Loans were
advanced to fishermen who were members of the Association for boats
and gear and they were bound to hand over their catches for sale on
their behalf. The Association, a forerunner of Bórd Iascaigh Mhara
(Sea Fisheries Board), took on the formidable task of marketing the
herring catches. Other actions included improvements in ice-making
and cold storage, and replenishment of oyster and mussel beds.

Tidal, inshore and inland fisheries

A small number of part-time inshore fishermen caught whitebait,
cod, plaice, sole, haddock and whiting. Salmon and sea trout became
more important as herring and mackerel catches declined. Fisheries
needed to be restocked and protected during the annual closed

season. Due to the breakdown of law and order between 1919 and 1923 there was widespread salmon poaching, and the Fisheries Act 1924 penalised salmon poachers and those who bought fish from them. In the debate on the bill Cumann na nGaedheal Deputy Eugene O'Doherty stated that 'salmon are scarce all over the country after three years of lawlessness'.[15] But the penalties were not a sufficient deterrent and poaching continued.

Fishing for shellfish (lobsters, crayfish, prawns, shrimps and crabs) and molluscs (periwinkles, oysters, mussels, scallops and cockles) remained at a low level. Lobsters, exported mainly to France, were a lucrative business and had a low cost of entry but entailed very hard work.[16] Fisheries failed to convince fishermen to use large French-style lobster pots or keep lobsters in ponds from which they could be released to the market when prices were good. Oysters continued to suffer from overfishing and a disease which occurred throughout the 1920s decimated stocks in all but Galway and Tralee bays. Inland salmon and trout fisheries were controlled by local boards of conservators and riparian owners. Many rivers and lakes needed restocking as these fisheries had tourist as well as commercial potential.

A British army commander threatened to blow local fishermen out of Lough Swilly in 1923. After protests by Cardinal Joseph MacRory and Cumann na nGaedheal Deputy P.J. McGoldrick the matter was resolved.[17] In 1929 Donegal fishermen in Lough Foyle clashed with the Northern Ireland-based Foyle and Bann fishery, which claimed it owned the fishing rights to the Lough. This was the subject of correspondence between Cosgrave, Lord Craigavon and Stanley Baldwin.[18] The Donegal fishermen were harassed by bailiffs and taken to court in Northern Ireland. They retaliated by damaging Foyle and Bann fishery boats and chaining bailiffs to a gate. The Irish government took a strong line, considering the matter to be a territorial dispute, and refused Craigavon's suggestion that the privy council should adjudicate. Despite meetings between the Irish and Northern Ireland attorney generals in 1929 and informal contacts between External Affairs and Dominions Office officials in 1931, the matter was not resolved until the two governments bought out the fishing rights on both sides of the estuary and set up a joint authority, the Foyle Fisheries Commission, in 1952.[19]

RURAL INDUSTRIES AND THE GAELTACHT COMMISSION

In 1926 calls were made for the abolition of the Department of Fisheries and for the closure of rural industries as many were not paying their way. These concerns, coupled with a fear that the Irish language was dying in the Gaeltacht, led to the establishment of the Gaeltacht commission in 1925. It reported on rural industries engaged in spinning and weaving of homespun yarns and recommended the establishment of carding and finishing mills, and a state trade mark for cloth of a particular quality. The commission also addressed housing, livestock, poultry, seeds, land reclamation, arterial drainage, forestry, kelp, carrageen moss, mineralogical survey and domestic training. It reported that there was a lack of sustained and systematic instruction in fishing and recommended that a brand for cured mackerel should be mandatory. An iodine factory was established in Galway in 1929 to process kelp and a start was made on collective marketing of carrageen in 1930. However, the prospects of many Gaeltacht industries were grim. Lace sales were hit hard by American tariffs, button-making had been discontinued, knitwear suffered from lack of designs and there was a misguided belief that woollen stockings and hose were 'not subject to the exigencies of fashion'.[20] There was a perceived need for marketing but the reality was that most of the products were unfit for a changing market. Renewed efforts were made to develop small-scale craft-based industries and in 1931 a Gaeltacht office was opened in Dublin to promote them under the Round Tower brand.[21] The commission recommended the replacement of non-Irish-speaking civil servants, first in Irish-speaking areas and later everywhere. The government concurred insofar as the recommendations were practical but there was no agreement on how to do it.[22]

The enthusiasm of the commission and the departmental sub-committee set up to co-ordinate actions was not met with a similar response in the Gaeltacht. The *Irish Times* commented, 'If the folk of the *Gaeltacht* had the zeal of the commission, there would be no need for a commission'. Canon Hegarty of Belmullet stated that it was[23] all very well to be constantly urging the government to do this and that for the people, but the people are going about with their hands in their pockets wasting their time, and are not inclined to do a single scrap for themselves ... Fishermen didn't take instruction, they know it all.

The commission found that in areas where Irish was strong, it was stronger than in 1911, but in areas where Irish was weak (seven counties), it was weaker and there had been a loss of Irish-speakers. Organisational difficulties arose as multiple state agencies were responsible for the Gaeltacht. An effort to start a Gaeltacht sweepstake was declared illegal by Justice Minister James Fitzgerald-Kenney in 1931. Fisheries was criticised by Lord Longford of the Gaelic League, who stated that 'if the Irish do not revive the language they would cease to be in any sense of the word a nation'.[24]

A SMALL UNDER-RESOURCED DEPARTMENT

Fisheries was a small department, most of its budget was spent on administration and the fisheries section was overshadowed by lands after 1928. Cumann na nGaedheal did not have a coherent fisheries policy. Griffith had been committed to developing marine resources but, when he died in 1922, the fishermen lost a valuable ally. His successors did not appreciate the potential of the sea and inland fisheries. The failure to invest in fisheries had long-term consequences when Ireland entered the EEC in 1973, as it was unable to claim the fishing rights it needed to belatedly develop its deep sea fishery.[25]

Rural industries got limited practical support. The Land Commission faced a mammoth task: to acquire and distribute the remaining land from landlords. It was pressurised by politicians and farmers, under-resourced, and faced with administrative and legal difficulties. The latter were largely resolved by legislation and by 1932 land was being acquired and distributed more efficiently and effectively.

Chapter 13 ～

TRADE, INDUSTRY AND
INFRASTRUCTURE

INTRODUCTION

Pre-treaty Sinn Féin trade and industry policy had been to introduce tariffs to protect existing and fledgling industries and substitute imports with home manufactures, thereby reducing the dependence on Britain. This approach had some short-term economic merit, but the downside was that Irish farmers and consumers would have to pay more and there was a risk that the British would impose retaliatory tariffs. After partition, Irish industry, trade and commerce declined as much of the country's industrial base was located in Northern Ireland. Agriculture, together with its ancillary industries—brewing, distilling and biscuit-making—accounted for most exports, along with Ford tractors. The government choose to retain free trade to maximise exports, minimise farm costs and keep the cost of living low, while the opposition inside and outside the Dáil advocated tariff protection. Neither side seems to have considered a compromise between the extremes of free trade and protection. Nevertheless, trade, commerce and industry recovered from the post-World War I economic depression and the civil war and made progress, until the Wall Street crash in 1929 led to a severe worldwide depression.

Trade and industrial development before 1922 had been the responsibility of a branch of the British Board of Trade, which did nothing to stimulate industry as Ireland was a captive and easily accessible market for British manufacturers. Voluntary bodies like the Cork Industrial Development Association (CIDA), founded in 1903, tried to fill the gap. CIDA helped bring the Ford Motor Company to Cork in 1917 and led to the formation of the Irish Industrial Development Association, which established the national trade mark to promote Irish products:

Yet services rather than agriculture or industry had been the fastest-growing sector of the economy between 1850 and 1920.[1] Sinn Féin promoted the myth that political independence would lead to economic independence and prosperity. But Ireland was the poorest, least developed part of the British Isles. The Irish had been entitled to a British standard of living while in the United Kingdom, but after independence they had to work for it as there was no divine right to prosperity.[2]

More people needed to be gainfully employed and tariffs offered a quick fix. But the long-term solution required entrepreneurs capable of identifying business opportunities, raising productivity, introducing new technologies, improving quality, and delivering products and services at competitive prices on the home and international markets. Foreign inward investment had to be attracted as Irish entrepreneurs did not have the necessary management skills, technologies or access to markets.

There was a high level of male employment during World War I. The country enjoyed a period of unprecedented prosperity between 1914 and 1920 during which farmers and merchants did very well, but wage-earners, despite greater opportunities for employment, suffered cost-of-living increases which were not always recompensed by pay rises. In the depressed economic situation after 1920, wages were reduced. Unemployment and under-employment became major problems despite the fact that emigration, which had been disrupted by the war, increased as many were attracted to the booming economy in the US. In the early 1920s, 43 per cent of Irish-born men and women were living abroad. This proportion was far higher than for other high-emigration countries like Norway (14.8 per cent), Scotland (14.1 per cent) and Sweden (11.2 per cent).[3]

The Irish Free State had an abundance of unskilled labourers but lacked skilled workers and managers; access to low-cost materials, energy and technology; and export markets other than the UK. The Cumann na nGaedheal governments did not encourage foreign investment as they wished to retain ownership in Irish hands. They were reluctant to intervene in the market, were short of money, were unwilling to borrow and believed that agriculture rather than industry would be the driving force in the economy.

While the government may appear to have accepted Ireland's economic dependence on Britain, it faced the harsh reality that economic independence was not possible in the short term. In the troubled times after 1922 it sought political and economic stability, made few radical changes and maintained the status quo where possible. This was particularly evident in the approach to agriculture, industry and trade.

THE DEPARTMENT OF INDUSTRY AND COMMERCE

The Irish Free State's industrial position in 1922 could be summed up as follows: brewing, distilling and biscuit-making holding their own; butter and bacon still important but declining; corn-milling and baking serving local needs; and flour millers facing competition from British millers with surplus capacity. Engineering plants were mainly small and low-technology apart from the Ford Motor Company and the railways. Woollen, linen and poplin textiles, hosiery, apparel and footwear businesses were under pressure from imports. There were a few mines and a struggling cement industry. Exports were mainly live animals, butter, bacon, eggs, other food products, Guinness stout, whiskey, Jacob's biscuits and

Ford tractors. Imports included manufactured goods, machinery, food, textiles and clothing. The retail banking and commercial sectors were adequately developed, the railways linked Dublin with the major cities and towns, the road system was extensive but in a poor state, and there were no shipping links other than to Britain. Electricity was available in urban areas but there was a low level of consumption and no national grid. Gas was an important source of energy in towns and cities.

The state had few innovators and entrepreneurs like William Martin Murphy, who before his death in 1919 had built electric tramways and light railways in Ireland, Britain, Argentina and the Gold Coast (Ghana). Yet economically, Ireland ranked tenth among 23 European countries: ahead of Norway, Finland and Italy and only a little behind France, Austria and Sweden. Per-capita income had grown since the famine as there were fewer people to share the nation's wealth. However, wealth was not distributed evenly and there were many poor and destitute people as social welfare benefits were minimal. Northern Ireland was not as prosperous as Britain and did not have a significantly higher per-capita income than the Irish Free State, which seems to have reached a reasonable standard of living without industrialisation and little growth in total output.[4]

The Ministers and Secretaries Act 1924 assigned the Department of Industry and Commerce responsibility for trade, commerce, industry, labour, statistics, transport, shipping, natural resources, energy, registration of companies and business names, and factory inspection. Dublin-born Joseph (Joe) McGrath was appointed Minister for Labour in January 1922 and took over the trade and industry portfolio, which included labour and economic affairs, in August. He was 34 years old, educated by the Christian Brothers and had worked as manager of the insurance section of the Irish Transport and General Workers' Union. He was a member of the IRB and Irish Volunteers, participated in the 1916 rising and war of independence, during which he served on Michael Collins's counter-intelligence staff. He reluctantly accepted the treaty and in its immediate aftermath was head of the CID and director of military intelligence.

Gordon Campbell, the son of James Campbell, Baron Glenavy, former unionist MP, lord chancellor of Ireland and first chairman of the Senate, was appointed department secretary. Aged 37, he was a barrister who had served in the British ministries of munitions and labour before becoming chief industrial conciliator in Ireland (1919–21). Campbell favoured state intervention in industry and played a key role in the Shannon hydroelectricity scheme. After succeeding his father as Lord Glenavy, he resigned before the 1932 election, being subsequently replaced by John Leydon, who later made a major contribution to Irish public life. Two former members of CIDA, Diarmuid Fawsitt and E.J. Riordan, joined the department, the latter being a committed protectionist. Industry and Commerce was biased towards intervention but did not reject free trade. It sought the best of both worlds but its freedom to manoeuvre was inhibited by the government's belief that agriculture would be the principal means of growing the economy.[5]

Trade policies
The Irish achieved political, financial and military independence in 1922, but economic independence did not follow, as the British and Irish economies remained interdependent. Ireland was Britain's fifth biggest customer, while the UK was in effect Ireland's only customer and the world's largest food importer. The Irish needed new export outlets but free access was difficult to achieve as European countries, hit hard by the post-World War I economic depression, protected their home markets by raising tariffs. Italy and Germany adopted a policy of autarky (extreme self-sufficiency). Irish exporters had no direct shipping routes to Europe and were unaccustomed to operating in non-English-speaking countries. Their best prospect was to export to the UK, where many had long-standing relationships. However, once Britain began to erect tariff barriers in 1931, Irish exports were threatened. Services, which had been the most rapidly growing sector in the economy, did not expand significantly again until the 1960s.

The 26 counties of the Irish Free State had had a considerable internal trade in goods and services with the six northeastern counties before 1922. The Belfast boycott of August 1920 had begun the destruction of the commercial unity of the country as it discouraged northern firms from doing business in the south and led to a counter-boycott of southern goods in the north. The boycott was a response to 10,000 'disloyal' (Catholic and socialist) workers being driven out of factories and shipyards in Belfast by loyalists, who also burned some of their homes. The erection of customs posts by the Irish Free State imposed a further barrier, and trade between the two parts of the country declined and has never fully recovered.[6] Dublin and border towns were worst hit and economies of scale were lost on both sides of the border. Some banks swapped branches as they opted to focus on either the Irish Free State or Northern Ireland.

Tariffs rather than industrial development were the major preoccupation of Industry and Commerce between 1922 and 1932. Import duties were perceived as undesirable because they would increase the cost of living and farm inputs, and could provoke retaliatory tariffs. This belief was shared by bankers, large farmers, and professional and business interests who supported the government when it needed help in its early days (and the ministers reciprocated). Business interests were represented by the chambers of commerce, independent deputies and senators, and the Cork Progressive Association, whose sponsored candidates won two seats in the Dáil at the 1923 election.

The Irish Free State lacked industrial strength. Labour unit costs were high, productivity was low, the home market was small, and many raw materials (and coal) had to be imported. The infrastructure was underdeveloped and there was little industrial tradition, skilled labour or technological expertise. There were few entrepreneurs, who were looked on with suspicion by politicians as profiteers. Nonetheless, some new businesses were promoted, such as knitwear company Sunbeam, established by William Dwyer in Cork in 1928, which later became the state's largest textile manufacturer. Monopolists, although willing to invest, were distrusted. The government wished to retain ownership in Irish hands. Any business investing in the Irish Free State had to be sure it could make profits or get state aid. The government sought to limit the former and did not provide the latter. Consequently the state was not an attractive place for investors.

Arthur Griffith was the leading proponent of industrialisation and tariffs but, after his death, Finance and Agriculture favoured free trade and made it difficult for Industry and Commerce to protect the industrial base from competition, encourage import substitution and promote new industries. The government was committed to free trade, while the Labour Party supported tariffs in the expectation that they would deliver jobs. But tariffs created difficulties, an example of which was the Ford Motor Company. It was an integral part of Ford's UK operations and had been built on the assumption that parts and equipment could move freely between the two countries. If duties were imposed, the Cork plant could be closed.[7]

The government set up the fiscal inquiry committee to consider tariffs in 1923. It was comprised of civil servants and academics who were biased in favour of free trade.[8] Its report did not favour tariffs and met with opposition, so Minister McGrath promised limited protection which would not injure agriculture. Assistant Secretary of Finance J.J. McElligott argued that protection, once granted, could never be reversed and would inevitably entail further tariffs. McGrath resigned from the government over the army mutiny and subsequently became labour advisor to Siemens Schuckert in Shannon, where he confronted trade unionist Jim Larkin and broke a strike by employing non-union army ex-servicemen. In 1930 Richard Duggan enlisted him to work for the hospitals sweepstakes and he embarked on a very successful career in business and horse racing. He was succeeded as Minister for Industry and Commerce by 35-year-old lawyer Patrick McGilligan, who was not enthusiastic about protection, believing that the poor economic situation was due to the apathy of producers, all of whom were looking for 'doles'. People were exhorted to work harder and drink less. 'Ireland sober would be Ireland free.'

The 1924 budget imposed tariffs on a range of goods and further duties were applied up to 1926. Fearing this would raise the cost of living, the government reduced the duty on tea. But pressure for tariffs mounted from the Labour Party and business interests. Minister for Posts and Telegraphs J.J. Walsh openly criticised government policy, arguing that manufacturing companies coming to Ireland needed protection. However, ministers Hogan and O'Higgins opposed tariffs together with the majority of the executive.

Department Secretary Gordon Campbell suggested a tariff commission, which was set up by Finance Minister Ernest Blythe in 1926 against Secretary of Finance Joseph Brennan's wishes. It was structured to make it difficult to secure tariffs. After the June 1927 election Campbell made the case for actively seeking inward foreign investment, investigating new export markets, state funding for a 'Buy Irish' campaign, assessment of the difficulties of setting up factories outside the major towns and the initiation of tariff proposals by Industry and Commerce. Only the 'Buy Irish' suggestion was implemented.[9]

J.J. Walsh resigned over tariffs in 1927. Between then and 1932 the major parties were diametrically opposed to each other on protection. Cumann na nGaedheal looked outward to free trade, expansion of exports to Britain and minimal tariffs, while Fianna Fáil looked inward to self-sufficiency, building industries behind tariff walls and a reduction of dependence on the British market. Yet self-sufficiency was, in Garret FitzGerald's view, an 'absurd' aspiration for a small, underpopulated, under-resourced state. The fact that its policies could diminish living standards was accepted by Fianna Fáil in what it perceived to be the national interest.[10] Its prominent deputies advocated solutions to unemployment which included protection (Seán Lemass), house-building (Seán T. O'Kelly), import substitution (Seán MacEntee) and not employing foreigners while Irish were out of work (Eamon de Valera).[11] Fianna Fáil was not a radical party. In many respects it was as conservative as Cumann na nGaedheal—but it was more pragmatic, flexible and willing to try alternative approaches. It differentiated itself from the government in its socioeconomic policies and contained more people committed to industrialisation. Fianna Fáil sought urban votes and attracted businesspeople and intellectuals who had become disenchanted with the government's policy on tariffs and industrial development and its lack of social policy.[12]

The 1927 World Economic Conference failed to secure a reduction in tariffs or the abolition of import quotas. The tariff commission initially granted protection on margarine and rosary beads but then procrastinated before raising further tariffs in 1930. UK manufacturers set up in Ireland to circumvent the tariffs and a British trade commissioner was appointed to Dublin in 1929. Ministers were infuriated when Irish shareholders made capital gains by selling out to British companies seeking to establish a presence in Ireland. Despite the tariffs, the inflationary effect of protection was minimised because of the depressed market, while levels of duty were not high enough to keep out all imports, thus preventing domestic producers from gaining monopolies.

Flour millers sought protection against dumping of British flour. The government opposed it, fearing higher bread prices. As there was over-capacity in flour milling in Britain and Ireland, Industry and Commerce tried to reorganise the industry along with the Irish flour millers' association by seeking higher levels of efficiency and price controls. They failed to agree and Ranks, a British milling consortium, bought control of much of the industry, thereby creating the virtual monopoly the government had sought to avoid.

Industry and Commerce did not intervene in the case of the insurance industry, which was dominated by unregulated British insurers who invested their funds outside the state. Irish-owned companies were subjects of acquisition bids by UK insurers and were losing business, leading to apprehension that some might collapse with a detrimental effect on national credit.[13] The department was concerned about the drain of £2.5 million per annum out of the country as there was no reinsurance business done in the state.[14] Solutions considered included a state monopoly, amalgamation of companies and a greater level of regulation, but no action was taken.

As the part-time tariff commission was not working satisfactorily by the late 1920s, Agriculture Minister Hogan proposed a full-time commission, which recommended more tariffs. Secretary of Finance McElligott called for them to be examined before being accepted but was ignored. However, the government had not been converted to tariffs as the reformed commission was used to protect agriculture rather than benefit industry. The Wall Street crash in 1929 and the worldwide trade depression in its aftermath forced governments worldwide to radically change their economic policies. In autumn 1931 the protectionist national government in Britain passed the Abnormal Importation (Customs Duties) Act, an anti-dumping measure. Weeks later the Irish Free State passed virtually identical legislation. The government, concerned with price-fixing, considered price controls for milk, bread, meat, porter and stout.[15] It also held trade talks with the British in an effort to protect its main export market.

Protection promised profits with low risk and was attractive to Irish industrialists, but did not lead to the long-term export growth that was needed as very few of the companies formed under it succeeded in developing foreign markets. Import substitution resulted in short-term employment gains but at the risk of retaliatory tariffs which could damage major exporters. Tariffs ultimately led Ford and Guinness to relocate parts of their production facilities to Britain.

Ireland was over-influenced by British industrial technology and style of business, which had been overtaken by the US, Germany and other nations. Scandinavian countries, which sought a mix of sustainable agricultural and industrial development, would have offered a better model. Long-term industrial development required a radical change in government policy together with intervention and substantial investment. This made 'solutions' like protection and import substitution attractive. However, when tariff barriers were raised worldwide after 1929, duties became justifiable to protect jobs and prevent below-cost selling.

There were few prospects of increasing industrial exports as most Irish manufacturers had little to offer and were ill-equipped to sell into Europe and the US. In 1926 the Irish Free State sent 83 per cent of its exports to Britain, 13 per cent to Northern Ireland and one per cent to the US.[16] Yet the Irish failed to maximise trade opportunities in Britain and Northern Ireland, its closest and most accessible markets. Unemployment remained high, emigration reached its highest level in 40 years and agricultural output was still four per cent below the pre-World War I figure in 1929/30.[17] Unemployment and under-employment remained major problems. Apart from the economic consequences of being unemployed in a state with minimal social welfare benefits, unemployment led to disillusionment. People expected prosperity after independence, and regardless of the fact that the expectation was unrealistic, they blamed the government when it failed to materialise.

Despite little formal industrial development or assistance by way of tariffs, subsidies or grants, industrial output rose from a low base by eight and a half per cent between 1926 and 1929, but fell to two per cent between 1929 and 1931.[18] When agriculture failed to deliver, the government had no alternative plan. It was badly advised by conservative civil servants who wished to maintain the status quo but were unaware of, or unwilling to consider, the need for long-term industrial development. The government sought the advice of academics, many of whom were as conservative and detached from economic and commercial reality as the civil servants. The end result was a series of bad decisions and lost opportunities.

Secretary Campbell criticised Hogan's policy and proposed assisting agriculture by protection, subsidies and loans together with guaranteed prices, stating, 'The idea is prevalent to a dangerous extent that if industry goes up agriculture goes down. A saner view would be that both must go up.' He advocated developing agriculture and industry simultaneously, looked at the potential of industries like chemicals and provided funds for the development of the Drumm electric battery.[19] But Campbell made little progress, proving that Industry and Commerce officials could not change government policy. Security of supply does not seem to have entered the government's considerations. A proposal to build an oil refinery was opposed and the only cement plant was closed after being taken over by Portland Cement.[20]

McGilligan combined Industry and Commerce with the External Affairs portfolio after 1927. He apparently asked for this as he wished to continue his involvement with electrification, his major project. Papers written by Campbell and T.J. Barrington suggested currency devaluation to ease the deflationary pressures and make Irish produce more competitive, coupled with selective tariffs, assistance in restructuring and marketing, and aid for agriculture.[21] This more radical approach might have achieved results if it had involved both the public and private sectors in partnership. But it would have needed a major change in attitude by Finance and Agriculture, while co-operation between the two main political parties in the national interest was unlikely. A compromise between the extremes of free trade and protection would have produced better results in the long term. Cumann na nGaedheal was driven from free trade to protection by the post-1929 depression. This was a major policy shift for a free-market party which previously intervened only where the alternative was price-fixing cartels or monopolies.

INDUSTRIAL DEVELOPMENT

In 1922 the average income in the Irish Free State was less than half of that in Britain. The population was just under 3 million, of which 57.3 per cent were in paid employment.[22] However, the 670,000 described statistically as 'being engaged in agriculture' included many so-called 'relatives assisting' on farms too small to afford them gainful employment. These people formed, in T.K. Whitaker's view, 'a reservoir of hopeless, poverty stricken under-employment which filled emigrant ships for decades'.[23]

An internal departmental memorandum dated winter 1923 indicated that there had been little viable economic development since the treaty. Unemployment was high, swelled by discharged ex-servicemen; business was depressed, bank deposits were falling, trade was poor, taxes and public expenditure were too high and the cost of living was increasing.[24] Labour unit costs were high, productivity was low and there was a shortage of skilled workers. Companies were going out of business. Industry was fragmented with too many small firms. The few big companies such as Guinness, Jacob and Ford were all export-oriented. Old industries like the naval dockyard at Haulbowline were difficult to revive as no buyer or alternative business could be found. Cumann na nGaedheal Deputy Michael Egan believed the government should hand over the dockyard to somebody free of rent. Industry and Commerce suffered from an absence of exact data, while employers were badly organised and had poor communications with the department. To improve this, advisory committees were set up for 30 industries.[25]

Apart from land and water, there were few natural resources. Small deposits of coal, copper and barites existed; slate, turf, stone and clay were abundant but timber was scarce due to the depletion of forests and woodlands.

Initiatives in promoting industrial development and transferring technology came from Irish people at home and abroad and from foreign industrialists. Examples include a Dr Nolan of Nobel Explosives, who offered to advise the army on ordnance; Dublin solicitor J. Plunkett Dillon, who promoted the manufacture of electrical appliances protected by tariffs; and Victor Zorn, who sought to interest Cork businessmen Liam de Róiste and Hugo Flinn in joint ventures with German industrialists.[26] Much of this activity was confined to individual initiatives and received minimal state support in the absence of a government policy on industrial development. However, the Industrial and Commercial Property Bill 1927 was introduced to protect trademarks and intellectual property in the state.

The postwar economic downturn, and damage done between 1919 and 1923, reduced the capacity of agriculture and industry to increase employment. The government began the process of reconstruction by paying compensation, extending relief and making investments in drainage, roads and housing using Irish bricks. Such investments were limited as there was a reluctance to borrow even for capital projects. Government contracts were awarded to Irish firms. After the civil war, the climate for industrial development improved and the government tentatively began to make a number of interventions in the economy.

A national supply of cheap energy was needed for industrial development and public consumption. Thomas A. McLaughlin, an engineer working for Siemens Schuckert in Germany, was the innovator of the Shannon hydroelectric scheme. He approached Siemens and the government with a carefully thought-out plan for generating electricity by harnessing the fall of the river Shannon at a single point in Ardnacrusha. He was opposed by the Institution of Civil Engineers, English interests, union leader Jim Larkin and a Dublin lobby group, all of whom favoured a scheme on the river

Liffey, together with the *Daily Mail*, which saw the plan as a bid by the Germans to take economic control of the Irish Free State.[27] McLaughlin had a wider vision, foreseeing the benefits of rural electrification. Siemens quoted a low price, to be paid for in Irish currency, and agreed to unfavourable conditions to secure the business at a time when German industry was severely depressed and urgently needed foreign exchange and prestigious projects. It was the largest foreign contract awarded to a German firm since the construction of the Berlin–Baghdad railway in the nineteenth century.[28] Siemens subsequently made a substantial loss on the project but the scheme's success earned the firm a worldwide reputation and provided a valuable reference for future business.

The government published a white paper in 1924 and accepted the Siemens proposal despite objections from politicians, business interests, farmers and newspapers. De Valera criticised the scheme even though it conformed to his ideas on self-sufficiency. The new minister, Patrick McGilligan, became an enthusiastic champion of electricity and piloted the project through the cabinet while Finance Minister Blythe was absent in 1925. Land was compulsorily acquired for the biggest construction project ever mounted in Ireland at that time, which employed 5,000 building and engineering workers. The plant was equipped with the most modern technology and much of the original generating machinery is still in use. It began to deliver electricity in October 1929 at an estimated cost of 0.53 pence per kilowatt hour, compared with the Dublin Corporation cost of 1.28 pence in 1923.[29]

The Electricity Supply Board (ESB) was set up in 1927, because Secretary of Finance Brennan did not want the state to become involved in business while the Oireachtas would not accept a private company. McLaughlin was appointed managing director of the ESB, whose brief was to operate and maintain the Shannon scheme and sell its output nationally. The Electricity (Supply) Act 1927 gave the ESB wide powers. The government-appointed board decided not to sell in bulk to distributors of electricity but to retail direct to the customer on a 'not for profit basis'.[30] The ESB acquired the 300 existing electricity producers and 91 stations and developed its own technical expertise in the design, construction and operation of electricity systems. The decision not to sell to public supply authorities was strongly opposed by them. It was a good decision as it allowed the ESB to focus on meeting national rather than local needs. The company persuaded energy consumers to change to electricity and began to connect urban areas where there was a critical mass. It did not follow up its initial success due to lack of finance, and rural electrification was not started until after World War II. The government was also slow to exploit the opportunities for electricity-related industrial development.

McLaughlin resigned from the ESB in May 1931 following 'differences of opinion on matters of policy' with the government. Accusations were made by both sides but the substance of the dispute seems to have been very poor accounting in the ESB, a 12 per cent cost over-run on the project (unforeseen extras, compensation to landowners for pylons, etc.) and insufficient funds for development. McGilligan insisted that proper accounting controls be introduced and this led to a dispute with the board and the resignation of Chairman John J. Murphy. He was replaced by R.F. Browne, who confronted McLaughlin and, under pressure from the government to accept equal status as joint managing director with director of civil works James M. Fay, McLaughlin resigned. After Fianna Fáil came to power McLaughlin was re-appointed to the ESB board as technical director in August 1932 and remained in that position for the next 25 years. In retrospect he believed that the history of the ESB would have been different if he had 'had the good sense to accept' McGilligan's proposal that Fay should be joint managing director.[31]

As electricity became the main source of energy, the gas companies declined in importance. Turf received short-term priority during the British coal strike in 1926 but its development, as advocated by the recess committee, did not occur until the 1930s and particularly in the 1940s, when energy shortages during World War II provided the necessary impetus.

The government supported the sugar beet industry to substitute imports and provide farmers with an attractive cash-crop. Large-scale sugar beet processing had been developed in Europe from the mid-nineteenth century and the British government had subsidised a number of sugar factories. Belgian, British, Czechoslovak, Dutch and French companies were interested in setting up in Ireland. The Sugar Beet (Subsidy) Act 1925 provided the necessary subsidies after the government agonised about the level sought, which in the end was only slightly above that in Britain. Fianna Fáil later complained that the subsidies were 'too generous'.[32] The government did not seem to understand that any business investing in the Irish Free State, which was still politically unstable, was taking a big risk. Instead of encouraging investors, it remained obsessed with foreign ownership, excess profits and monopolies. Lippens, a Belgian manufacturer, commenced sugar production at Carlow in 1926. An average sugar content of 17.3 per cent was achieved by 1927. Only in Czechoslovakia was the content higher, proving that Ireland was ideally suited to sugar beet production.[33]

The Trade Loans (Guarantee) Act 1924 empowered the government to guarantee repayment of approved loans advanced by the banks subject to a maximum of £750,000. While 337 applications were received and 47 were approved, little money was advanced as the banks were reluctant to lend over a five-year term. One recipient of funds was the glass bottle industry, which was restructured in 1925 by means of tariffs and finance from trade loans. However, Secretary of Finance Brennan referred the arrangement to the Comptroller and Auditor General and the initiative was not repeated.[34]

The banking commission recommended the termination of the trade loans guarantee scheme. It received little evidence in favour of industrial banking because there was no shortage of capital for worthwhile projects.[35] The commission indicated that finance could be obtained from the Industrial Trust Company, which had been set up in 1926 with funds provided by Irish and Irish-American private investors and the state to advance long-term finance for industry, and to take over the trade loan guarantees in the face of a virtual boycott by the banks. Some loans were made but the balance was invested in British and foreign shares as 'a temporary measure,' pending opportunities to lend. The company became insolvent after the 1929 stock market crash and, when wound up in the early 1930s, 87 per cent of its investments were in British or foreign shares and only 13 per cent in Irish stocks. Its investments proved in retrospect to have been highly speculative. Nevertheless, in 1926–27, Irish people had £195 million invested abroad, while foreigners had £75 million invested in Ireland, indicating that there was enough capital but too few entrepreneurs to use it.[36]

INFRASTRUCTURAL DEVELOPMENT

Roads came under the Department of Local Government and were funded out of the road fund introduced in 1920 (into which petrol and oil duties and traffic fines were paid), and by grants from central funds and local authorities. Grants had been curtailed during World War I and few road improvements were made in its aftermath. During the period 1919–23, councils pursued the line of least resistance and little work was done. The destruction of roads and bridges during the civil war and the increase in motor traffic meant that roads needed to be upgraded and maintained, while concerns were already being expressed at the level of traffic in Dublin. The Local Government Act 1925 legislated for road improvement and classification. After 1927, grants, which had hitherto been limited to improvements, were extended to include maintenance and by 1928 £2 million had been spent on road construction. Reservations were expressed regarding the impact of road-building on the railways and an awareness of the need to co-ordinate rail and road traffic led to the Road Traffic Act 1931. Legislation for town and infrastructural planning was initiated but was not enacted until the Town and Regional Planning Act 1934.

Most of the railways had been built during the nineteenth century. There were 30 rail operators and 3,500 miles of track in 1922. However, many companies were in financial difficulties due to the growth in road transport, high wages and excess track. Yet the railways had been profitable up to 1913, when they made a profit of £1.1 million.[37] They suffered damage during the war of independence and civil war when trains were derailed, signal cabins burned and bridges blown up. The government, realising that the railways needed rationalisation, set up the railways commission in 1922, and passed the Railways Act 1924, which forced 26 companies to amalgamate as Great Southern Railways (GSR). The railways lost subsidies from local authorities and were inadequately compensated by the state. Line closures and poorer service levels followed as the gravitation of the population to the eastern side of the country deprived many rural lines of passengers.[38] GSR passenger numbers declined from 15.5 million in 1926 to 11.9 million in 1931, leading Fianna Fáil to call for state control of the railways.[39] The Railways Acts and the Transport Act 1932 permitted the closure of unremunerative services. However, rationalisation did not solve the problems; decades of under-investment followed and rail freight volumes declined. The railways were not empowered to operate road transport until the Railway (Road Motor Services) Act 1927, enabling private carriers to secure a head start. Canal use continued to decline, as did the tramway systems in Dublin and Cork, which ceased operating on 30 September 1931.

Unregulated private bus companies competed with each other. The railways faced increasing competition from private road carriers which offered more flexible and cheaper services. The number of cars increased slowly, while horse-drawn hackney cabs were gradually replaced by motor taxis.

The Irish shipping fleet remained small and mainly coastal, and part of it was acquired by British operator Coast Lines. The ports and harbours tribunal (1930) recommended state control over ports, grants, appointment of general managers and the creation of a free port. Air traffic regulations were introduced in 1922 and an air link between Dublin and London commenced in 1926. The government refused to subsidise it in 1930.[40]

Tourism was closely linked with the railways, transatlantic liners and cross-channel steamers. The railways had developed resorts such as Killarney in the nineteenth century and their hotels were promoted in Britain and the US. A Tourist Bill was introduced and in 1925 the Irish Tourist Association was formed, which co-operated with its sister organisation in Northern Ireland to develop all-Ireland tourism. In the 1920s the standard of hotels and catering needed upgrading but the state did not invest in training or in the development of the industry, which had considerable potential.

LABOUR

Unemployment was a major problem. Two groups of workers in particular found it difficult to get jobs: British ex-servicemen and anti-treaty prisoners released after the civil war. The former were more numerous than the latter and received little assistance in the anti-British mood following partition and the treaty. Farm labourers also suffered from wage reductions and job losses due to increasing mechanisation. Between 1922 and 1932 trade unions found it difficult to gain ground in a predominantly agricultural country with little industry. The movement was fragmented and membership declined significantly due to internal dissention and fewer agricultural labourers. Industry and Commerce had responsibility for labour and industrial relations but did little to resolve trade disputes, although some legislation was passed and three joint industrial councils were set up. Trade disputes continued to be governed by the Trade Disputes Act 1906.[41]

Workers were concerned that the government's 'one remedy for economic ills' was reduced wages and complained that arable land was untilled, native industries were dying, foreign goods were being sold below cost and profiteering was rampant. They quoted Pope Leo XIII, who stated that a worker's wage must be sufficient to keep himself and his family in 'frugal comfort'.

Over 80 groups of workers set up 'workers' soviets' during 1922, taking over businesses, factories and creameries and running them on co-operative lines. They were disowned by the trade unions, most of which were non-syndicalist and opposed to 'political' strikes, and because they were sued for damages by angry owners. One such business, the Condensed Milk Company of Ireland, threatened to cease trading with a consequent loss of jobs and outlet for milk suppliers. The soviets were condemned by the government and anti-treaty sides and did not survive long.

The beginning of the 1920s was a time of industrial strife. Wages had risen during World War I and the boom years afterwards, but by 1922 the economy was in depression. In a period of deflation employers sought to reduce wages to remain competitive. Workers fought to retain their earnings and in the unstable political conditions industrial action was occasionally violent. Days lost due to strikes and lockouts in 1922 were 794,642, rising to 1,208,734 in 1923 and falling to 231,577 in 1925. The causes were reduced wages, working hours, closed shop disputes, working arrangements, holidays, trade union principles and sympathetic strikes. Settlement outcomes were 94 in favour of employers, 151 in favour of workers, with 164 reaching an uncertain conclusion.[42]

The Apprenticeship Act 1931 arose from a recommendation of the Commission on Technical Instruction 1926–27. It was based on the South African and Queensland Apprenticeship and Trade Board Acts 1909 and 1918. But its operation was hampered by poor co-ordination between the Departments of Education and Industry and Commerce. Employers were hostile, trade unions operated closed shop practices, and there were too many rules and no definition of apprentices. The act also included 'learners', widening its scope unnecessarily. Employers and trade unions do not seem to have been consulted and the act imposed legal sanctions for non-compliance with a voluntary scheme. As a result, little was achieved.[43]

State unemployment insurance was deducted from pay by employers, who also made contributions. As benefits were related to the number of contributions made and ceased when they were used up, the system was designed for short- rather than long-term unemployment. But some employers, including local authorities, failed to stamp employees' unemployment insurance cards. The outcome was that some unemployed workers could not claim insurance benefits. Unemployment increased as army demobilisation after the civil war put large numbers back on the labour market. Labour exchange managers were instructed to submit former national army soldiers for all jobs and they were favoured for civil service posts. There was a further rise in unemployment in 1931 as emigration stalled and emigrants returned from Britain, Canada and the US due to the trade depression.

While the government made few initiatives on labour during the 1920s, it was influenced by the International Labour Organisation (ILO) after the Irish Free State joined in 1924. One of the organisation's senior officials was Irish-born Edward Phelan (later secretary-general), who provided considerable assistance to the government in its initial dealings with the ILO and League of Nations. The ILO provided information and recommended legislation on labour issues.

CONSOLIDATION RATHER THAN PROGRESS

In its 1931 special report Industry and Commerce listed its achievements as sourcing materials, marketing, transport, new industries, trade development, the *Irish Trade Journal*, factory and workshop inspection, Irish preference for public contracts, resolution of industrial disputes, unemployment insurance, statistics, trademarks, geological survey, and company and business name registration.[44] This seemingly impressive list obscured the fact that there was little industrial development; manufacturing exports had not grown, while services remained static.

Governments must balance consumption with investment. To stimulate the economy by consumption they tax the rich and redistribute the revenue. If they invest they reduce present living standards in order to improve future standards of living. The Cumann na nGaedheal governments failed to stimulate the economy by either consumption or investment.

The introductions of hydroelectricity and sugar production were significant achievements but more foreign inward investment was needed. Barrington felt that well-managed foreign firms which might transfer knowledge would be better than no development.[45] But the government did not create conditions where business could flourish. It was slow to raise tariffs, was suspicious of profit-seekers and monopolists, wanted Irish control of industry and did not promote investment or raise productivity. It made minimal investments in infrastructure and did not set up an effective means of industrial credit. Industrial development, tariffs, import substitution and security of supply should have been part of an integrated economic programme. Instead, business developed slowly, due mainly to tariff-supported import substitution.

The Irish ended up buying dear and selling cheap. The government remained convinced that agriculture would be the engine of growth despite the fact that it had failed to deliver in the nineteenth and early twentieth centuries. The solution was to either commercialise agriculture like Denmark or build an industrial base while simultaneously intensifying agriculture. Land, labour and capital were available but entrepreneurs were needed to productively utilise them. The net result of the government's efforts was to conserve and consolidate rather than make progress. Yet Ireland was still a relatively prosperous state in 1929. Thereafter the decline set in and by 1949 it was a poor one.[46]

Chapter 14 ~

HEALTH AND SOCIAL WELFARE

INTRODUCTION

A number of significant developments in public health occurred after 1910. Until then women's health had not been a priority and the maternity benefit under national health insurance was widely welcomed in 1911. From 1916 onwards dental care, hospital services for children, convalescent care for nursing mothers and children, and health visitors were introduced irrespective of means on a non-compulsory basis. This arose because a large number of volunteers for service in World War I were rejected on medical grounds, prompting the British government to fund improved medical services, particularly for mothers and children. The Midwives (Ireland) Act 1917 led to registration of midwives, whether trained or not. The Public Health (Treatment of Children) Act 1919 provided for inspection and treatment of children in school.[1] The Ministry of Health Bill 1919 brought all public health under one department in Britain but not in Ireland. The Irish health system came under pressure due to the demobilisation of large numbers of British soldiers, who were often in poor health, and the 'Spanish' influenza epidemic of 1918–19, which resulted in about 23,000 deaths.[2] There were few improvements in social welfare between 1922 and 1932.

PUBLIC HEALTH

The dispensaries were the basis of the public healthcare system. They had been in existence since the eighteenth century and had been statutorily established under the Dispensaries Act 1805 and the Medical Charities Act 1851. There were 558 dispensary districts in 1925, which provided free access to doctors and medicines for the poor, and they continued to fulfil that function until the introduction of medical cards in 1970. In 1922, hospital services were not co-ordinated centrally and were divided between public (infirmaries, fever hospitals, 'lunatic asylums' and dispensaries) and voluntary (maternity, acute care, teaching and medical research).[3] At that time the voluntary system was broadly similar to that in Britain. The public sector dealt with infectious diseases, the most significant of which were tuberculosis (TB), typhoid, paratyphoid, diphtheria, scarlet fever and measles. There had been a major expansion of public health services between 1913 and 1922, but health was not seen as an important issue during the struggle for independence. The first task of the new government was to separate public health from the Poor Law and shift the emphasis from the poor to those in need of medical treatment.

The major reform of public health was the introduction of the county schemes, which were designed to reorganise the admin-istration of Poor Law indoor and outdoor relief efficiently and sympathetically. The boards of guardians, county hospital and infirmary committees were abolished and administration was centralised under one authority at county level. The exception was Dublin city and county, where the boards of guardians remained in place until the enactment of the Local Government (Dublin) Act 1930.[4] By the time the Local Government (Temporary Provisions) Act 1923 was passed, 22 such schemes had already been initiated by local authorities. The act provided for the schemes to be amended and modified, and county boards of health established. Workhouses were closed or converted into county homes and in some cases into hospitals. There was some disruption of public hospital services in the changeover, while destruction of workhouses occurred during the civil war when some were used as military barracks. From 1925 public medical services were centralised under the Department of Local Government and Public Health (Local Government), which had no authority over the voluntary health sector. After the changeover the public healthcare system consisted of county homes (for the destitute and elderly), county hospitals (acute care), cottage and district hospitals (primary care), TB sanatoria, fever and mental hospitals.

The government needed to cut costs to bring the state's expenditure into line with revenue. Basic maternal and infant welfare, which had been introduced before 1922, and venereal disease services were reduced. The former lost out because the Catholic Church did not approve of the state's involvement in mother and child care. The commission on venereal disease 1926 recommended compulsory notification, imprisonment of prostitutes, examination of women prisoners and treatment for seamen. The Catholic Archbishop of Dublin, Edward Byrne, was surprised that the 'chief disseminators of the infection were non-prostitutes' and sought to delay the report.[5]

The rationalisation of the workhouses took place without a corresponding investment in county hospitals to allow them to handle the extra cases, so the sick poor suffered in the short term. Local authorities would not spend extra money as it would increase the rates, while the government would not spend it because it would increase taxes. Preventative health measures were cut back. Local authorities tried to stop county hospitals sending patients to voluntary hospitals as they would have to pay for their care. The changes were hastily implemented with varying results and in face of opposition.

The Local Government Act 1925 provided for county medical officers of health, health nurses and sanitary inspectors. County boards of health, elected by the county councils, were given responsibility for public health. Homes run by religious orders and charities continued to provide most special care services, including those for unmarried mothers, orphans and children in care. In 1927 the report of the Commission on the Relief of the Sick and Destitute Poor, Including the Insane Poor condemned the disorganised and chaotic implementation of the reforms but had no sympathy for those who wanted hospitals in every small town. The commission recommended the repeal of all existing mental health laws and their replacement with new legislation, together with provision for voluntary admission and modern methods of treatment.

Local Government reported an improvement in health in 1927. Typhus had practically disappeared in urban areas but remained a problem in the west due to poverty, congestion and bad housing. Yet the department had difficulty persuading local authorities to appoint county medical officers. TB continued to be a major health problem. There was a downward trend in mortality, but a large number of cases were still not reported (except in areas where county medical officers were functioning) and compulsory notification was needed. Mental hospitals remained largely unchanged, but maternal mortality was reduced and cancer treatment was in its early stages.[6] Midwives were regulated but midwifery homes were not inspected until 1934. Up to the end of the 1920s the high infant mortality in Ireland was accepted with 'a curious mix of apathy and stoicism.' The main reasons for mortality were poverty, ignorance and the poor nutrition of mothers and children. The state provided some relief for poor mothers but did not financially assist unmarried mothers to keep their babies.[7] Voluntary bodies and charities such as the Society of St Vincent de Paul gave support and assistance.

Local authorities remained responsible for the implementation of the Sale of Food and Drugs Acts and continued inspections of milk and meat. The Public Relief (Dublin) Act 1931 placed the onus on the state to provide a greater level of assistance. Improvements in public medical care occurred during the 1920s due to better qualified staff being hired through the local appointments commission and increasing specialisation in medicine and surgery, while more vaccinations were provided despite resistance.

Nevertheless, it was a hard time to be poor and sick. Hospitals in the early twentieth century were a last resort rather than places of cure. There were no antibiotics so people kept away from infected patients. Most people were born and died at home and the sick were mainly treated in their own homes. People expected the state to provide only the bare minimum and they contributed to benevolent and friendly societies to get some health insurance. Dispensaries provided basic health care for the poor, while hospital outpatient departments gave medical attention at little or no cost. Voluntary hospitals and consultants charged according to patients' means and treated the poor free of charge. The state concerned itself mainly with medical care of the poor and infectious diseases, and made no significant investments in health. Farmers Party leader D.J. Gorey was in favour of the state subsidising and taking control of health. Medical ability to combat illness was improving and pressure was being put on the state to provide access to medical treatment based on need rather than ability to pay.

Medical doctors registered under the Medical Registration Act 1858 became apprehensive that a post-independence Irish medical council would damage their chances of employment in Britain and could lead to a reduction in students attending Irish medical schools. Bills were put through the Dublin and Westminster parliaments to allow Irish doctors to obtain registration in Britain. The Dentists Act 1928 addressed similar regulatory matters.

THE VOLUNTARY HEALTH SECTOR

The voluntary health sector did not come under Local Government. Voluntary hospitals delivered most of the acute care and maternity services in the major urban areas and also treated patients referred to them from public hospitals. They were hit hard by inflation during World War I and had no money for capital expenditure. Voluntary hospitals had originally been funded in the eighteenth and early nineteenth centuries by lotteries, which had subsequently been prohibited. Many people were unable to pay the full cost of medical treatment and complaints were made that private fee-paying patients were getting preference. Voluntary hospitals argued that their charters did not oblige them to provide unlimited treatment for the poor, while Local Government would not increase the small grants (limited to some Dublin hospitals) which had been fixed in the 1850s.

The voluntary hospitals began to run sweepstakes, which were illegal, but the government took no action to prevent them. Justice Minister Kevin O'Higgins opposed legalising lotteries because he believed they could not be run without fraud. Church of Ireland Archbishop of Dublin John Gregg asked, 'what shall it profit the State if its hospitals heal the bodies of its citizens, and heal them at the cost of their souls?' He argued, 'The Lottery Acts will go by the board, and it is almost certain that some future Government, hard pressed for cash, will be tempted to take refuge in all the demoralising devices of State lotteries and premium bonds.' Jesuit John Hannon was, however, of the view that nothing in the Ten Commandments forbade lotteries.[8]

Holles Street maternity hospital threatened to close in 1929 after failing to raise funds for essential repairs. The government relented and the Public Charitable Hospitals Act 1930 authorised a monopoly for the promotion of sweepstakes on horse races for hospitals which could show that at least 25 per cent of their beds were allocated to non-paying patients.[9] The first sweep was run in 1930 and by the following summer £1 million was raised, 90 per cent from overseas subscribers.[10] This was an enormous sum at the time and minister Richard Mulcahy immediately appropriated 25 per cent of it for the development of county hospitals.[11] The sweepstakes were the beginning of sustained hospital funding but they undermined the independence of the voluntary hospitals. Sweepstake organisers issued reports on the state of the voluntary hospitals, one of which criticised the lack of unified policy and co-ordination between voluntary hospitals, poor community planning and surveying of precise needs, inadequate provision of paediatrics, obstetrics, orthopaedics, fever treatment and services for middle-class patients (the poor and rich private classes were deemed to be catered for) and advocated co-ordination between general, special, poor law and fever hospitals; better clinical recording; a follow-up system for discharged patients and an end to duplication of services.[12] Voluntary hospitals, many of which were run by charities and religious orders, were gradually upgraded as medical technology advanced and sweepstake funds became available, while private nursing homes, usually located near voluntary hospitals, became popular with the middle class.

SOCIAL WELFARE

After 1922, the government made minimal changes in social welfare. German Chancellor Bismarck had introduced the first state social welfare benefits between 1883 and 1889 and the British followed from 1897 onwards. In 1922, national health insurance in the Irish Free State was administered locally by friendly and benefit societies such as the Ancient Order of Hibernians and centrally by the National Insurance Commission. It was compulsory for all workers aged between 16 and 70 and was funded by members' contributions and an annual state grant. The National Insurance Commission was chaired by Sir Joseph Glynn, a solicitor, Catholic social activist and former chairman of Galway county council. The National Health Insurance Act 1924 reduced the state's contribution and Labour Party opposition prevented further cuts. The National Insurance Commission was strongly in favour of retaining insurance cover but held off recommending a state medical service pending a valuation of the insurance societies in 1925. The Commission's recommendations that promised economy were implemented in 1929 while those costing money were ignored. Secretary of Finance J.J. McElligott stated that 'only in exceptional circumstances is direct intervention by the state desirable'.[13]

Ireland had very large numbers of old-age pensioners relative to the working population, due to high emigration. After 1922 the Irish Free State had difficulty funding pensions, which were reduced in 1924, and means testing was enforced more rigorously. Claims for pensions were assessed by pension officers who were Revenue Commissioners staff.

Unemployment benefits were based on the number of contributions made by workers. Once the benefit period expired no further payments were made as the system was designed for short-term unemployment. Thereafter, home assistance and relief works were the only source of income for out-of-benefit workers.

Pre-treaty Sinn Féin had no coherent policy on the Poor Law. The first Dáil had promised to replace it but offered no alternative. After independence the government was under financial pressure and local authorities' annual grants were reduced by £1.5 million. Workhouses were closed and amalgamated. The Local Government (Temporary Provisions) Act 1923 determined that public assistance would be administered on a county basis, except in some urban areas, and statutory restrictions on relief granted to certain classes outside the workhouse were removed.

Home assistance, as poor relief had been renamed, was still needed in the 1920s, as exemplified by the plight of people in areas such as Cape Clear, Hare and Sherkin islands in west Cork. Labour Deputy Timothy Murphy reported that the people did not have enough food while on the mainland 'children of honest respectable working men have been looking for bread from door to door'.[14] He quoted a clergyman on one of the islands saying that 'without immediate help, there will be starvation and deaths due to cold and hunger' and reported that Gardaí were making enquiries regarding the removal of a number of children of destitute parents to industrial schools.[15]

Former British garrison towns like Athlone, Buttevant, Fermoy, Kildare and Newbridge lost significant sources of employment and trade after 1922 and sought relief. One such relief scheme was the drainage of the Awbeg river, which flooded 5,000 acres each year. Despite many representations, the Office of Public Works was slow to commence work. The lack of accurate statistics on unemployment made targeting relief works to the worst-hit areas difficult.

The Irish social welfare and healthcare systems were developed piecemeal over decades. Advances were hampered by the anti-interventionist stance of the Catholic Church, which exerted a profound influence until the 1960s and, while trade unions campaigned for change, they got little support from the general public.

Public Housing

The British government embarked on a house building programme after World War I, erecting over 200,000 publicly built houses between 1919 and 1922. In Ireland there was an urgent need for reconstruction after the civil war as many public and private buildings had been destroyed. Reconstruction work was carried out by the Office of Public Works and local authorities. The provisional government announced a £1 million public housing scheme in March 1922 and the Dublin Reconstruction (Emergency Provisions) Act 1924 gave wide powers including compulsory purchase to begin work in the capital. Housing was a major issue with 46,416 houses needed, one third to replace unfit habitations.[16]

Many houses in Ireland were small and overcrowded, with inadequate heating, bad ventilation and poor sanitation. The 1926 census showed that there were 781,000 people living in overcrowded conditions. Local Government focused on building houses in urban areas after 1922 as rural housing had been the priority from the latter part of the nineteenth century. The initial housing schemes were funded by central government, local authority rates and short-term loans. By 1924, 959 dwellings had been built, some in imaginative designs influenced by the British 'garden city' architectural movement. However, the government shifted the focus to encouraging the private sector to build houses. The Housing (Building Facilities) Act 1924 provided substantial grants, enough to cover one-sixth of building costs. Local authorities could supplement the grants with loans, free or cheap sites and remission of rates, but their social housing programmes were curtailed due to lack of finance and the cost of servicing loans. The Housing Act 1925 reduced the grants. Housing growth slowed and did not increase significantly until 1929, when low-interest loans were made available for public housing.

The high cost of public housing and the low level of rents achievable were major concerns. Wages were considered high and productivity in the building trade low but no action seems to have been taken to reduce costs by improving building methods. Only 14,000 houses were built in the public sector between 1922 and 1929, while a total of 26,000 private and publicly funded houses were constructed.[17]

The Housing (Miscellaneous Provisions) Act 1931 introduced new measures for slum clearance. Lump sum grants were replaced with annual subsidies towards loan charges, and local authorities were allowed to advance loans to persons intending to build and to private sector tenants wishing to buy the dwellings they rented. This act laid the foundation for a radical expansion of house-building during the 1930s.[18] The Housing (Gaeltacht) Act 1929 provided for grants and loans for house building in Irish-speaking areas. A large proportion of the population rented accommodation and many of their needs were addressed by the Landlords and Tenants (Town Tenants) Bill 1932. The Local Government (Rates on Small Dwellings) Act 1928 made owners rather than occupiers liable for rates where rateable valuations were below a certain limit.

Chapter 15 ∿

EDUCATION AND THE IRISH LANGUAGE

INTRODUCTION

The Irish Free State government inherited an under-resourced education system from the British. Primary education was the best-developed part. Technical education, a relatively new innovation, did not meet the needs of industry or agriculture. Secondary education was poorly funded and not accessible to the majority. University education was attainable only by a small minority.

The post-1922 Department of Education made a number of administrative reforms, bringing all sectors of education and related areas into a single department, and introduced the Primary, Intermediate and Leaving Certificate examinations. Much of the resources committed at primary and secondary level were devoted to the revival of Irish, and the standard of other subjects fell. Technical training was starved of resources until a basis for future development was established in 1930. The reformatories and industrial schools were managed by religious orders and funded by the state on a capitation basis. They remained largely unchanged after 1922, but the standard of inspection fell as the Catholic Church's stewardship was not effectively monitored by the state after independence. As a result conditions for the children in care deteriorated. Teacher training was mainly focused on the Irish language. The universities remained poorly funded with low student numbers.

The Department of Education Report for 1923–24 gave the following information:

	Schools	Teachers	Pupils	%
Primary	5,636	13,043	493,382	84.9
Secondary	278	2,133	22,897	3.9
Technical	77	1,035	59,105	10.2
Reformatories	4	26	111	
Industrial Schools	52	496	5,663	1.0
Total	**6,047**	**16,733**	**581,158**	**100.0**

Notes:
1. Technical pupils included 33,625 students attending classes elsewhere than in 'established technical schools'.
2. Between 1922 and 1932 the maximum number of primary pupils attending was 518,355 in 1926–7 after the Christian Brothers joined the system and school attendance numbers improved. The number fell to 502,393 in 1930–31 and to 444,132 by 1946–7.

Student numbers at Trinity College and the three National Universities (Dublin, Cork and Galway) increased from 1,977 male and 277 female students in 1909–10 to 2,126 males and 911 females in 1926–27. The number of clerical students at Maynooth was between 500 and 600.

THE NATIONAL EDUCATION PROGRAMMES
The first national school education conference concluded in January 1922 that there should be a minimum national programme. Its recommendation that Irish be taught for one hour a day was immediately implemented by the provisional government under Public Notice Number Four on 1 February 1922. While not all of the conference's other recommendations were accepted, its proposed approach set the tone for the next 50 years and a second conference in 1925 endorsed them.

The focus on language was not unique to Ireland. Newly independent Finland placed the emphasis on Finnish at the expense of Swedish, which had been the dominant language for 700 years until Russia annexed Finland in 1809. The Estonians, Latvians and Lithuanians, who also gained independence from Russia after World War I, sought to undo the effects of nineteenth-century Russification.

THE DEPARTMENT OF EDUCATION
The Department of Education was set up under the Ministers and Secretaries Act 1924 and was given responsibility for primary, secondary and vocational education, teacher training, endowed schools, reformatories and industrial schools. The three education boards (national, intermediate and technical instruction) were merged into a single department but continued to be administered separately within it. Reformatories and industrial schools had already been taken over from the Local Government Board in 1922. Education was also given responsibility for the universities, which were funded under a separate vote until 1957.

History professor Eoin MacNeill, a founder member of the Gaelic League and Irish Volunteers who had been born at Glenarm, County Antrim in 1868, was appointed Minister for Education in August 1922 (succeeding Fionán Lynch, who had held the post since January before returning to the army during the civil war). MacNeill resigned from the government over the boundary commission in 1925 and was succeeded by Killarney-born 44-year-old John Marcus O'Sullivan, professor of modern history at University College Dublin (UCD), who had been educated at UCD, Bonn, Berlin and Heidelberg. O'Sullivan, whose brother was a former MP, had little involvement in politics during the war of independence—although the pre-treaty Dáil cabinet often met at his house. He was elected to the Dáil in 1923 and was later appointed parliamentary secretary for the Department of Finance. He succeeded J.J. Walsh as chairman of Cumann na nGaedheal but lacked his dynamism and organisational expertise. Because of his linguistic skills O'Sullivan was frequently chosen to represent Ireland as a delegate at the League of Nations.

Joseph O'Neill served as secretary of the department from 1923 to 1944. Born at Tuam, County Galway, in 1878, the son of an RIC policeman, he spent his childhood on the Aran Islands. Educated at St Jarlath's College, Maynooth, Manchester and Freiburg, he rose to be chief inspector of education, was acquainted with Michael Collins and a close associate of UCD Jesuit Professor Timothy Corcoran, whose views on education and the Irish language had considerable influence over government policy. O'Neill served on the local appointments commission between 1926 and 1946 and was the author of a number of books.

Michael Collins fought a rearguard action on education in Northern Ireland when he arranged for nationalist teachers, who refused to accept salaries or grants from the Northern Ireland government, to be paid by the department in an effort to maintain control over education and to influence events, but after his death the Irish Free State ceased making payments.

Minimal educational reform
The government made no attempt to achieve greater control over primary and secondary schools, which were largely controlled by the Catholic Church. Public written examinations were retained, payment by results was dropped in 1924, scant attention was paid to school meals, medical services and textbooks, and there was no expansion in the role of parents. Very little was invested in children with disabilities and it was left to the religious orders to provide special care. Books by English writers were replaced by those of Irish writers or translations of the classics.[1]

The Catholic Church insisted that parents should be responsible for their children's education. It opposed free education and secured a dominant position as the government wanted control over the curricula rather than the schools. In 1922 national schools organised at parish level catered for primary students in a rudimentary manner. Secondary schools were either private or run by the clergy or religious orders. Secondary examination failure rates were high: 49 per cent failed to pass a single subject in 1919–20, because all students were entered for examinations in the hope that as many as possible would pass, as state aid was based on results.[2] To improve this situation, two examinations recommended by the viceregal commissions before independence, the Intermediate (15–16 years) and Leaving Certificates (17–18), were introduced. The changes made were initially more apparent than real, as cramming continued, while teachers resented the publication of examination results for each school. Nevertheless, by 1930, 76.9 per cent of students sitting the Leaving Certificate passed the examination. At second level the emphasis was on languages, history and geography, with mathematics and science neglected. The technical schools run by the county committees of education were not geared to industrial or agricultural needs. Third-level education was only available to the privileged few. In the opinion of W.B. Yeats, 'The old *regime* left Ireland, perhaps, the worst educated country in Northern Europe'.[3] Nevertheless, education reforms were confined to changes in administration and examinations, and the revival of Irish.

PRIMARY EDUCATION

Ireland had the highest illiteracy rate in the UK, with 13.2 per cent in the 1901 census which reported the rate in England and Wales as 2.8 per cent. The real rate of illiteracy was probably higher, as the census regarded people who signed their names on the census form to be literate. Rural illiteracy was higher than that in urban areas. After independence the government saw little need to reform the primary curriculum; it just added the emphasis on Irish. The division of national schools along denominational lines continued. Eighty per cent of them had only one or two teachers. The Catholic Church unsuccessfully opposed the amalgamation of boys' and girls' schools which the government considered necessary for educational and financial reasons. The Catholic Church objected to Irish National Teachers Organisation (INTO) proposals that the state should bear the cost of buildings and that maintenance should be funded by local authorities. Labour deputy and INTO activist T.J. O'Connell complained that schools only got £3 for maintenance per annum, voluntary effort was needed to raise funds, sweeping of schools was done by children, books were costly, and teachers were dependent on numbers for their jobs and could be 'thrown out' no matter how efficient they were. He believed national teachers should have the benefit of university education.[4]

In 1924–25 there were 5,636 primary schools and 13,043 teachers (lay and clerical).[5] As many were one-teacher schools with under 50 pupils, teachers were stretched to provide lessons for six or seven standards simultaneously.[6] School attendance was a serious problem with only 69 per cent attending in 1922, compared with 90 per cent in England and 86 per cent in Scotland. This was in part because attendance had never been properly enforced. Attendance between six and 14 years was made compulsory in 1927 and efforts were made to enforce the law. These bore fruit and by 1930–31 the figure had risen to 83 per cent.[7] A small number of schools remained outside the national primary school system. Some were privately owned and managed, and could decide their own curriculum but received no state aid. Private schools were not subject to state supervision except in respect of school attendance. There were few nurseries or kindergartens.

Primary school starting ages were between four and six. Once children reached sixth standard by age 12–14, they were expected to be able to read and write Irish and English and have a basic knowledge of arithmetic, Irish history after 1600, geography (a general knowledge of Ireland, Britain, Europe and North America), singing, and needlework (girls only). The ability to communicate in Irish and English was considered paramount but oral Irish was hard to teach in large classes. A minority of boys were taught algebra and geometry while some girls studied cookery and domestic economy. All pupils were given instruction in religion, health and hygiene. While music and nature study could be taught, no funding was allocated. Some school meals were provided by the state and for 'necessitous children' by the Society of St Vincent de Paul. A student leaving a primary school was expected to be aware of[8]

> duties towards his parents, love for his country, obedience to lawful authority, respect for private and public property, belief in dignity of work and need for service, good manners, courtesy and a sense of order, and regard for all God's creatures.

The Christian Brothers, who had remained outside the national school system, joined it in 1925–6, adding 19,574 students. Primary schools in urban areas were overcrowded, with class sizes in the 40s and 50s not unusual. As children were deemed fit to go to work at 14, a minority of national school pupils advanced to second level and even as late as 1952, only 14,655 students transferred from primary to secondary.[9]

A committee of inspection of primary schools made up of department officials, INTO and Christian Brothers recommended the introduction of the Primary Certificate examination in 1927. They were supported by the Commission on Technical Education. The 'primary' was first set in 1929, it was not made compulsory, and only 25 per cent of students sat it.

SECONDARY EDUCATION

While there were 493,382 national school pupils, there were only 22,897 attending secondary school in 1923–24, despite the fact that fees in most secondary schools, particularly those run by the Christian Brothers, were low and many pupils were educated free of charge. Secondary school students were concentrated in the lower years and less than one third of those sitting the Intermediate progressed towards the Leaving Certificate. Males predominated and it was not until the 1960s that females would equal them. Of the 1,058 sitting the Leaving Cert in 1929, only 313 were girls.[10] The 278 secondary schools in 1924 offered courses in Irish, English, French, Latin, classical Greek, domestic science, mathematics, history, geography and other subjects including chemistry and physics. In 1931–32 15,173 students took French, 2,985 took Greek and 14,682 took science subjects other than domestic science. School and pupil numbers increased and by 1931–32 there were 306 schools and 30,004 students, of which 34 schools used Irish as their ordinary medium.[11]

The courses were over-academic with little to orient students towards agriculture, industry or commerce. This was detrimental in a state where entrepreneurs were in short supply and educated people were needed to innovate and develop the available resources to increase the state's wealth and create employment. Education in the 1920s was seen mainly as a means of getting a secure job rather than acquiring life skills or contributing to the economy.

Some parts of the community were opposed to spending on education. Farmers Party leader D.J. Gorey argued that too much money was being spent on it and that education 'ought to be directed to fit us for the position in life which we have to occupy'.[12] Farmers saw Ireland as an agricultural country where the majority did not need second-level education, but independent Deputy Richard Henrik Beamish appealed for farmers' children to get a good education, stating that the sooner children were 'brought within a system of organised thought the better'.[13] The belief that Ireland was an agricultural country was to hold back advances in education until the 1960s. The Catholic Church opposed conveying rural children to central secondary schools, arguing as late as 1954,[14]

The physical strain involved and the general inclemency of our climate are bound to have ill-effects on their health. Moreover, long absence from the immediate control of parents and teachers and the want of reserve likely to be encouraged by travel in groups, are not conducive to moral well-being.

Poor children received no assistance to go to secondary schools apart from a few local authority scholarships, although the department supported children from *an fíor-Ghaeltacht*.

Industrial schools and reformatories
Poor children and unmarried mothers 'did not get independence in 1922'.[15] Most children of single parents were not reared by their mothers in a disapproving society. Some were adopted, generally by overseas parents as adoption was not legal in the Irish Free State, a few were fostered and the majority ended up in industrial schools. After independence the state and society allowed the Catholic Church almost complete control of the industrial schools and reformatories. The church willingly took on the task of operating them and was paid by the state on a capitation basis. Rev. Br. Ryan of the Christian Brothers, Artane, gave a 'vigorous and logical' defence

of the industrial school system in evidence to the Commission on the Relief of the Sick and Destitute Poor in 1925.[16] During the 1920s children could be admitted to industrial schools for many reasons apart from the necessity of taking them into care for their own protection, including failure to attend school, under the School Attendance Act 1926. The industrial schools and 'Magdalen' homes had been established by religious orders as part of the process of reforming the Poor Law by moving mothers and children out of the workhouses into institutions more suited to their care. But after independence, conditions in the industrial schools and reformatories worsened as Education failed to inspect them as effectively as the local government board had before 1922. It also failed to follow up children over 16 who left the schools as it would require 'a very large staff of inspectors' to do so.[17] In an effort to cover up the evident neglect, the relevant files between 1922 and 1939 appear to have been destroyed. The majority of Catholic unmarried mothers went to homes run by nuns to have their babies rather than remain at home. Some mothers stayed in the homes for longer periods, often becoming institutionalised over time. Older children deemed to need further 'protection' were transferred to the laundries attached to the homes, often for extended periods. The reformatories, industrial schools, and Magdalen homes became in effect concentration camps where children and adults were incarcerated, poorly fed, clothed and educated, and subjected to severe discipline, and in some cases to violence and sexual abuse.[18]

The British began phasing out institutional care in the 1920s. No corresponding reform took place in the Irish Free State as the Catholic Church opposed it. The issue of how to deal with unmarried mothers and their children was hotly but inconclusively debated. Legion of Mary founder Frank Duff argued that the breaking up of mothers and children was the root cause of many problems later in life.[19] The Carrigan committee's report on sexual crimes and juvenile prostitution, completed in 1931, was kept secret and the debates on it by a private Dáil committee were not published. Neither politicians nor journalists investigated the schools, homes or laundries, or enquired into the level of domestic child sexual abuse. The industrial schools continuously sought more children to increase their revenue and the Children's Act 1929 made it easier for children to be committed to them. There were no visiting committees so the state was the children's only protector. It failed them miserably between 1922 and 1932 and for many decades afterwards.

Technical education

After independence, technical schools were under-resourced and, in Jesuit Thomas Finlay's view, most students entering them lacked sufficient general education to take full advantage, so resources and time were wasted bringing them up to the required standard.[20] The technical schools taught mathematics, woodworking, metalwork, drawing, commercial subjects, domestic economy, English and physical training. When Irish was introduced in 1922, it was assumed that students would sacrifice one of their other subjects if they took it. However, little Irish was taught until after Fianna Fáil came to power.

The Commission on Technical Education reported in 1927 that schoolwork had very little relevance to the needs of trade and industry and recommended increasing the school leaving age from 14 to 16, compulsory attendance (14–16) if not working, continuation of part-time education for those employed under 16, and for the first two years of apprenticeship at a minimum of 180 days a year. It criticised the national school system from which students emerged 'functionally illiterate' and called for legislation on apprenticeship and intensive training for teachers.

The commission's report led to the Vocational Education Act 1930, which was Minister O'Sullivan's major contribution. It provided a blueprint for technical school development for the next 40 years and led to the Apprenticeship Act 1931. The Vocational Education Act replaced the technical instruction committees with 38 new vocational education committees and changed their composition by adding trade unionists, employers and individuals with an interest in education, while reducing the number of councillors. The Catholic bishops did not approve of the technical schools as they were non-denominational and co-educational, expressed reservations that teachers could be dispersed over too many types of schools, opposed night schools on moral grounds, and ensured that vocational schools would not compete with secondary schools by limiting their curriculum. The clergy were pacified by being given seats on the new committees and in many cases became their chairmen. The act led to a high degree of uniformity of technical education throughout the state, and 46 new schools were built and 21 extended by 1936.[21]

Continuation education was added to the existing full-time education programme on a non-compulsory basis but was gradually made obligatory. Two-thirds of students finished school at primary level in the 1920s, a figure that remained almost constant until the 1950s, so technical schools were important for low-income families as they were free. However, they were considered socially inferior and compared unfavourably (for no good reason) with secondary schools. There was no access to third-level education from the technical schools. Education set up a training scheme for new industries, but little use was made of it. By 1931 there were 63,426 students in vocational schools, of whom 19,503 were in urban areas.[22]

The Vocational Education Act built on the experience gained in technical education since 1900 and was a success, but the Apprenticeship Act was ineffectual as it was based on imported laws grafted on to a poorly developed existing system, with little modification to make them suitable to Irish conditions.

THE UNIVERSITIES

After independence, the universities were fee paying, had low student numbers and were short of money. The Commission on Industrial and Scientific Research report in April 1922 emphasised the need to start on the right note by raising the level of training and third-level education. Cumann na nGaedheal deputy Liam de Róiste asked in the Dáil in 1923 what the universities had done for agriculture, to improve the education of the ordinary people or in scientific research. He urged them to turn the minds of their students to the development of the country and not to prepare them for emigration. He agreed that the amount of money being given to the universities was small but if they put up a proper case they would get more.[23]

Trinity College found it hardest to adapt to the new state. The Government of Ireland Act 1920 had proposed that Trinity be granted £30,000 per annum but the Irish Free State provided only £3,000 a year. Consequently its finances were in a poor condition and its source of students dwindled as the Protestant population had declined due to war losses and emigration. Catholics remained banned from attending Trinity, Archbishop Edward Byrne of Dublin stating that 'It is still an institution to which a Catholic can go only at grave peril to his faith'.[24] Minimal investment was made by the state, although the University (Agriculture and Dairy Science) Bill 1926 provided funds for agriculture at University College Dublin and dairy science at University College Cork. Expenditure on the National Universities ranged from £111,000 in 1922–23 to a high of £175,000 in 1926–27, falling back to £155,000 by 1932–32.

University College Galway led the development of Irish from 1929, but the lack of Irish textbooks handicapped the teaching of the language at third level.[25] Maynooth remained a Catholic university for the education of priests. There were around 3,200 students in the Irish universities in 1900 (including Queen's University, Belfast) and by 1930 there were 5,000 in the Irish Free State.[26] Third-level technical education was not introduced until the establishment of the regional technical colleges from the 1960s onwards.

TEACHER TRAINING

National teacher training did not change after 1922 apart from training teachers to speak Irish. The Marlborough Street training college was closed, which meant that all remaining colleges were denominational. These had been established under British rule: St Patrick's, Drumcondra (1882), Our Lady of Mercy, Blackrock (1883), Church of Ireland, Kildare Place (1884), De La Salle, Waterford (1891) and Mary Immaculate, Limerick (1901). A training college for Christian Brothers was set up at St Mary's, Marino, in 1930.

Primary teachers trained at the expense of the state had to repay the cost of their training before they were allowed enter the civil service. More teachers were being trained than could secure employment in Ireland.[27] The Commission on Technical Education commented on the lack of technical teacher training, which was not obligatory, and stated that nothing had been done apart from providing short-term courses.

The immediate problem with regard to teaching Irish and other subjects through Irish was that in 1922 only 1,107 out of 12,000 lay teachers were qualified to teach bilingually and 2,845 were qualified to teach Irish.[28] Most teachers had little knowledge of the language and as a result teachers with poor language skills had to teach it because the revival of Irish was a government priority. Education sought to address the problem by ensuring that newly qualified teachers had sufficient Irish while at the same time training existing teachers in the language. Native Irish speakers were favoured and non-native speakers had to secure high marks in oral Irish to qualify for training places. Summer courses in the Gaeltacht and at universities were organised to train existing teachers. Those below 45 years of age were obliged to attend. By 1926 almost 50 per cent of teachers were deemed to have learned enough Irish to teach it. Seven residential preparatory colleges were established, six Catholic (three each for men and women) and one Protestant (mixed gender). The number of school days, which was already low by European standards, was reduced to facilitate teacher training in Irish. By 1929 the department decided that teachers had sufficient Irish and summer courses were discontinued. Secondary teacher training in Irish was encouraged by financial incentives and from 1924 secondary schools received 25 per cent extra funding if Irish was used in teaching all subjects and 10 per cent if used in half the subjects. Graduate qualification and secondary teacher training were introduced in 1924–25.[29]

Teachers' pay and conditions
Teachers' pay and pensions were contentious issues. Primary teachers received a pay rise in 1921 but salaries were reduced by 10 per cent in 1924. Further pay cuts were made in the 1931 supplementary budget while an over-supply of teachers depressed pay rates. National teachers had bad relations with inspectors. An enquiry in 1927 found an over-emphasis on control but nothing was done to rectify matters. However, primary teachers were treated more favourably than

secondary teachers. They had salary scales, contracts of employment and pension rights.

Labour Deputy T.J. O'Connell argued that secondary teachers were inadequately paid and scandalously treated. Their average salaries were not much more than a starting national school teacher's; they had no guarantee they would be paid and no pension rights.[30] Lay teachers in clerically run schools had few promotional opportunities. The Association of Secondary Teachers in Ireland (ASTI) lobbied Dáil deputies, seeking minimum salaries, improved increments, pensions and security of tenure. The union complained in 1924 that grants were lower than 1913 (despite a significant rise in the cost of living), accommodation was inadequate, and the best teachers were emigrating.[31] A pension scheme was implemented from 1929 onwards, but secondary teachers had to wait until 1937 before they received contracts of employment.

Secondary schools were private and before independence had received minimal state support. The British had tried to increase state involvement between 1900 and 1920 but had been opposed by the schools and the churches. After 1922 capitation grants were given to 'recognised schools' and incremental salaries were paid to 'recognised teachers', but most schools remained free to operate as they wished, provided they followed department rules. The commission on technical education called for standard conditions of employment and salary scales for whole-time technical teachers in 1927.

THE IRISH LANGUAGE

The percentage of people speaking Irish as a first language in Ireland had declined from 24.5 per cent in 1861 to 17.6 per cent by 1911 (these figures are derived from the census figures for Ireland as a whole). Sinn Féin and the Gaelic League wished to revive the use of Irish. Arguments put forward to support that objective included the ideas that a nation without a language is not a nation, that full independence and sovereignty would not be achieved unless Irish was restored to everyday use, and that the Irish people had been alienated from the English state for centuries and needed to be reconciled with a new Gaelic state. The emphasis on Irish, together with the increasingly

Roman Catholic character of the new state, antagonised many Protestants and unionists, and discouraged them from perceiving the Irish Free State or a united Ireland in a positive manner.

From 1922 onwards the state took over responsibility for the Irish language from cultural pressure groups like the Gaelic League with the intention of preserving and extending the Gaeltacht and using education to spread the language in non-Gaeltacht areas. The problem was that Irish outside the Gaeltacht was an academic rather than a living language. Some opposition came from Protestants, who accounted for less than 10 per cent of the population, were scattered geographically and were also ideologically unprepared for independence. Many of them had been employed in the civil service, police and army before independence. After 1922, they saw the Irish language as a barrier to continued employment opportunities in sectors where they had previously enjoyed preference. They were anxious to co-operate in schools but feared Irish would drive out other subjects. Protestants gradually reached an accommodation with the state despite having reservations about the 'Catholic' flavour of textbooks. But not all Protestants were against the Irish language. Senior department inspector George Nicholls was a 'complete revivalist' who stated that 'every hog, dog and devil' would have to learn it.[32] Catholics were reluctant to react against the Irish language and there were few vocal critics, although an unnamed senator was reported to have stated that expenditure on Irish was 'an abuse of money'.

The Catholic Church saw the revival of Irish as a contribution towards countering the impact of the Hollywood and Fleet Street media.[33] But concern was expressed about the threat posed by Irish to classical languages, mathematics and commercial subjects. Of the 488 students sitting the Leaving Certificate in 1925, only 70 took mathematics.[34] The INTO was worried about teaching subjects through Irish as it was leading to a drop in standards. Independent Deputy James Dillon stated that Irish governments did more damage than the British and that ramming Irish down the throats of schoolchildren was not sensible. Class sizes were large and students' attention was divided between subject and language. Subjects that should have been interesting became tedious tasks.[35] Those who protested were ignored by the government. School inspectors soon reported poorer results in other subjects.

Teaching infants through the medium of Irish was to be the foundation of restoring the language. The theory was that they would acquire early knowledge which would enable them to receive increasing amounts of their education through Irish as they progressed through school, and would continue to use the language as adults, thereby bringing it back into everyday life. Irish was promoted through newspaper articles, bilingual town and street names, Irish titles for officials, encouraging civil servants to use Irish and making official forms available in both languages.[36] However, the children were mainly living in an English-language environment. Once school ended each day, and during holidays, they had little opportunity of practising the language unless they lived in the Gaeltacht, as few parents spoke Irish. Consequently they were badly educated in a language they did not fully comprehend, by teachers who often had a poor knowledge of it and little or no training in teaching through Irish.

The majority of the general public did not learn Irish because they were not motivated to do so or rejected the possibility that it could replace English. Paradoxically, there was more interest before the treaty than after it, as people believed that once independence had been achieved it was no longer necessary to learn Irish. This contrasts with the Welsh, who have been much more successful in retaining and expanding the use of their language, perhaps because it differentiates them from the English. Membership of the Gaelic League declined in the 1920s.[37] Neither Cumann na nGaedheal nor Fianna Fáil politicians set a good example. Very few spoke fluent Irish; the majority just had 'cúpla focail' (a few words). There was no economic incentive for the population to change its language. In fact the reverse was the case. Yet the possibility of two languages coexisting does not seem to have been actively considered. The revivalists insisted that Irish must replace English, while the majority of the population was either unwilling to make the necessary sacrifice or was simply apathetic. The people would have had to make a huge effort to re-Gaelicise Ireland. They had neither the motivation nor the commitment to do so.

Education officials privately admitted that few teachers were qualified to teach any subject in Irish.[38] There was a shortage of Irish textbooks, general literature, magazines, periodicals and newspapers. An Gúm, Education's publications branch, partially filled the gap after 1926 by paying special bonuses to authors to write and translate books suitable for seven-to-eleven-year-olds. However, it seems to have been difficult to sell them.[39]

Education considered whether Gaelic script should be replaced with Roman script, which was less costly to print, but a decision was postponed, possibly to the detriment of the language. While there was apparently a rule that one-third of original works should be in Roman type, many new books were printed in it. No serious effort was made to standardise the Irish dialects. Finance minister Ernest Blythe, a northern Protestant and fluent Irish-speaker, promoted the establishment of the Gaeltacht Commission in 1925, but few of its recommendations were implemented.

After Fianna Fáil's entry into the Dáil in 1927, Irish became a more significant political issue as the party tried to explain its objectives in terms of a republican, Irish-speaking united Ireland. But when it got into power it was no more successful than Cumann na nGaedheal. Fianna Fáil did, however, spur the government to finance Irish in University College Galway, and to strengthen the language in the civil service by making passing of an oral examination mandatory, and ruling that civil servants under 30 would be ineligible for promotion without knowledge of Irish. Suggestions like paying older people to instruct their grandchildren and supporting the Gaelic League and the Gaelic Athletic Association to teach Irish came to nothing. Eoin O'Duffy made a significant effort to encourage members of the Garda to learn Irish, but he was a rare exception. While applicants needed Irish to enter the civil service, its business was conducted almost entirely in English.

There was no coherent language policy and there seems to have been no understanding of the need to 'sell' the language. This was a lost opportunity as people were initially well-disposed towards Irish: the link between Irish and separatism was still strong in their minds. The Council of Education subsequently reviewed the progress in the revival of the Irish language, expressed concerns with the level of achievement and quoted from the Welsh central advisory council:[40]

> Unless the acquisition of the second language can be related to a purpose beyond the mere learning of the language, unless the general community or the school can supply incentives, and unless language is regarded by the teacher as a tool to be used more and more freely and imaginatively, the language lesson may remain a series of pointless verbal tricks. There is little value in learning a language merely in order to have acquired it and indeed in such conditions there is very little likelihood that the child will ever learn it.

Irish could not be revived through the schools alone. The public had to be convinced of the necessity for its revival, motivated to make the sacrifices to learn it, given incentives to use it and provided with the tools to enable people to change their everyday language, which was one of the most widely spoken languages in the world and the international language of commerce. The language revival was initiated by government *diktat* and failed because the majority was not convinced of its need.

EDUCATIONAL PROGRESS—FORWARD OR BACKWARDS?

The department, in its 1931 special report, noted the improvements in teacher training and the increased number of textbooks available. It stated that it had 'made an effort un-paralleled in history to restore the native language of the country to its proper place in the national life'. It had attempted to improve the standard of education in the two reformatories and 52 industrial schools, which in the year 1929–30 had 110 and 6,677 pupils respectively.[41] But the reality was that the already poor standard of education fell, the Irish language was not revived, teachers were not well treated, and students, particularly those in the reformatories and industrial schools, were ill-served by the state, while little improvement was made in equality of opportunity or access to second and third levels.

Educational development was neglected mainly because resources were concentrated on reviving the Irish language. The government laid down the law that Irish was to be restored but its actions never translated into intelligent implementation or practical support. Compulsion was the most consistent trait. No justification for the revival was provided on economic or social grounds, nor was there an understanding that Irish culture could be expressed through English. The department did not apparently have any constructive ideas about what kind of education was needed. Few educational innovations were made, advice and criticism were ignored and international best practice was rarely considered worth investigating, let alone implementing.

A huge amount of time and resources were spent on Irish, but the outcome was a poor return on the money spent and damage done to the teaching of other subjects. The revivalists were obsessed with the fear of losing an idealised Gaelic Ireland that had never existed, were convinced that time was running out and were culturally exclusive to the extent that they fell out with the majority of the Irish people. Education was hijacked in an attempt to create a new Irish national identity. Cumann na nGaedheal delegated the almost impossible task of reviving the language to the teachers and children without adequate resources, regardless of the damage inflicted on education. The end result was that Irish was killed off by a native government more effectively than by the British. Students learned it at school because they were compelled to and never spoke it afterwards.[42]

However, some progress was made. Average school attendance and examination pass rates improved, numbers attending secondary schools increased, £600,000 was invested in school buildings, 531 national schools were amalgamated between 1928 and 1931 and the Vocational Education Act 1930 provided a sound basis for the future development of technical schools.[43]

Chapter 16 ～

POSTS, TELECOMMUNICATIONS AND RADIO

INTRODUCTION

In 1922 the principal means of internal and external communications—posts, telecommunications and wireless—were delivered by the Post Office, which also provided money transfer, banking and counter services. It administered the savings bank and savings certificates on behalf of the Department of Finance and purchased, inspected and stored goods and uniforms for other government departments. The Post Office came into direct contact with more people than all other government departments and aimed to preserve a balance between government requirements, staff interest and public demand. Unlike other departments, its headquarters' staff was a fraction of its total establishment, most of whom were in departmental grades specific to the Post Office. No other government department had as much continuity, as its core business remained largely unchanged after independence.

THE DEPARTMENT OF POSTS AND TELEGRAPHS

The Post Office in Ireland was formally established in 1774. After the granting of legislative independence in 1782, an independent Irish Post Office took over its operations in 1784. This situation prevailed until 1831, when concerns over financial mismanagement led to control being transferred to the postmaster-general in London. In 1922, the Irish Free State took back its operations in the 26 counties, while those in Northern Ireland remained part of the British Post Office.

James J. (J.J.) Walsh was appointed Postmaster-General in April 1922 at the age of 42 years. Born near Bandon, County Cork, he had formerly worked in the Post Office and been active in the GAA and served as chairman of its Cork county board. He joined the Irish Volunteers and Sinn Féin and was elected to Cork city council. Walsh was transferred by the Post Office to Bradford in England and was subsequently dismissed after 20 years' service due to his political activities. He returned to Ireland and commenced business as a tobacconist in Dublin, where he joined the Irish-American (separatist) wing of the Ancient Order of Hibernians and participated in the 1916 rising as a member of the Hibernian Rifles, after which he was sentenced to death. Elected an MP in 1918, he was imprisoned frequently during the war of independence. Walsh considered the treaty to be the better of two bad alternatives. Unlike other Cumann na nGaedheal ministers, he believed the party should be a mass movement and favoured patronage. He was dynamic, opinionated and argumentative, and antagonised many of his colleagues, particularly Kevin O'Higgins.

P.S. O'Hegarty was appointed by Walsh as secretary of the department. The son of a Fenian, he was born at Carrignavar, County Cork, in 1879 and together with his brother Seán, later a leading IRA commander in the war of independence, was educated at North Monastery, Cork. O'Hegarty joined the Post Office and worked in London between 1900 and 1914. He was prominent in IRB circles and was involved in the recruitment of Michael Collins into Sinn Féin and the Gaelic League. He was dismissed in 1918 for refusing to take an oath of allegiance to the crown and established a bookshop in Dublin. O'Hegarty opposed the attempt to force Northern Ireland into the Irish Free State, and was a prolific writer, outspoken critic of the anti-treaty side, and 'great decision maker' who remained secretary until he retired in 1944.[1]

The Post Office was the largest employer in the Irish Free State, with a workforce of 13,500 in 1922. However, it was unprofitable and needed to reduce its costs while simultaneously maximising investment in telephones to meet demand and increase revenue. The postal and counter services were expected to grow as the economy expanded; telegraphs were declining, while telephones had great potential. Making a profit required good commercial and operational management, but the Post Office was run by bureaucrats who, while competent at administration, had neither the training nor the expertise to manage a complex business. Fianna Fáil Deputy Hugo Flinn suggested that management consultants be engaged to improve efficiency in 1928.[2]

Under the Ministers and Secretaries Act 1924, the department was assigned responsibility for posts, telegraphs, telephones and wireless together with the government's central purchasing function. Walsh's title was changed to Minister for Posts and Telegraphs. He was an external minister, one of the few members of the government with business skills, and became the main driver of change in the Post Office until he left politics over the issue of tariffs in 1927. Subsequently he set up a bus company, supported Fianna Fáil in the 1932 election and, after his business was bought out by Dublin Tramway, he invested in Clondalkin Paper Mills, Solus Teo., Belbulben Barytes and other companies, becoming a very successful businessman.

Following Walsh's departure the department was downgraded when the Minister for Finance was assigned the portfolio, leaving a parliamentary secretary in charge.

After independence, good relations were maintained between the Irish and British Post Offices. Most of the mail from Ireland continued to be despatched to the UK, while Ireland probably remained the major recipient of mail from Britain. The Post Office network was extensive, consisting of 55 head post offices, 34 departmentally staffed offices and 2,000 sub-offices, together with sorting offices, telegraph and telephone exchanges, wireless stations, engineering depots, a factory and stock-holding facilities together with management, back-office, establishment, and accounting functions at its headquarters in Dublin.[3] High-level engineering, purchasing, accounting and general management functions, formerly carried out in London, were rapidly transferred to Dublin.

Posts and telecommunications were among the first examples of large-scale international co-operation to deliver a worldwide service. In 1922 traders in Dublin and Cork had similar rapid access to goods as merchants in Glasgow and Aberdeen since they could order from English suppliers by mail, telegraph or telephone for next day delivery by parcels transported overnight by steamers and the railways.[4]

The Post Office was a monopoly with the exclusive privilege of carrying letters, transmitting telegrams and controlling the use of wireless apparatus, telegraphy and telephony. It remitted its revenue to Finance and received voted money for its expenditure like other government departments. The Post Office had more discretion in making certain payments without Finance sanction due to the 'commercial character of the business'. It was the only government department that produced commercial accounts which presented its financial results in a format similar to those of private business. The tension between running a commercial undertaking and providing public and social services was one which soon became apparent but, while it was frequently debated, it was never resolved.

Irish and British ministers and Post Office officials met on 10 February 1922 to discuss temporary over-printing of stamps, new stamps, extra costs during the transitional period, a £1 million claim for damage to the GPO in Dublin arising from the 1916 rising, and administrative matters such as appointments, staff transfers between Britain and Ireland and telephone agreements.[5] During the civil war post offices were robbed (an average of 150 monthly), mail was stolen, telegraph and telephone lines were cut, exchanges wrecked and services disrupted by the irregulars.[6] Code markings were changed in Crown Alley exchange, causing confusion in switching calls.[7] The main sorting office at the Rotunda ice rink was destroyed by fire in November 1922. Postal records were burned, adding to those already lost at the GPO in 1916. The Valentia and Clifden transatlantic cables were cut and station instruments damaged, leading to fears that the cables would be moved to Britain 'to place them out of the reach of Mr de Valera's friends'.[8] The holding of wireless, telegraph and telephone apparatus was banned by the government and all equipment had to be surrendered; contraband equipment was confiscated and penalties imposed.

The Post Office was a patronage department and the minister had power to appoint sub-postmasters/postmistresses from a list of suitable candidates vetted by officials; there were many other positions where political influence could deliver jobs. Consequently Dáil deputies vigilantly watched all appointments. Apart from staff dismissed during the civil war and the army mutiny, personnel issues in the Post Office were mainly pay and conditions related. Disputes arose over the time taken to revise and rewrite the rule books, reclassification of grades, and promotions.[9] Irish staff in the UK and British staff in Ireland wished to be repatriated but the Post Office insisted on exchanging staff on a one-for-one basis, which disadvantaged the Irish, many of whom wished to return home. Complaints were made that the Post Office gave preference to recruiting ex-army men, but that was in line with government policy. The Post Office trade unions maintained links with their northern brethren, making excursions to Northern Ireland and arranging a joint visit to Paris in 1930.[10]

Post Office services were subjected to 'wholesale destruction' during the civil war and repairs took about a year to complete, using up scarce resources and delaying development.[11] Thereafter postal and counter services remained expensive operations due to high staff numbers and the imperative to provide similar service levels throughout the state regardless of customer density. The Post Office performed a vital social function but it was expected to operate on a commercial basis. Telegraphs were inherently loss-making, while the extension of the telephone service, which had considerable revenue-generating potential, was delayed due to shortage of skilled staff in the early years and insufficient capital investment thereafter.

The Irish Post Office was granted independent recognition at the International Postal Congress in Stockholm in 1924 and achieved voting rights at the International Telegraph Conference.

The 1922 Post Office strike

The British Post Office lost £7.3 million in 1920–21, of which £1.1 million was attributable to the Irish Free State, the Irish Post Office having been run at a loss since 1897.[12] The government could not sustain losses of that magnitude, so it sought to reduce payroll costs by cutting the cost-of-living bonus awarded during World War I to compensate for high inflation. The cost of living had dropped sharply after the war without a corresponding decrease in wages, while sick leave was high as a day could be taken without a medical certificate. Employees were worried that gains made during the war would be lost and threatened strike action in March 1922.[13] Similar pay cuts were implemented in Northern Ireland without a strike. Walsh, an ex-trade unionist and former left-wing radical, conceded that the workers were badly paid, but was annoyed at strike action so soon after independence. This was the first public service strike faced by the new government and Walsh believed there was a political agenda as it occurred during the civil war. He refused arbitration and sent a telegram to the Postmaster-General in London asking him to ascertain the number of Irish who wanted to transfer back to Ireland. The executive prevented him from bringing staff home to break the strike.

The strike began on 10 September 1922 and lasted less than three weeks. It became more contentious after shootings at Amiens Street telegraph office and Crown Alley telephone exchange. Arrests were made, employees were threatened and one, Miss Olive Flood, was wounded by gunshot.[14] The unions claimed a 'quasi-military junta' had taken over the Post Office.[15] A skeleton service was provided by 'volunteers' aided by the chambers of commerce and businesses. Unskilled labour was recruited and prisoners in Mountjoy gaol were promised early release if they helped break the strike. Workers who continued at their duties took temporary residence in sorting offices and were given armed escorts.

The strike was generally backed outside Dublin, although some staff continued working. The three Post Office trade unions united on a temporary basis and attempted to place advertisements in newspapers. The newspapers adopted a hostile attitude towards the strike because they depended on business advertising and were losing revenue as many newspapers were delivered by post. The unions had daily strike bulletins printed to present their case to the public. Labour Deputy T.J. O'Connell argued that postal workers did not wish to challenge the authority of the state and were non-political.[16] The government's reaction to the strike upset Labour Party activists who supported the Irish Free State, as the struggle for independence and social revolution had been closely linked since James Connolly and the Irish Citizen Army's participation in the 1916 rising. The government was annoyed by Labour Party-inspired Dáil debates on the strike which delayed the passing of the constitution. Most of the anti-treaty side remained aloof from events. The government adopted a hard line, particularly Minister for Industry and Commerce (and Labour) Joe McGrath, who insisted that civil servants did not have the right to strike.[17]

The strike ended with agreement that the wage cuts be made in two phases while the postal commission, set up under the chairmanship of James Douglas in June 1922 to enquire into pay, organisation of work and conditions of employment, would resolve the remaining issues. After the strike, the Post Office was reorganised and sought additional work including rate collection, licensing, outdoor relief and old age pension investigation to occupy staff being displaced. This was rejected by the government as 'external Ministers were not to be given extended powers'.[18]

The strike left a legacy as 'volunteers' had continued to work and officials who kept the system running were promoted. Despite allegations of victimisation, nobody was dismissed. The postal commission felt 'strongly that the spirit of distrust at present prevailing amongst many sections of Postal employees is not conducive to either efficiency or improved organisation'. The government disregarded or materially altered most of the commission's recommendations and the unions complained at the 'unwarrantable' delay in implementing them.[19] A lasting consequence was the amalgamation of the Irish Postal Union and the Irish Postal Workers Union to form the Post Office Workers Union in 1923.

Cost reduction

After reconstruction, cost reduction took precedence over expansion or upgrading of services. Farmers Party leader D.J. Gorey offered three reasons for losses: overstaffing, overpayment and the cost of rural deliveries, neatly summarising the areas that were to receive attention. Walsh promised that all goods purchased by the Post Office would be sourced in Ireland provided they did not cost over 20 per cent more than foreign suppliers.[20] Commercial account surpluses and deficits after operating costs, depreciation and other non-cash charges demonstrate the steady reduction of losses:

	£000s	£000s	£000s
Year	Posts	Telegraphs	Telephones
1922–23	-656	-406	-46
1923–24	-404	-344	-26
1924–25	-290	-179	-3
1925–26	-217	-163	-34
1926–27	-170	-165	-44
1927–28	-71	-142	-49
1928–29	-9	-148	-35
1929–30	-19	-127	-16
1930–31	+69	-106	-8
1931–32	+117	-89	+39

Source: Department of Posts and Telegraphs Commercial Accounts, 1922–32.

The support for cost reduction was not unanimous. Fianna Fáil Deputy Seán Lemass stated in 1928,[21]

> if we have to accept the fact that the Post Office is not a paying concern and cannot be under the present circumstances, then let us do so frankly and not talk about it as a semi-commercial institution when, in fact, it is a semi-charitable institution.

However, among his party colleagues, Seán MacEntee saw no reason why the Post Office could not be run at a profit, while Hugo Flinn suggested that uneconomical services be eliminated.[22] Much of management's focus in the first decade was on cost reduction in order to restore profitability. This was largely achieved by cutting employee numbers to 12,200 (a decrease of about eleven per cent), changing work practices and duties, substituting lower-paid staff for higher-remunerated personnel and reducing services and outlets.[23] Walsh achieved major savings before leaving office in 1927. Afterwards the Post Office continued to reduce costs and by 1932 postal and telephone services were making a surplus of revenue over expenditure, which more than offset the loss on telegraphs.

COUNTER SERVICES

There was little change in counter services after independence. During the civil war, counter staff faced danger as irregulars robbed post offices and threatened and, in some cases, injured staff. Older people often received their pensions late when sub-offices, mail vans or trains were held up and looted. Many sub-post offices were destroyed during the civil war and not all were brought back into service. This resulted in diminished access to counter services in sparsely populated areas.

The GPO in Dublin had not been rebuilt after its destruction during the 1916 Easter rising. A tender for reconstruction and extension was issued in 1925 to include an arcade of shops running from Henry Street to Princess Street, and the new building was opened in 1928.

Irish depositors were encouraged to move their money from the British Post Office to the Irish Post Office. Once the state became stabilised after the civil war and people were convinced that the Irish pound would remain on par with sterling, deposits were transferred to the Post Office savings bank, national savings certificates and national loan stock, reducing the balance in Britain from £9 million in 1925 to less than £5 million in 1929.[24]

POSTS

The postal system was quickly adapted with British stamps and postal orders being over-printed *Rialtas Sealadach na hÉireann (Irish Provisional Government)*. Early indications of government policy were Walsh's stated intention to appoint Irish-speaking sub-postmasters in Gaeltacht areas, and post boxes being repainted green. Work began immediately to repair the damage inflicted during the civil war. Postal cost cuts were achieved by reducing the number of postmen and sorters, leading to a lower frequency of deliveries. Retiring employees were not replaced; 'temporary' staff were recruited and paid 'miserable pittances'.[25]

The postal service in 1922 was considerably better than it is today. Deliveries in cities occurred two or three times a day and in towns twice a day over a six-day week. Delivery times of letters were shorter due to sorting in travelling post offices on night mail trains and cross-channel steamers. While postal service levels were reduced at home, they were improved internationally as mail was despatched direct from Ireland rather than via Britain. Airmail services were expanded worldwide. However, the imbalance of overseas mails remained a significant problem. The Irish Free State received far more mail than it despatched and was not recompensed for the cost of sorting and delivering the surplus. Other countries, notably Australia, had a similar problem and both administrations tried to have this addressed at Universal Postal Union conferences. To raise extra revenue, the Post Office imposed a delivery fee of sixpence on most non-dutiable parcels while the government levied sixpence (statistical tax) on all parcels coming in by sea in an effort to discourage imports.

Postal deliveries were reduced to thrice weekly in rural areas, once a day in towns and twice a day in cities. The postal commission recommended new rates of pay and changes in work practices. Work done by sorting clerks was transferred to lower-paid postmen. Sorting clerks and telegraphists were redeployed as post office assistants to perform all clerical work except that done by executive officers. The cutbacks were not radical as most rural postmen still delivered very little mail and even when delivery frequencies were reduced many remained under-employed. The first cutbacks resulted in 60 sub-offices out of 2,000 being closed, 555 out of 7,000 postal staff dismissed or having their jobs modified, and 400 postal districts changed to alternate day delivery.[26] Costs were also reduced through increased use of motor transport, using Ford vans built in Cork.

Businesses exerted pressure for a reduction in the price of stamps when the British Post Office lowered its prices in 1923. That pressure was resisted although some rates for parcels and inland postcards (used mainly for commercial purposes) were reduced. Attempts to innovate by introducing the collection of cash on delivery in 1924 were criticised on the grounds that it would encourage imports by facilitating mail order sales. The British Post Office did not introduce cash on delivery until 1928. Post boxes on buses and trams were tried out on an experimental basis. Stamp vending machines were provided and stamps designed by Irish artists were printed in Ireland.

The Dublin postal district was responsible for postal services in the capital and for most foreign mails. This situation became a major issue in 1927. The postal commission had highlighted poor management and lack of supervision and direction. After an internal enquiry found that 'higher control has almost ceased to function and that control generally has become ineffective', Walsh made three appointments, one of whom was his brother, in an effort to sort out the problems.[27] He was challenged in the Dáil but was unrepentant, quoting from an internal report that under the British 'The men controlled themselves and got completely out of hand.'[28] The unions do not seem to have denied that problems existed and focused on favouritism. Walsh countered, 'I do not promote men for friendship's sake. I know no friend, either in politics or outside.'[29] He left office some months afterwards and the problems in the Dublin postal district remained unresolved.

The Posts and Telegraphs portfolio was combined with Finance in 1927 and the minister was replaced by a parliamentary secretary, Farmers Party leader and former rugby international Michael Heffernan. The unions complained about his lack of knowledge of the Post Office and saw him as an advocate of retrenchment.[30]

In 1928 Seán Lemass raised the question of letters opened by the Post Office between 1923 and 1928. Cumann na nGaedheal Deputy Bryan Cooper countered by asking for a list of letters removed from post offices in 1922 and delivered marked 'censored by the I.R.A.'. The Post Office did not have power to censor, but could 'look at specific letters'. This was frequently done in the case of circulars and lottery letters.[31]

TELECOMMUNICATIONS

It was difficult to reduce telegraph costs as the service was inherently loss-making and nothing had been done to upgrade it since 1914. Telegrams declined in volume terms by 20 per cent between 1923 and 1928.[32] The press, which received reduced rates, strongly resisted price increases. Repairs to war-damaged parts of the system were carried out and a direct link was arranged with US telegraph companies. A regular source of complaint was porterage (delivery charge) on telegrams, which increased based on the distance customers were located from post offices. Losses were reduced by a combination of staff cuts, automation (such as the introduction of Baudot data entry equipment and Creed teleprinters), and the use of motorcycles for telegram delivery, while prices were kept high to discourage users. Business sense indicated that the service should be run down and closed, but that could only be done when telephones were more widely available. Walsh, who disapproved of gambling, would have liked to stop the telegraph service being used to place bets.

A reconstruction committee was set up in autumn 1923 and repairs to the telephone system began as soon as the army cleared the irregulars out of the towns and cities. In secretary P.S. O'Hegarty's opinion the system taken over from the British was in a 'most scandalous state' and it suffered further damage during the civil war.[33] The repair was a lengthy and costly process and delayed the expansion of the telephone service. Many technically qualified staff moved to the British Post Office after independence, causing further delay. Telephones required significant new investment. The telephone exchange system needed to be upgraded from manual to automatic. The automatic telephone system had been patented by Almon Brown Strowger, a Kansas City undertaker, in 1891, and offered major productivity gains as it required no local call operators, enabled a greater volume of call handling and was accurate and cost-efficient. Exchanges were upgraded slowly and Dublin was not completely automated until 1930. The Strowger system remained in use until 1989, although it was gradually being replaced by the cross-bar system from 1957 onwards.

The Post Office tried to popularise telephones but in the early 1920s they were expensive and not widely available outside urban areas.

Charges for installation of new telephones were high, but phones were urgently needed, and the ability of farmers in Norway and Denmark to keep abreast of market prices, and French fishermen receiving weather forecasts over the phone prior to sailing, were mentioned in the Dáil in June 1923.[34] Both of these issues were later addressed by radio. Dairy co-operatives needed phones to compete on the British market but were mainly located in rural areas where there were few if any telephones. In response to an allegation by Clann Éireann Deputy William Magennis that telephone calls were being intercepted in 1927, Walsh replied that he had forbidden telephone and telegram tapping. Seán Lemass asked in 1928 if copies of telegrams received or sent by political opponents were given to the minister and was informed they were not.[35]

Demand would grow as more telephones were installed but the initial capital cost of exchanges, wiring and switchboards was high. It was difficult to get critical masses of users to justify the cost of installing connections in more towns or districts so, in order to secure a return on the investment quickly, areas of high demand were satisfied first. This left the less-populated parts of the country at a disadvantage and even as late as 1978 there were still 63,000 on the waiting list.[36] In 1928 the number of telephones per 1,000 people was 0.7 in the Irish Free State compared with 14.8 in the US, 9.2 in Denmark and New Zealand and three in Britain.[37] Even by 1973 Ireland had only 12 telephones per 100 people, the lowest figure in Europe.[38] Nevertheless, some progress was made. In 1924–25, 56 new exchanges were opened, 218 Garda stations connected, 51 call offices set up, and 57 miles of underground cable and 2,537 miles of single wire laid. Automatic exchanges were installed in Dublin and Cork, and telephone subscribers increased to 22,500. Progress was hampered by the shortage of technical staff and lack of capital.[39] The Post Office factory, which repaired telegraph and telephone apparatus, was criticised by the Comptroller and Auditor General, who reported that the cost of repairing some articles was greater than that of buying them on the open market.[40] Nevertheless, the factory was extended and took over the printing of stamps along with additional work on telephone equipment.

The Telephone Capital Act 1924 authorised the minister for finance to issue money from central funds to be repaid by terminable annuities over periods generally not exceeding 25 years. This was to be the method used to finance telephone capital until 1984. Walsh announced that 'It is our intention … to push the telephone service into every town and village in the country'.[41] But telephone capital investment fell far short of what was needed and it was to be over four decades before adequate funds were invested. However, between 1922 and 1932 telephones were provided to 556 previously unserved towns and villages together with public telephone kiosks erected mainly in urban areas. Overseas calls could be made to most European countries along with the US, Mexico, Canada, South America, Australia and New Zealand.

WIRELESS AND RADIO

The treaty imposed restrictions on international cables and wireless stations. Communication with places outside Ireland could not be established or submarine cables landed without agreement, existing wireless concessions could not be withdrawn, but the British were entitled to land additional submarine cables.[42] There was disagreement regarding wireless stations which communicated with ships at sea. The Post Office operated the stations at Valentia and Malin, but the British paid for them. The British were concerned with imperial defence, the Irish with sovereignty. The Irish accepted the defence arguments but insisted that no military or commercial control would be acceptable. After 1930 advances in technology considerably lessened the strategic importance of Valentia and Malin.

Radio technology made rapid advances in 1920, but broadcasting was not a priority of the government. Walsh decided that radio should be run by the private sector and issued a white paper in 1923 proposing a consortium of business interests similar to that which operated the then privately owned British Broadcasting Company (BBC).[43] A Dáil committee was set up to examine the white paper. There was minimal public demand for radio but once the BBC started broadcasting, and particularly when Belfast 2BE came on the air, the government felt it had to respond. It was also impelled to act because radio sets were being smuggled into the country or being manufactured without licence, while a few amateurs had set up their own broadcasting stations. The government advertised the radio concession for an Irish Broadcasting Company. Interested parties included former Dáil Deputy Liam de Róiste, independent Deputy Andrew O'Shaughnessy, and Cork businessmen Hugo Flinn and Senator T.P. Dowdall. They had links with British-based property developer Andrew Belton. Cumann na nGaedheal Deputy James McGarry, an electrical engineer, also wished to be considered.[44]

The broadcasting committee set up by the government presented its report in 1924. Its proceedings were controversial. Walsh, an ex-telegraph operator who understood the technology, alleged that two members of the committee were in contact with a foreign manufacturer (probably Marconi). But the main dispute broke out over the dealings between committee member and independent Deputy Darrell Figgis and Andrew Belton, who had used Figgis as a front man in a number of potential property deals because of his long association with Sinn Féin.[45] Belton denied any undue or corrupt influence, but his association with Figgis was controversial as they had been accused of running independent candidates in the 1922 election against the spirit of the Collins/de Valera pact supported by Lord Midleton, head of the southern unionists, with a view to building up a business party. The committee deemed Belton an unsuitable person to be in charge of the state radio station.[46]

The committee's final report recommended that the station should be run by the Post Office. Irish language and education would have priority over entertainment, operations would be financed by licence fees and advertising, and news sourced from existing news agencies. A director and a non-paid board would be appointed, and material relayed from other stations as a cost-efficient way of providing broadcasts. The government wished to achieve optimum value from radio and consideration was given to it as a means of low-cost education. The newspapers, fearing they would lose advertising, attacked the report, suggesting that the people should listen to the BBC.

The British confidentially provided advance details of the Wireless Telegraphy and Signalling Bill 1925 and the Irish Free State promptly

passed the Wireless Telegraphy Act 1926.[47] The British admiralty and
war office expressed concern about services for ships and planes in time
of war and British forces at Berehaven, Haulbowline and Lough Swilly
were exempted from Irish control under the act. The British proposed
wartime censorship of cable and radio stations in 1924, but apart
from setting up a committee, the government did nothing. Following
pressure from the British, it appointed the first interdepartmental
committee on censorship in time of war in 1931 but it did not complete
its work or make a report.[48] The Wireless Telegraphy Act authorised the
minister to receive, transmit, relay or distribute such broadcast matter
as he should 'think proper', thereby giving ministers untrammelled
powers over radio until 1960. Finance Minister Ernest Blythe and
Labour Party leader Tom Johnson expressed reservations about the
scope of these powers.[49] They were ignored by the government, which
had high expectations for the station. Its subsequent Director, Maurice
Gorham, wrote that Radio Éireann (Irish Radio) was expected to do
a great many things that were not demanded of other national radio
services, most of them far better equipped:[50]

> It was expected to revive the speaking of Irish, to foster a taste for
> classical music, to revive Irish traditional music, to keep people
> on the farms, to sell goods and services of all kinds, from sausages
> to sweep tickets, to provide a living and a career for writers and
> musicians, to unite the Irish people at home with those overseas,
> to end partition.

The above comment suggests that politicians and interest groups had
unreasonable expectations of what the station should deliver over and
above a normal broadcaster's duty to inform, educate and entertain.

2RN, the new radio station, was opened by Douglas Hyde on
1 January 1926. Seamus Clandillon was appointed Director and 2RN
quickly made its mark by being the first station outside the US to relay a
sporting event, on 29 August 1926, and the first to announce Lindbergh's
successful New York–Paris air crossing in 1927. On 26 April 1927 another
station, 6CK, was opened in Cork. Most of its content was relayed from
2RN and programme production ceased in 1930.[51] An 80kw, later 100kw,

station was built at Athlone and formally opened in 1933.[52] This station was needed to get maximum coverage. Yet the expenditure of £48,000 was considered 'spendthrift' by Fianna Fáil Deputy Seán MacEntee.[53]

Radio was seen as a means of fostering Irish culture and protecting it from harmful outside influences. When 2RN began broadcasting, 80 per cent of air time was devoted to music, with language lessons, gardening, poultry-keeping, historical talks, news and weather forecasts taking the remainder of the time. The Irish language took pride of place but French, German and Spanish lessons were also provided. The programmes brightened rural life but many people could not receive them due to lack of radios, sets with limited reception and poor coverage.

2RN helped save traditional music from extinction.[54] In the 1920s Ireland was exposed to more external culture than ever before, particularly through the radio and cinema. It is paradoxical that radio was the means of importing foreign culture while at the same time preserving and revitalising Irish culture. (This was similar to the Finnish experience.) The identity projected by the Irish Free State was Gaelic, Catholic, rural and Irish-speaking. The language was seen as a vital component in nation-building. Irish songs, dance music and games were broadcast, supporting Gaelic culture as a central prop of national identity. As that identity was an ideal not shared by all, the government attempted to socialise the people to accept it. Radio was used to preserve what was left of Gaelic culture and to lay a foundation for its restoration while providing an alternative listening option to foreign stations. This gave support to the argument that radio should be an instrument of state policy. Yet only five per cent of radio time at most was devoted to programmes in Irish and a dedicated Irish station was not established until 50 years afterwards.[55]

Public opinion was 50 per cent favourable to 2RN, while responses to surveys included complaints of too little/too much Irish, too much/ not enough jazz, lack of variety and too much music. At Deputy Bryan Cooper's request, rugby matches were broadcast in addition to GAA and soccer. The first sponsored programme was made for Euthymol toothpaste in December 1928. A heated Dáil debate took place concerning sponsored programmes, which had been pioneered by the popular Hilversum and Luxembourg stations; deputies did not want foreign suppliers to be allowed advertise if they were in competition with Irish manufacturers.[56]

Radio made a huge impact on people hearing it for the first time but the novelty soon wore off on a diet of plays, lectures and almost endless music. 2RN gradually built up a symphony orchestra which helped develop an audience for classical music. Programmes in Welsh were broadcast once a month for the benefit of listeners in north Wales. There was no proper news service. Buying one from the newspapers was considered too costly so one journalist haphazardly gathered material from newspapers, government departments, Oireachtas reports, postmasters, the stock exchange and the BBC. 2RN came to an arrangement with the Dublin correspondent of the Cork Examiner in 1929 and he provided two news bulletins nightly. This was acceptable to his employers as he included no news from Cork.[57] Accommodation was a problem. Radio moved to the newly rebuilt GPO in 1928. It was not an ideal location as the studios were not purpose-built and were subject to noise interruptions. The stations suffered from frequent changes in wavelength as international regulation of the wave bands did not keep pace with the rapid expansion of radio.

The government was in favour of tight control over broadcasting as exercised by J.C. Reith at the BBC. Radio was considered a dangerous medium and there was apprehension about its future.[58] No political broadcasting or public involvement by radio personnel in politics was allowed.

The Department of Finance was against the commercialisation of radio but expected it to pay for itself. The station's first operating budget was £120 per week including fees for relays and copyright. It was to be funded by radio licences, duty on imported equipment and radio sets, and advertising.[59] But only 10 per cent of an estimated 40,000 sets were licensed.[60] The original licence fee was halved as many could not or would not pay it. Few prosecutions were successful as district justices were lenient. By the end of 1926 licence numbers had increased to 15,000 and the licence revenue stream improved, although duty on imports fell as Irish companies began making radio sets. There was little advertising, which Clandillon considered a nuisance. It was not until sponsored programmes were introduced in 1931 and Athlone came on air that advertising began to generate significant revenue.

The Department of Finance kept tight control over expenditure. Staffing levels were low with many part-timers being used. Investment was focused on getting coverage for the Irish Free State. Plans were made to set up stations in Galway and the northeast but nothing came of them, perhaps because Athlone considerably increased coverage. John Logie Baird, the inventor of television, came to Dublin in 1929 to promote TV—but Clandillon did not have him on the radio as he believed television was not feasible.[61] In 1927, Ernest Blythe became minister and Michael Heffernan, leader of the Farmers Party, parliamentary secretary. This combination was not seen as favourable to 2RN as Finance and the Farmers Party were both against increased public expenditure. However, Heffernan was disposed towards advertising and encouraged sponsored programmes. Between 1928 and 1932 the station was run with too few staff, and while it occasionally had successes with GAA, soccer and rugby broadcasts, Commandant James Fitzmaurice's appearance after his transatlantic flight, hammer-thrower Dr Pat O'Callaghan's gold medal at the Amsterdam Olympics and world heavyweight champion boxer Gene Tunney's interview at the Tailteann Games, it was hard work for the under-resourced station to meet expectations.

THE TAILTEANN GAMES

Mention should be made of Aonach Tailteann (the Tailteann Games), which were largely the creation of J.J. Walsh. The games were an effort to encourage Gaelic culture, attract the Irish from abroad and bring economic and political benefit to the new state. The first Tailteann Games were believed to have been held around 600 BC and the last traditional event had taken place in 1169 during the reign of Rory O'Connor, the last high king of Ireland, shortly before the Norman invasion. Walsh and the government wished to 'create a fresh image of the nation' and encourage the 'organisation, cohesion and solidarity of the Gaelic race at home and in particular abroad'. The games, which were a demonstration of triumphant nationalism and a celebration of Irishness, attracted 36,000 foreign visitors in 1924.[62] International competitors, many of whom had competed at the Paris Olympics, represented Ireland north and south, England, Scotland, Wales, US, Australia, New Zealand, Canada and South Africa. Competitions included hurling, Gaelic football, shinty, handball, boxing, car and cycle racing, yachting, tennis, athletics, swimming, rowing, archery, gymnastics, tug-of-war, golf, water polo, clay pigeon shooting, steeplechasing, motorboat racing, and aerial displays. Cultural events included plays, song and band recitals, operas, dancing, art and chess. Irish goods were exhibited. The opening of this 'mini Olympics' at Croke Park was a spectacular event with distinguished visitors including John Devoy, John McCormack, C.G. Fry, Augustus John, G.K. Chesterton, Compton McKenzie, Sir Edwin Lutyens and the Maharajah of Nawanagar.[63] The games, which were confined to Dublin, were boycotted by some of the anti-treaty side. They were still a great success and some events were very well-attended, with 100,000 watching the aerial display at the Phoenix Park. Critics complained that the most popular sports (motor racing and aerial displays) were not Irish. The Tailteann Games were a boost to the morale of the new state less than a year after the civil war and received huge press coverage in Ireland and abroad. They were repeated in 1928, when a higher percentage of women competed than at the Amsterdam Olympics, and less successfully in 1932. The government reluctantly provided financial support for the 1924 games. Afterwards Ernest Blythe unsuccessfully tried to recover the money advanced, arguing it was a loan, and the state sought to collect entertainment tax. After Walsh left politics in 1927, the games received little support from the government. They were postponed in 1936 and were finally killed off in 1938 by an interdepartmental committee set up by de Valera.

Chapter 17 ⌒

| CONCLUSION

T he Irish achieved freedom when the southern separatists seized
the opportunity afforded by the Great War and British military
over-commitments in its aftermath to escape from the British
Empire. Had the Irish remained part of the United Kingdom they
would have found it increasingly difficult to leave, as British welfare
state benefits were improving and the fear of a reduction in living
standards and poorer state services could have diminished majority
support for breaking the Union.

However, freedom was obtained at a high price as the country was
partitioned under the Government of Ireland Act 1920. The treaty
resulted in dominion status for 26 counties but confirmed partition
as the six northeastern Ulster counties remained within the United
Kingdom. After the treaty the separatist movement split between
those who wanted a republic immediately and those who knew that
was not possible but were willing to accept 'the freedom to achieve
freedom'.

After 1922 the Irish Free State government had the freedom to
make its own decisions and the liberty to develop an Irish civil society.
The people of the Irish Free State secured political independence
from Britain with some terms and conditions attached. These did

not impede the creation of a new state as they pertained to Ireland's relationship with Britain. But partition, dominion status and the oath of allegiance left many people deeply dissatisfied. A minority took up arms against the state, leading to civil war and sporadic violence in its aftermath.

Michael Collins and the provisional government took control of a state where there was little respect for government, administration and law as these had been closely identified for centuries with English rule. The terror tactics of the Black and Tans and Auxiliaries further undermined respect for the rule of law. Partition damaged the country's economy, divided its population and led to trouble on both sides of the border. The civil war resulted in further disorder, deaths, injuries, and destruction of property and infrastructure. It wasted an enormous sum of money which could have been invested in development projects, undermined civic trust and left a legacy of bitter division which lasted for decades. The imperatives of defending the state and achieving a rapid return to normality changed the government's focus from reform and development to firm military action, pragmatic administrative change, consolidation, centralisation and fiscal stringency. Consequently there was much more continuity than change in public policy, government, administration and law.

Collins saw the treaty as a stepping stone along the way to sovereign independence and national unity. But after the civil war, the Irish Free State was considerably weaker politically, economically and financially. William T. Cosgrave and Kevin O'Higgins became preoccupied with defending the state against internal revolt and focused on law and order, reconstruction and stability at a time when the world economy was depressed and money was in very short supply. They were less aggressive than Collins, and were reluctant to confront the British, due to the state's dependence on the UK market for its exports. Instead they concentrated on addressing internal problems and extending Irish sovereignty by stealth as opportunities arose. With the enactment of the Statute of Westminster in December 1931, they achieved most of their objectives with regard to sovereignty, as the statute gave the Irish *carte blanche* to remove the remaining objectionable provisions of the treaty without British interference. The government had no economic incentive to leave the British Commonwealth, as continuing membership guaranteed Irish exports duty-free access to the UK at a time when there were no alternative markets. Its ministers contributed little to the evolution of the Commonwealth, other than where it furthered Irish ends, with the exception of O'Higgins, who perceived it as a potential vehicle for achieving a united Ireland.[1] Eamon de Valera also chose to remain in the Commonwealth, despite adopting a more aggressive line after 1932.

Most of the changes in public policy, government and administration were made out of necessity and for pragmatic rather than ideological reasons. They were driven by the need of the Cumann na nGaedheal governments to defend the state; restore law and order; recruit a new civil service, army, police force, judiciary and diplomatic corps; achieve fiscal stability; recover business confidence; and begin reconstruction after years of conflict. Cosgrave's governments did not introduce radical reforms and minimised change because farmers, business and professional interests, civil servants, the Catholic Church and, indeed, the majority of the population were conservative and wished to build a new state and reap the benefits of independence. The continuing anti-treaty armed resistance also discouraged reform, which is fraught with danger at times of military, political and economic turmoil.

The democratisation of the British state during the late nineteenth and early twentieth centuries provided a working model of government and administration which met the needs of the independence movement. Its objective had been to take over the state as a going concern rather than to revolutionise or radically reform it, despite pre-treaty aspirations, many of which may have been devised more for propaganda than policy reasons. Despite civil war and subsequent intermittent armed resistance, the Free State survived because the government retained the support of the majority of the people and faced down anti-democratic elements, even where they were ex-comrades or former allies.

Cosgrave was a chairman rather than a chief. As a sensible, hard-headed businessman, he was a good choice to be the architect of the new state. He was a conservative, and after the deaths of Arthur Griffith and Michael Collins, the resignations of Joe McGrath and Eoin MacNeill, and the departure of J.J. Walsh from politics, the more radical members of the government were gone. Cosgrave was deeply religious and instinctively sought to build a close relationship with the Catholic Church, recognising the political advantages of such a connection. In return for the church's support, he was prepared to concede it the right to be the arbiter on public morality, education, health and social welfare. This meant there would be no change in these areas as the church was committed to maintaining the status quo. Its leadership was not homogenous as individual bishops occasionally broke ranks, but in general it remained supportive of the Irish Free State. Like Cosgrave, de Valera understood the importance of good relations with the church and courted the bishops in an effort to make Fianna Fáil politically respectable. Cosgrave epitomised the conservative leadership of the Irish Free State. He was firm and cautious and these qualities were reflected in the government's style of decision-making.

Many government decisions were influenced by the treaty and civil war. In the early years of the state the emphasis was on what the government needed to do rather on what it wished to do. The pressures of armed resistance, shortage of money, inexperience of ministers and fear of failure heavily influenced decisions. Most were made for pragmatic reasons, such as the retention of the existing civil service and courts. After the civil war the government remained cautious. It avoided radical decisions, intervening only when it was impelled to do so. As it had to vigorously defend the internal security of the state, it was reluctant to intervene in the economy, while in social and educational matters it avoided actions that might antagonise the Catholic Church.

Government policy choices and actions were always made with reference to its three core objectives: defending the state against internal revolt, maximising returns from agriculture, and balancing the budget. Money was an overriding consideration as the government was determined to live within its means—even at the cost of inhibiting the development of human and natural resources and keeping wages and social welfare benefits low. The government opposed tariffs and did not relax its tight grip on the state finances. As a result, opportunities for reform and development were lost, particularly because the state lacked a coherent and co-ordinated economic plan including a judicious mix of free trade and selected tariffs together with tax incentives, subsidies and supports to focus investment in the most productive areas. More government intervention was required to grow the economy and to create a climate where farmers, entrepreneurs and workers could co-operate with the government to exploit the state's resources to their full potential. Foreign inward investment was also needed.

Ministers, department secretaries, senior civil servants and commissions made significant inputs into government decisions, which do not appear to have been much influenced by Cumann na Gaedheal backbenchers or the Farmers Party and independent deputies who supported the government in the Dáil. A few senators were consulted, while the opposition was generally ignored. Vested interests like the larger farmers exercised influence, as did the Catholic Church, whether or not it was consulted formally.

The background of the key decision-makers was significant. The ministers who served between 1922 and 1932 included six lawyers, three former Post Office officials, two journalists, two university professors, two merchants, a teacher and a farmer. Many were university graduates at a time when very few Irish people achieved that level of education. Some of the ministers were 1916 Easter rising veterans. Almost all had actively participated in the war of independence, served as members of the pre-treaty Dáil, or acted as judges in Dáil courts. The department secretaries appointed were former Dublin Castle or British public servants, with the exception of Joseph Walshe. Few senior civil servants participated in the Easter rising or war of independence. As the senior civil servants were accustomed to working in the old British system, they made few changes in administrative methods. The majority of ministers had experience of local government, public administration or law. This equipped them to quickly grasp the reins of power and, as they were under pressure, they continued to use the systems, processes and procedures with which they were familiar, making changes only where necessary.

Effective implementation is vital to achieve successful policy outcomes. The Irish Free State government took over the British administrative system, which had been designed to run Ireland as a crown colony rather than as an integrated part of the UK, and adapted it to suit the needs of an independent state. However, while policies can be formulated, legislation enacted, regulations made and orders issued, action has to be taken to convert them into concrete results. The government and the civil service do not seem to have appreciated that there was a gap between policy-making and execution that needed to be bridged. The Cosgrave administration was poor at public relations and failed to promote its policies or build a partnership with the majority of the people. The British had ruled Ireland by making decisions with little or no input from Irish public representatives. After independence, the executive governed with the consent of the people, who could remove it at the next general election. The government enacted much legislation, often, it seems, in the *hope* that the public would comply. It did not plan, fund, communicate, implement or co-ordinate its policies effectively. This was particularly evident in relation to agriculture, lands, fisheries, industry, education and telecommunications. The failure of the government and the civil service to appreciate the need for systematic implementation meant that many laws, orders, commission reports, regulations and instructions were rejected, ignored or only partially accepted by the public.

The constitution set out the rules for the government of the Irish Free State. As many of its articles were influenced by the treaty it did not command universal respect. Nevertheless, it was a useful document which could have been improved had there been a consensus after independence. Dominion status was a problem, mainly because nobody knew what exactly it meant. While in reality the government was free to do as it pleased, the insertion of the king into the constitution antagonised many people even though he was a figurehead with no real influence. George V, who was personally well disposed towards the Irish, never interfered in Irish Free State affairs.

While the oath of allegiance remained a contentious issue for some, pragmatists viewed it as a temporary nuisance or simply the price of admission to the Oireachtas. They took it and got on with creating a new state.

In many states which gain independence following an armed struggle, the army is the stabilising force afterwards. In Ireland it was the main source of instability. The civil service provided the stability in the new state. Collins understood this and, before his death, created an effective administration. After the army mutiny, the military was significantly reduced in size, depoliticised and brought under civilian control.

Opportunity to make radical change occurs rarely and needs to be seized. The creation of the new state in 1922 was an opportunity to make alterations which could have been implemented without major opposition, as changes were expected by the public and might have been welcomed by many. However, the circumstances surrounding the birth of the new state discouraged radical change and afterwards the focus was on reconstruction, consolidation and stability rather than reform and development. Examples of what might have been achieved between 1922 and 1932 include root and branch reform of the public service, courts, legal profession and local government to make them more efficient, effective and responsive; assigning responsibility for policing to a police authority; delegating more powers to local bodies; beginning the process of creating a national health system; achieving a sustainable balance between agriculture, marine resources, industrial development and services; using taxation policy to ensure more equitable distribution of wealth and adequate funding for local authorities; and raising the standard of education, improving equality of opportunity, and providing technical and commercial training to support business. Entrepreneurship required encouragement and more investment was needed in industry, the physical infrastructure, housing and telephones. Many of the above tasks still remain to be completed eight decades after Cosgrave left office. The governments between 1922 and 1932 did not do all they wished to do; nor did they do all they could have done.

The Cosgrave governments performed well when the range of military, political, security, economic, fiscal and social difficulties they faced are taken into consideration. Cosgrave took a strong line against the enemies of the state, supported strict financial control and retrenchment, and guided the state through its formative years. Along with his ministers, he was not motivated by the desire for popularity or wealth and left a legacy of personal integrity. Yet he was not always in control at times of crisis. During the army mutiny O'Higgins took charge and made the hard decisions. Afterwards he became the strongman in the government. Following his death, the executive became increasingly beleaguered, particularly after Fianna Fáil entered the Dáil in 1927, vigorously opposed it on almost every issue, and gradually began to be seen by the public as a credible alternative to Cumann na nGaedheal.

The Cumann na nGaedheal governments legitimised the state and increased sovereignty; overcame armed revolt; established a new civil service, army, police force, court service and diplomatic corps; restored law and order; maintained strict management of finance; controlled inflation; supported agricultural production and developed electricity generation and sugar production, but otherwise marked time on the economy. By 1932 the state was stable politically, strong administratively, sound financially, in better shape economically than many of its European counterparts and law-abiding apart from a minority of subversives. But agriculture needed intensification and improved marketing. Industry, marine resources, roads, housing, healthcare and telephones needed investment and the standard of education needed to be raised. The focus on preserving the state and its hard-won independence resulted in insensitivity toward the needs of the poor and disadvantaged, while the arrangement with the Catholic Church meant that important social issues were contained rather than resolved. Given the circumstances of the state's foundation, the civil war, the government's aversion to risk, the shortage of money, the extreme stress under which ministers worked, competing sectional interests, the persistent underlying level of violence, and the economic depressions in the early and late 1920s, the Cosgrave governments' achievements were remarkable. Much more could have been done, but the civil war divided the people, distracted the government, dissipated scarce resources, diminished the possibility of making radical change and delayed long-term development.

Cosgrave and his governments managed the problems that confronted them better than any of the newly formed states that were created from the ruins of the Austro-Hungarian, German, Ottoman and Russian empires in the aftermath of World War I. Law and order were restored, the population was fed, the state remained solvent, and inflation was controlled. The state did not succumb to internal revolt or financial ruin and strengthened its democracy at a time when totalitarianism was on the rise in Europe. The ministers between 1922 and 1932 had to learn on the job and served a hard apprenticeship. Those that succeeded them in 1932 inherited a civil service which had administered the state for 10 difficult years, an army that took its orders from the government, an established police force, and a population which accepted parliamentary politics as the norm. The greatest achievement of Cosgrave and his governments was the establishment of a workable democratic state. After losing at the polls in 1932, Cosgrave handed over power peacefully to those he had defeated in the civil war. He had always upheld the principle that the people alone had the right to elect those who governed them, and passed on a democratic state where it was clearly accepted by all but a small extremist minority that the ballot box was the sole means of changing governments.

REFERENCES

Chapter 1

1. John M. Regan, *The Irish Counter-Revolution, 1921–36* (Dublin, 1999), 378. 'Phases of Revolution', lecture delivered by John Marcus O'Sullivan to the ard-cumann of Cumann na nGaedheal on 21 November 1923.

Chapter 2

1. Basil Chubb, *The Government and Politics of Ireland* (London, 1982), 6.
2. Garret FitzGerald, *Reflections on the Irish State* (Dublin, 2003), 4.
3. David Fitzpatrick, *The Two Irelands* (Oxford, 1998), 16.
4. D. George Boyce, *Nationalism in Ireland* (London, 1982), 252–4.
5. John M. Regan, *The Irish Counter-Revolution, 1921–36* (Dublin, 1999), 17.
6. Michael Laffan, *The Resurrection of Ireland: The Sinn Féin Party, 1916–1923* (Cambridge, 2005), 231.
7. James Casey, *Constitutional Law in Ireland* (London, 1992), 3–4.
8. Brian Farrell, 'The drafting of the Irish Free State Constitution', *Irish Jurist*, vol. 5 (1970), 115.
9. J.J. Lee, *Ireland, 1912–85: Politics and Society* (Cambridge, 1989), 79.
10. Martin Maguire, 'The Civil Service, the State and the Irish Revolution, 1886–1938' (PhD thesis, TCD, 2005), 2, 34, 140–48, 166–9.
11. *Irish Times*, 29 June 1921.
12. William J. Flynn, *The Oireachtas Companion and Saorstát Guide for 1929* (Dublin), 12–13.
13. William Sheehan, *British Voices from the Irish War of Independence, 1918–21* (Cork, 2005), 151–2. Montgomery to Lt-General A.C. Percival, York, 14 October 1923.
14. Piaras Béaslaí, *Michael Collins and the Making of Modern Ireland*, vol. 2 (New York, 1926), 258.
15. Paul Canning, *British Policy Towards Ireland, 1921–1941* (Oxford, 1985), 3.

16. Kevin Matthews, *Fatal Influence: The Impact of Ireland on British Politics, 1920–1925* (Dublin, 2004), 7; 'The Council of Ireland', Commonwealth Relations Office memorandum, 19 April 1949, UKNA, HO 45/23466; Waterfield to Upcott, 6 April 1923, T160/163/F6282.

17. Casey, *Constitutional Law in Ireland*, 7–8.

18. Donal McCartney, 'Hyde, D.P. Moran and Irish Ireland', F.X. Martin (ed.), *Leaders and Men of the Easter Rising* (London, 1967), 47–52; *The Leader*, 23 June 1906.

19. Michael Tierney, *Education in a Free Ireland* (Dublin, undated), iv, vi, 15–26, 33, 62, 66, 83.

20. Aodh de Blácam, *Towards the Republic* (Dublin, 1919), vii, ix, 23–6, 29–35, 42–55, 60, 86, 102.

21. P.S. O'Hegarty, *Sinn Féin, An Illumination* (Dublin, 1919), 21.

22. Richard P. Davis, *Arthur Griffith and Non-Violent Sinn Féin* (Dublin, 1974), 129–49.

23. Arthur Mitchell, *Revolutionary Government in Ireland: Dáil Éireann, 1919–22* (Dublin, 1995), 49, 54–7.

24. Brian Farrell, 'The First Dáil and its constitutional documents', Brian Farrell (ed.), *The Creation of the Dáil* (Dublin, 1994), 66.

Chapter 3

1. Provisional government minutes, 16 January 1922, NAI.

2. Donal O'Sullivan, *The Irish Free State and Its Senate* (London, 1940), 16.

3. Brian Farrell, 'The drafting of the Irish Free State Constitution', *Irish Jurist*, vol. 5 (1970), 117.

4. Barra Ó Briain, *The Irish Constitution* (Dublin, 1929), 44–6.

5. Note on constitution, Kennedy Papers, P4/1680.

6. J.G. Swift MacNeill, 'Thoughts on the Constitution of the Irish Free State', *Journal of Comparative Legislation and International Law*, 3rd ser., vol. 5, no. 1 (1923), 53.

7. Constitution Committee, *Select Constitutions of the World* (Dublin, 1922).

8. Memorandum on special constitutional developments under the Treaty (1932), John A. Costello Papers, P190/55 (1).

9. Dáil debates (DD), vol. 1, col. 386, 18 September 1922.

10. DD 1, 648–9, 25 September 1922.

11. DD 1, 766, 26 September 1922.

12. DD 1, 773–6, 26 September 1922.

13. DD 1, 874, 27 September 1922.
14. Ó Briain, *The Irish Constitution*, 62, 82.
15. Nicholas Mansergh, *The Irish Free State: Its Government and Politics* (London, 1934), 50.
16. Ó Briain, *The Irish Constitution*, 69.
17. *Ibid.*, 124.
18. DD, 1, 1211.
19. The military installations under the general heading of Queenstown included the facilities on Haulbowline and Spike Island, and Fort Camden and Fort Carlisle.
20. The Constitution of the Irish Free State Act, 1922.
21. Legal opinion, Costello Papers, P190/58.
22. Gerard Francis Torsney, 'The Monarchy in the Irish Free State, 1922–32' (MA thesis, UCD, 1980), 39, 63.
23. Bill Kissane, *The Politics of the Irish Civil War* (Oxford, 2005), 12, 55.
24. *Irish Times*, 25 September 1936.

Chapter 4
1. Warner Moss, *Political Parties in the Irish Free State* (New York, 1933), 23.
2. *Ibid.*, 205.
3. Letter from Rev. Dr Brian P. Murphy OSB to the *Irish Examiner*, 29 February 2008; DD, 8 June 1922.
4. Minutes of Comhairle na dTeachtaí, 18–19 December 1926, NAI, DJ, JU58/675.
5. Richard Dunphy, *The Making of Fianna Fáil Power in Ireland, 1923–1948* (Oxford, 1995), 5–23.
6. *Irish Independent*, 25 January, 7 April 1927.
7. Anthony J. Jordan, *William Thomas Cosgrave, 1880–1965: Founder of Modern Ireland* (Dublin, 2006), 153.
8. *Irish Times*, 12 August 1927.
9. Dunphy, *The Making of Fianna Fáil*, 65, 74, 114, 125.
10. Mark O'Brien, *De Valera, Fianna Fáil and the 'Irish Press'* (Dublin, 2001), 11.
11. Letter from Frank Walsh to potential donors, 30 January 1930, Blythe Papers, P24/145.
12. *Irish Independent*, 4 June 1929.
13. W.K. Hancock, *Survey of British Commonwealth Affairs: Problems of Nationality* (Oxford, 1937), 322–4.

14. Nicholas Mansergh, *Britain and Ireland* (London, 1942), 70.
15. Ronan Fanning, 'The British dimension', *Crane Bag*, vol. 8 (1984), 42–4.
16. Jordan, *Cosgrave*, 182–3; Padraic Colum, *The Commonweal*, 23 March 1932.

Chapter 5

1. DD 1, 83, 11 September 1922.
2. Basil Chubb, *Cabinet Government in Ireland* (Dublin, 1974), 29.
3. James McGuire and James Quinn (eds), *Dictionary of Irish Biography* (Dublin, 2009). This is the main source of biographical information on ministers and secretaries.
4. Brian A. Reynolds, *William T. Cosgrave and the Foundation of the Irish Free State, 1922–25* (Kilkenny, 1998), 39, 54.
5. Anthony J. Jordan, *William Thomas Cosgrave, 1880–1965: Founder of Modern Ireland* (Dublin, 2006), 7, 159–61; *Irish Times*, 21, 23, 24 January, 1 February 1928.
6. Provisional government minutes, 5–22 July, 2, 5 August 1922, NAI.
7. Ernest Blythe, witness statement 939, IMA.
8. Memorandum, 15 November 1923, Blythe Papers, P24/192.
9. Bill Kissane, *The Politics of the Irish Civil War* (Oxford, 2005), 84.
10. Nicholas Mansergh, *The Irish Free State: Its Government and Politics* (London, 1934) 213–14, 317, 330.
11. *Irish Times*, 13 October 1923.
12. Basil Chubb, *The Government and Politics of Ireland* (London, 1982), 26.
13. *Ibid.*, 171, 207.
14. Donal O'Sullivan, *The Irish Free State and Its Senate* (London, 1940), 7, 87, 120, 208, 233–4.
15. Muiris MacCarthaigh, *Accountability in Irish Parliamentary Politics* (Dublin, 2005), 1.
16. *Ibid.*, 11–12, 22, 49–53, 65, 98, 103, 295.
17. Kissane, *The Politics of the Irish Civil War*, 168.
18. Dermot Keogh, 'Ireland and "Emergency" culture: Between Civil War and normalcy', *Ireland: A Journal of History and Society*, vol. 1, 1995, 4.
19. Martin Maguire, 'The Civil Service, the State and the Irish Revolution, 1886–1938' (PhD thesis, TCD, 2005), 345.
20. DD 16, 129–36, 1 June 1926.
21. Richard Haslam, 'Origins of Irish local government', Mark Callanan and Justin F. Keoghan (eds), *Local Government in Ireland Inside Out* (Dublin, 2003), 28–33.

22. Martin Maguire, *Servants to the Public: A History of the Local Government and Public Services Union, 1901–1990* (Dublin, 1998), 65.

23. John J. Horgan, 'City management in America', *Studies*, vol. 9, 1920, 41–6.

24. Aodh Quinlivan, *Philip Monahan: A Man Apart* (Dublin, 2006), 1–27.

25. *Cork Examiner*, 12 November, 1924.

26. DD 21, 1596–99, 17 November 1927; *Irish Independent*, 3 September 1929.

27. Eunan O'Halpin, 'Origins of city and county management', *City and County Management, 1929–1990* (Dublin, 1991), 119–20.

28. Mansergh, *The Irish Free State: Its Government and Politics*, 231.

29. J.J. Lee, *Ireland, 1912–1985: Politics and Society* (Cambridge, 1989), 162.

30. Letitia Dunbar Harrison file, NAI, DT, S2547a; *Irish Times*, 29 December 1930; *Irish Independent*, 3 January 1931.

31. Pat Walsh, *The Curious Case of the Mayo Librarian* (Cork, 2009), 11, 82–185.

32. Cabinet Papers, 22 December 1931, NAI.

33. Ruth Barrington, *Health, Medicine and Politics in Ireland, 1900–1970* (Dublin, 1987), 100.

34. DLGPH *Special Report*, NAI, DT, S2227.

35. *Irish Independent*, 7 September 1926.

36. T.J. Barrington, *From Big Government to Local Government* (Dublin, 1975), 99–119.

Chapter 6

1. Patrick Keatinge, *The Formulation of Irish Foreign Policy* (Dublin, 1973), 1–6, 13–14.

2. DD 5, 931, 16 November 1923.

3. Zara Steiner, *The Lights That Failed: European International History, 1919–1933* (Oxford, 2005), 1–48, 182–240.

4. Clare O'Halloran, *Partition and the Limits of Irish Nationalism* (Dublin, 1987), xi–xii.

5. Dermot Keogh, *Ireland and Europe, 1919–1948* (Dublin, 1988), 11; Aengus Nolan, *Joseph Walshe: Irish Foreign Policy, 1922–1946* (Cork, 2008), 18.

6. DD 5, 940, 16 November 1923.

7. Memorandum, Walshe, 1 June 1927, Desmond FitzGerald Papers, P80/594.

8. Nolan, *Joseph Walshe*, 334.
9. Waller, admission to League of Nations, 24 March 1923, NAI, DT, S3332.
10. Michael Kennedy, *Ireland and the League of Nations, 1919–1946*: *International Relations, Diplomacy and Politics* (Dublin, 1996), 27–38, 64; Keatinge, *The Formulation of Irish Foreign Policy*, 1.
11. Arthur Berridale Keith, *The Sovereignty of the British Dominions* (London, 1929), 347–50.
12. Donal O'Sullivan, *The Irish Free State and Its Senate* (London, 1940), 171.
13. Kevin Matthews, *Fatal Influence: The Impact of Ireland on British Politics, 1920–1925* (Dublin, 2004), 111, 136.
14. Kennedy to Cosgrave, 9 May 1924, Kennedy Papers, P4/414.
15. Northern Ireland policy, Blythe Papers, P24/70.
16. North-Eastern Boundary Bureau files, Blythe Papers, P24/76–7.
17. Boundary commission notes, Blythe Papers, P24/204–5.
18. Committee to consider offer to Northern Ireland, note 21, October 1924, Blythe Papers, P24/131.
19. Memoranda, O'Higgins, 29 September 1924, and O'Hegarty, 15 October 1924, NAI, DT S4084; report of committee on offer to Northern Ireland, 22 October 1924, Blythe Papers p24/131; Executive minutes, 1 December 1924, NAI, DT, S1801L.
20. Draft article, 21 December 1932, Costello Papers, P190/56.
21. Memoir dictated by MacNeill, McGilligan Papers, P35b/144.
22. Matthews, *Fatal Influence*, 231, 244; *Irish Independent*, 15 April 1926.
23. *Irish Independent*, 15 April 1926.
24. Frank Callanan, *T.M. Healy* (Cork, 1996), 604–13.
25. *Irish Times*, 27 March 1931.
26. Callanan, *T.M. Healy*, 610–24.
27. Request for a judge to sit on Privy Council, P24/219, Imperial Conference file, Blythe Papers, P24/111, 219.
28. *Irish Times*, 14 November 1929.
29. McDunphy to O'Hegarty, 7 November 1930, NAI, DFA unregistered papers; Leo Kohn, *The Constitution of the Irish Free State* (London, 1932), 362.
30. Lorna Lloyd, 'Loosening the apron strings: The Dominions and Britain in the interwar years', *Round Table*, vol. 92, issue 369, 2003, 281–7.
31. *Irish Independent*, 12 September 1925.

32. Gerard Francis Torsney, 'The Monarchy in the Irish Free State, 1922–32', (MA, UCD, 1980), 75.

33. *Irish Independent*, 19 December 1929.

34. Special constitutional developments under the treaty (1932), Costello Papers, P190/55(1); Note on meeting with Hertzog, FitzGerald Papers, P80/600.

35. DD 39, 2300, 16 July 1931.

36. *Irish Times*, 6 February 1926; Healy to Thomas, 3 June 1924, NAI, DT, S1801H.

37. DD 8, 167–84, 1 July 1924.

38. *Irish Press*, 21 November 1931, 19 January 1932.

39. *Irish Press*, 21 November 1931.

40. Dermot Keogh, *The Vatican, the Bishops and Irish Politics, 1919–39* (Cambridge, 1986), 80, 103–16, 127–34.

41. Cosgrave to Amery, 23 February 1927, NAI, DT, S4731.

42. DEA Special Report 1931, NAI, DT, S2220; *Irish Times*, 28 April 1928.

43. *Irish Times*, 6 January 1927.

44. Constitutional developments, Costello Papers, P190/55 (1).

45. Deirdre McMahon, *Republicans and Imperialists: Anglo-Irish Relations in the 1930s* (New Haven, 1984), 183–4.

46. Dermot Keogh, *Twentieth-Century Ireland: Nation and State* (Dublin, 1994), 51.

47. Keatinge, *The Formulation of Irish Foreign Policy*, 18–19.

Chapter 7

1. J.J. Lee, *Ireland, 1912–85: Politics and Society* (Cambridge, 1989), 67–8.

2. Capt. Austin Pender (ed.), *Irish Defence Forces Handbook* (Dublin, 1988), 90–91.

3. Department of Defence Special Report 1931, NAI, DT, S2223.

4. Risteard Mulcahy, *Richard Mulcahy (1886–1971): A Family Memoir* (Dublin, 1999), 111.

5. Tom Garvin, *1922: The Birth of Irish Democracy* (Dublin, 1996), 115 124.

6. Kevin Matthews, *Fatal Influence: The Impact of Ireland on British Politics, 1920–1925* (Dublin, 2004), 79.

7. John P. Duggan, *A History of the Irish Army* (Dublin, 1991), 89–91.

8. Memorandum, 26 July 1922, Mulcahy Papers, P7/B28.
9. *Irish Times*, 31 January, 2 February 1923; J.B. Lyons, *Oliver St. John Gogarty* (Dublin, 1980), 127.
10. Eunan O'Halpin, *Defending Ireland* (Oxford, 2000), 16–17.
11. Maryann Gianella Valiulis, *Portrait of a Revolutionary: General Richard Mulcahy and the Founding of the Irish Free State* (Dublin, 1992), 177.
12. Liam de Róiste Diaries, 47, CAI.
13. *Irish Times*, 9 December 1922.
14. *Irish Times*, 15 December 1922.
15. *Irish Times*, 20 January, 17 February 1923.
16. Captured documents found in Ernie O'Malley's possession, 25 July 1923, Kennedy Papers, P4/661.
17. Ronan Fanning, *Independent Ireland* (Dublin, 1983), 44; Mulcahy, *Richard Mulcahy*, 134, 193, 202.
18. E.M. Hogan, 'James Hogan and the Irish Civil War', Donnchadh Ó Corráin (ed.), *James Hogan* (Dublin, 2001), 10.
19. Brian A. Reynolds, *W.T. Cosgrave and the Foundation of the Irish Free State, 1922–25* (Kilkenny, 1998), 87.
20. Duggan, *Irish Army*, 131.
21. Memorandum on army re-organisation, 2 May 1924, Blythe Papers P24/208.
22. Fearghal McGarry, *Eoin O'Duffy: A Self-Made Hero* (Oxford, 2005), 130–32.
23. John M. Regan, *The Irish Counter-Revolution, 1921–36* (Dublin, 1999), 173–5.
24. Confidential report from Eoin O'Duffy regarding the army mutiny, 7 April 1924, Blythe Papers, P24/221.
25. Regan, *The Irish Counter-Revolution*, 196.
26. Harold O'Sullivan, *A History of Local Government in the County of Louth* (Dublin, 2000), 123.
27. DD 18, 384–402, 8 February 1927.
28. Military intelligence file, IMA, MP 9/10.
29. Army confidential reports, 22 October 1924 and 8 July 1925, Blythe Papers, P24/222, 223.
30. Council of Defence minutes, 28 July 1925, IMA.
31. DD 5, 956, 16 November 1923.
32. *Dáil Estimates, 1922–32*; Duggan, *Irish Army*, 157–65.
33. *Irish Press*, 12 November 1931.

34. Memorandum on defence policy, 22 July 1925, Blythe Papers, P24/107; memorandum, Costello Papers, P190/100.
35. Extract from minutes of informal conference at Admiralty on Free State Coastal Defence, 26 April 1927, NAI, DFA, 205/122; Cosgrave to Amery, 18 May 1927, NAI, DT, S5428.
36. Duggan, *Irish Army*, 149–51.
37. *Irish Independent*, 25 October 1928, 2 May 1929.
38. *Irish Times*, 31 August 1926.
39. *Irish Independent*, 11 May 1929.
40. McGarry, *Eoin O'Duffy*, 187–90.
41. Memorandum on Constitution (No. 17) Bill (1931) Blythe Papers, P24/201.
42. *Freeman's Journal*, 13 August 1923.

Chapter 8
1. V.T.H. Delany, *The Administration of Justice in Ireland*, 4th edition, Charles Lysaght (ed.) (Dublin, 1975), 79–89.
2. John P. McCarthy, *Kevin O'Higgins: Builder of the Irish State* (Dublin, 2006), 288.
3. *Irish Independent*, 11 July 1927.
4. W.B. Yeats, *Uncollected Prose II* (New York, 1975), 476.
5. Basil Chubb, *The Government and Politics of Ireland* (London, 1982), 319; Notes on court changes, May 1923, Kennedy Papers, P4/1095, 1097.
6. Mary Kotsonouris, *Retreat from Revolution* (Dublin, 1994), 48–51.
7. Memoranda, MacNeill and Hogan, Blythe Papers, P24/72–73; winding up of Dáil courts, July 1923, Kennedy Papers, P4/1068, 1071.
8. *Irish Times*, 17 January, 8 February 1924.
9. Eunan O'Halpin, *Defending Ireland* (Oxford, 2000), 4.
10. Liam McNiffe, *A History of the Garda Síochána* (Dublin, 1997), 11.
11. Protection Corps file, NAI, DJ, H197/27.
12. Gregory Allen, *The Garda Síochána* (Dublin, 1999), 6.
13. Jim Herlihy, *The Royal Irish Constabulary* (Dublin, 1997), 109–11.
14. Conor Brady, *Guardians of the Peace: Policing Independent Ireland* (Dublin, 1974), 41–8.
15. O'Halpin, *Defending Ireland*, 7.
16. *Irish Times*, 2 May 1922, 8 March 1923.
17. Brady, *Guardians of the Peace*, 73; Tim Pat Coogan, *A Memoir* (London, 2008), 22.

18. Brady, *Guardians of the Peace*, 73; Coogan, *A Memoir*, 22.
19. Fearghal McGarry, *Eoin O'Duffy: A Self-Made Hero* (Oxford, 2005), 117–20.
20. Brady, *Guardians of the Peace*, 76–81; Allen, *The Garda Síochána*, 85.
21. Police reports, 1922–3, NAI, JUS H 99/109.
22. Brady, *Guardians of the Peace*, 83, 94–5.
23. O'Halpin, *Defending Ireland*, 9.
24. Allen, *The Garda Síochána*, 46.
25. *Irish Independent*, 15 December 1926.
26. Brady, *Guardians of the Peace*, 128–41; file on David Neligan's transfer, 1932–4, NAI, DT, S2396.
27. Poteen reports, NAI, DJ, H 67/5, 9, 23; *Irish Times*, 8 March 1929.
28. Brady, *Guardians of the Peace*, 111–19.
29. Allen, *The Garda Síochána*, 100–101.
30. Brady, *Guardians of the Peace*, 165–7.
31. Seosamh Ó Longaigh, *Emergency Law in Independent Ireland, 1922–1948* (Dublin, 2006), 16.
32. DD 5, 1986, 1996, 2006, 15 June 1923.
33. Donal O'Sullivan, *The Irish Free State and Its Senate* (London, 1940), 255–6, 264.
34. *Irish Independent*, 8 November 1928, 18 May 1929.
35. Constitution (No. 17) Bill (1931) file, Blythe Papers, P24/201; Brady, *Guardians of the Peace*, 143–60.
36. James M. Smith, *Ireland's Magdalen Laundries and the Nation's Architecture of Containment* (Notre Dame, 2007), 183.
37. Lindsey Earner-Byrne, *Mother and Child: Maternity and Child Welfare in Dublin, 1922–60* (Manchester, 2007), 185, 187, 193.
38. Diarmaid Ferriter, *The Transformation of Ireland, 1900–2000* (Woodstock, 2004), 325–8.
39. Rosemary Cullen Owens, 'The machine will work without them', Myles Dungan (ed.), *Speaking Ill of the Dead* (Dublin, 2007), 60–63.
40. Complaint from North Dublin Licensed Vintners, Mulcahy Papers, P7/61.
41. *Irish Times*, 25 February, 1929.
42. Diarmaid Ferriter, *Occasions of Sin: Sex and Society in Modern Ireland* (London, 2009), 138.
43. Earner-Byrne, *Mother and Child*, 45, 177.

44. Peter Martin, *Censorship in the Two Irelands, 1922–1939* (Dublin, 2006), 57–8.
45. Kevin Rockett, *Irish Film Censorship* (Dublin, 2004), 71–93.
46. Michael Adams, *Censorship: The Irish Experience* (Tuscaloosa, 1968), 36, 49.
47. Donal Ó Drisceoil, *Censorship in Ireland, 1939–45: Neutrality, Politics and Society* (Cork, 1996), 2, 30.
48. *Irish Times*, 13 August 1926; *Irish Independent*, 1 February 1927, 19 October 1928; memorandum re: evil literature, McGilligan Papers, 35b/186.
49. Adams, *Censorship*, 91–3; Martin, *Censorship in the Two Irelands*, 89–92.
50. *Irish Times*, 25 and 28 August 1928.
51. *Irish Times*, 23 November 1928.
52. Sandra Larmour, 'Aspects of the State and Female Sexuality in the Irish Free State, 1922–1949' (PhD, UCC, 1998), 85–104.
53. Dermot Keogh, *Twentieth-Century Ireland: Nation and State* (Dublin, 1994), 55; Larmour, 'State and Female Sexuality', 131–9, 149–73.
54. *Irish Times*, 7 November 1929.
55. Ian O'Donnell, Eoin O'Sullivan and Deirdre Healy (eds), *Crime and Punishment in Ireland, 1922 to 2003* (Dublin, 2005), 3–4.
56. Cabinet Papers, 1922–32, NAI; *Irish Times*, 15 December 1927, 3 October 1928, 11 February 1929, 7 November 1929.
57. Legitimacy Bill (1929) file, NAI, DJ, H213/2.
58. O'Sullivan, *The Irish Free State and Its Senate*, 161–70.

Chapter 9

1. Martin Maguire, 'The Civil Service, the State and the Irish Revolution, 1886–1938' (PhD, TCD, 2005), 239.
2. Basil Chubb, *The Government and Politics of Ireland* (London, 1982), 266.
3. Peter Pyne, *The Irish Bureaucracy* (Londonderry, undated), 32–4.
4. Andrew McCarthy, 'Financial Thought and Policy in Ireland, 1918–45' (PhD, UCC, 1996), 233.
5. *Ibid.*, 231–6.
6. T.J. Barrington, *The Irish Administrative System* (Dublin, 1980), 15; Pierre Massé, 'French planning', *Administration*, vol. 10 (1962), 280.

Chapter 10

1. J.J. Lee, *Ireland, 1912–85: Politics and Society* (Cambridge, 1989), 107–8.
2. Ronan Fanning, *The Irish Department of Finance, 1922–58* (Dublin, 1978), 45–7.
3. J. Maher, 'The control and audit of public expenditure', Frederick C. King (ed.), *Public Administration in Ireland*, vol. 1 (Dublin, undated), 69–77.
4. *Irish Times*, 5 January 1924; Seanad Éireann, 4, 189–200, 23 January 1925.
5. DD 6, 1817, 7 March 1924.
6. Seán Réamonn, *History of the Revenue Commissioners* (Dublin, 1981), xi, 56, 105–15.
7. Kieran Coleman, 'The 1925 Cork Campaign to Abolish Income Tax' (MA, UCC, 2004).
8. *Irish Independent*, 11, 13, 27 February 1925.
9. DD 12, 700, 10 June 1925; 737, 11 June 1925; 16, 298, 3 June 1926.
10. Revenue Commissioners: Estimates of Irish Free State capital investments, 11 January 1929, NAI, P35A/19.
11. Seanad Éireann, 7, 762–9, 7 July 1926.
12. *Saorstát Éireann Official Handbook* (Dublin, 1932), 89–90.
13. Brian A. Reynolds, *William T. Cosgrave and the Foundation of the Irish Free State, 1922–25* (Kilkenny, 1998), 76.
14. DD 6, 1298–307, 21 February 1924.
15. Cork Employers' Federation pamphlet (1924), 17, UCC Special Collections, 593b.
16. Fanning, *The Irish Department of Finance*, 118.
17. *Ibid.*, 189.
18. Heffernan to Blythe, 'Interim report of the committee on government expenditure', 30 November 1931, NAI, DF E 121/2/27.
19. DD 23, 531–2, 26 April 1928; memorandum on economic committee, 1929, Blythe Papers, P24/212.
20. Dunn to Healy, 10 January 1924, Kennedy Papers, P4/732.
21. Memorandum, J.J. McElligott, 9 September 1931, Blythe Papers, P24/99.
22. *Irish Times*, 11 and 19 October 1923.
23. Memorandum from Michael Collins, 18 August 1922, and other memoranda related to control of the state's finances, NAI, DT, S8282–9568; Fanning, *The Irish Department of Finance*, 50–57; *Irish Times*, 24 November 1923, 29 April 1930.
24. *Irish Times*, 21 August 1926.

25. *Irish Times*, 8 January 1924.
26. File on financial agreements, UKNA, T160/702.
27. *Ibid.*
28. Financial Agreement between British and Irish Governments, Blythe Papers, P24/127; note on meeting between British and Irish Governments, 3 December 1925, Blythe Papers, PP24/142; file on financial settlement, UKNA, T160/239.
29. Costello to Minister/Secretary of Department of Justice, memorandum on criminal conspiracy, 16 December 1926, Costello Papers, P190/52 (16); Donal Ó Drisceoil, *Peadar O'Donnell* (Cork, 2001), 58–69.
30. *Irish Times*, 28 November 1931.
31. File on financial settlement, UKNA, T160/702.
32. DD, 74, 708.
33. Brian Girvin, *Between Two Worlds: Politics and Economy in Independent Ireland* (Dublin, 1989), 43.
34. Cormac Ó Gráda, *Ireland: A New Economic History, 1780–1939* (Oxford, 1994), 370–75.
35. John L. Pratschke, 'The establishing of the Irish pound: A backward glance', *Economic and Social Review*, vol. 1, October 1969, 74.
36. Maurice Moynihan, *Currency and Central Banking in Ireland* (Dublin, 1975), 21, 25.
37. Pratschke, 'The establishing of the Irish pound', 68, 74.
38. Moynihan, *Currency and Central Banking*, 173.
39. *Journal of the Institute of Bankers in Ireland*, April 1926, 43.
40. *Report of the Currency Commission, Year Ended 31 March 1932*, 6.
41. Moynihan, *Currency and Central Banking*, 167, 178.

Chapter 11

1. James Meenan, *The Irish Economy since 1922* (Liverpool, 1971), 280.
2. Robert O'Connor and E.W. Henry, 'Estimates of gross and net output and income', *Irish Economic and Social History*, vol. 23 (1996), 68.
3. J.J. Lee, *Ireland, 1912–85: Politics and Society* (Cambridge, 1989), 111–17.
4. Churchill to Collins, 20 July 1922, Blythe Papers, P24/65.
5. D. Hoctor, *The Department's Story: A History of the Department of Agriculture* (Dublin, 1971), 128.
6. DD 1, 440, 19 September 1922.
7. Raymond Ryan, 'Farmers, Agriculture and Politics in the Free State Area, 1919–1936' (PhD, UCC, 2005), 50.

8. Mary E. Daly, *The First Department: A History of the Department of Agriculture* (Dublin, 2002), 107.

9. DD 4, 1983, 8 August 1923.

10. DD 9, 574, 31 October 1924.

11. Terence Dooley, *"The Land for the People": The Land Question in Independent Ireland* (Dublin, 2004), 85.

12. DD 9, 2590, 12 December 1924.

13. DD 3, 1946–74, 14 June 1923.

14. Hogan, note dated 29 January 1924, McGilligan Papers, P35b/2.

15. DD 3, 2007, 15 June 1923.

16. Peadar O'Donnell, *There Will Be Another Day* (Dublin, 1963), 6.

17. *Irish Times*, 30 May, 12, 15, 19, 20, 21, 22, 30 June, 16, 23 July 1923.

18. Kevin O'Shiel and T. O'Brien, 'The Land Problem in Ireland and Its Settlement', paper presented at Congress on Agrarian Law, Florence, 1954.

19. *Report of the Land Commissioners, Year Ended 31 March 1932*, 13.

20. DD 5, 1153, 22 November 1923.

21. *Report of the Commission on Agriculture*, NAI, DA, AGF 2005/68/403.

22. DD 7, 2671–81, 2692, 19 June 1924.

23. DD 9, 1022, 7 November 1924.

24. Henry Kennedy, 'Our agricultural problem', Frederick C. King (ed.), *Public Administration in Ireland*, vol. 2, 53.

25. *Irish Times*, 23 July 1928.

26. *Irish Times*, 19 November 1928, 15 January 1930.

27. Patrick Hogan, memorandum on dairy industry, 5 January 1927, Blythe Papers, P24/175.

28. Patrick Bolger, *The Irish Co-operative Movement: Its History and Development* (Dublin, 1977), 217.

29. *Irish Times*, 7 February 1928, 3 December 1929.

30. Maurice Henry (ed.), *Fruits of a Century* (Dublin, 1994), 11.

31. DD 11, 314, 24 April 1925.

32. DD, 5, 453, 31 October 1923.

33. Daly, *The First Department*, 148–52.

34. Flax file 1922–3, NAI, DA, AGF 92/2/1689.

35. *Irish Trade Journal*, May 1928, 87.

36. *Irish Times*, 30 April, 29 October 1928.

37. DD 24, 410, 13 June 1928.

38. J.B. O'Connell, *The Financial Administration of Ireland* (Dublin, 1960), 180.

39. Hoctor, *The Department's Story*, 164.
40. DD 15, 2413, 28 May 1926.
41. Kennedy, 'Our agricultural problem', 51–3.
42. R.C. Ferguson, 'Industrial policy and organisation', *Public Administration in Ireland*, vol. 1, 48.
43. Kennedy, Kieran A., Thomas Giblin and Deirdre McHugh, *The Economic Development of Ireland in the Twentieth Century* (London, 1988), 202–4.

Chapter 12

1. John de Courcy Ireland, *Ireland's Sea Fisheries* (Dublin, 1981), 90–91.
2. DD 5, 938, 16 November 1923.
3. *Report of Committee on Allocation of Functions among Government Departments* (M & S Act), NAI, DOT, S1932a.
4. *Irish Times*, 16 September 1924.
5. John Molloy, *The Herring Fisheries of Ireland, 1900–2005* (Dublin, 2006), 26.
6. John Molloy, *The Irish Mackerel Fishery and the Making of an Industry* (Killybegs, 2004), 56–7.
7. DD 1, 2490, 30 November 1922.
8. *Irish Press*, 16 September 1931.
9. *Report of the Sea Fisheries Conference*, 1927, 5–26.
10. Donal Ó Drisceoil, *Peadar O'Donnell* (Cork, 2001), 58.
11. Mícheál Ó Fathartaigh, 'Cumann na nGaedheal, sea fishing and west Galway, 1923–32', *Irish Historical Studies*, vol. 36, May 2008, 96.
12. *Report of the Department of Agriculture on Sea and Inland Fisheries*, 1935, 4.
13. *Irish Independent*, 6 September 1928.
14. Fisheries Loans file, 1926 onwards, NAI, DLF, BV36.
15. Memorandum re Fisheries Bill, 1924, Kennedy Papers, P4/792.
16. *Report of the Sea Fisheries Conference*, 1927, 8.
17. Lough Swilly file, IMA, A9424.
18. Lough Foyle correspondence, 1929–32, Blythe Papers, P24/160.
19. Cabinet Minutes, 14 April, 1927, NAI; Michael Kennedy, *Division and Consensus: The Politics of Cross-Border Relations in Ireland* (Dublin, 2000), 26–35.
20. Memorandum on Gaeltacht Industries, McGilligan Papers, 35b/12.
21. *Irish Press*, 10 October 1931.

22. Letter explaining recommendations of Gaeltacht Commission, 14 January 1928, NAI, DF, FIN 2/2/28.

23. *Irish Times*, 13 January 1927.

24. *Irish Times*, 27 February 1929.

25. D.J. Maher, *The Tortuous Path: The Course of Ireland's Entry into the EEC, 1948–73* (Dublin, 1986), 270–346.

Chapter 13

1. E.J. Riordan, *Modern Irish Trade and Industry* (London, 1920), 265–86; L.M. Cullen, *An Economic History of Ireland since 1660* (London, 1987), 164.

2. Patrick Lynch, 'The economics of independence', *Administration*, vol. 7 (1959), 93.

3. Terence Brown, *Ireland: A Social and Cultural History, 1922–2002* (London, 2004), 10.

4. Kieran A. Kennedy, Thomas Giblin and Deirdre McHugh, *The Economic Development of Ireland in the Twentieth Century* (London, 1988), 13, 23–4.

5. Brian Girvin, *Between Two Worlds: Politics and Economy in Independent Ireland* (Dublin, 1989), 23–7.

6. Dennis Kennedy, *The Widening Gulf: Northern Attitudes to the Independent Irish State, 1919–49* (Belfast, 1988), 88.

7. Statement by Henry Ford & Son, Ltd, 9 March 1923, Mulcahy Papers, P7/C54.

8. Mary E. Daly, *Industrial Development and Irish National Identity* (Syracuse, 1992), 21.

9. *Ibid.*, 29–34.

10. Garret FitzGerald, *Reflections on the Irish State* (Dublin, 2003), 18.

11. *Irish Times*, 20 October 1929.

12. Girvin, *Between Two Worlds*, 58–9.

13. *Irish Independent*, 5, 12, 15 September 1925.

14. *Irish Times*, 16 April 1928.

15. Memorandum on food price control, 6 February 1924, Blythe Papers, P24/100.

16. Hugh D. Butler, *The Irish Free State: An Economic Survey* (Washington, 1928), 73.

17. DD 17, 274–80, 18 November 1926; Kennedy *et al.*, *The Economic Development of Ireland*, 37.

18. Kennedy *et al.*, *The Economic Development of Ireland*, 38.
19. Gordon Campbell: memoranda seeking foreign investment, April 1925, and minute, 18 January 1927, McGilligan Papers, P35b/5.
20. Proposals for the establishment of an oil refinery, Blythe Papers, P24/116.
21. Daly, *Industrial Development*, 57.
22. *Irish Trade Journal*, September 1926, 229; November 1928, 32.
23. T.K. Whitaker, *Protection or Free Trade: The Final Battle* (Dublin, 2006), 3.
24. Unsigned memorandum dated winter 1923, McGilligan Papers, P35b/2.
25. *Irish Trade Journal*, November 1925, 29.
26. Correspondence re industrial development and army ordnance, A2942, Irish Military Archives; Liam de Róiste Diaries, 47, 50, CAI.
27. Brendan Delany, 'McLaughlin, the genesis of the Shannon scheme and the ESB', 16; Lothar Schoen, 'The Irish Free State and the electricity industry', 34, Andy Bielenberg (ed.), *The Shannon Scheme and the Electrification of the Irish Free State* (Dublin, 2002), 16; file on anti-Shannon meeting held by Jim Larkin, NAI, AG, AGO/218/25.
28. Gerald O'Beirne and Michael O'Connor, 'Siemens-Schuckert and the electrification of the Irish Free State', *Shannon Scheme*, 73–5, 90–99.
29. Michael J. Sheil, *The Quiet Revolution: The Electrification of Rural Ireland, 1946–76* (Dublin, 1984), 16–18; Butler, *The Irish Free State*, 44.
30. DIC *Special Report*, 1930–31, NAI, DT, S2225.
31. T.A. McLaughlin, 'The first five years of the ESB', *Engineers' Journal*, vol. 21, no. 16 (1968).
32. *Irish Independent*, 9 November 1928.
33. *Irish Trade Journal*, November 1927, 5.
34. Daly, *Industrial Development*, 48–9.
35. Banking Commission memorandum, McGilligan Papers, P35b/20.
36. J.J. Lee, *Ireland, 1912–85: Politics and Society* (Cambridge, 1989), 109.
37. DD 6, 3291, 11 April 1924.
38. Girvin, *Between Two Worlds*, 27.
39. Ruth Dudley Edwards with Bridget Hourican, *An Atlas of Irish History* (London, 2005), 179.
40. Memorandum on air services, 25 April 1922, Blythe Papers, P24/240; *Irish Independent*, 29 October 1926, 22 April 1930.

41. DIC *Special Report*, 1930–31, NAI, DT, S2225.
42. *Irish Trade Journal*, May 1926, 152; Emmet O'Connor, *A Labour History of Ireland* (Dublin, 1992), 99.
43. Daly, *Industrial Development*, 18.
44. DIC *Special Report*, 1930–31, NAI, DT, S2225.
45. Daly, *Industrial Development*, 54.
46. Brian Girvin, 'Nationalism, Catholicism and democracy: Hogan's intellectual evolution', Donnchadh Ó Corráin (ed.), *James Hogan: Revolutionary, Historian and Political Scientist* (Dublin, 2001), 145.

Chapter 14
1. Mel Cousins, *The Birth of Social Welfare in Ireland, 1922–52* (Dublin, 2003), 75–80.
2. Ruth Barrington, *Health, Medicine and Politics in Ireland, 1900–1970* (Dublin, 1987), 80.
3. Lindsey Earner-Byrne, *Mother and Child: Maternity and Child Welfare in Dublin, 1922–60* (Manchester, 2007), 26.
4. Desmond Roche, *Local Government in Ireland* (Dublin, 1982), 52.
5. Cabinet Minutes, 17 May 1927, NAI.
6. *Saorstát Éireann Official Handbook* (Dublin, 1932), 173; DLGPH *Report*, 1930–32, 56.
7. Earner-Byrne, *Mother and Child*, 15, 40, 60–70, 177.
8. DD 2, 1989, 2015, 2 March 1923; *Irish Times*, 26 February 1923, 24 February 1930; *Irish Independent*, 2 May 1930.
9. Marie Coleman, 'The origins of the Irish Hospitals Sweepstakes', *Administration*, vol. 23 (1975), 42.
10. *Irish Independent*, 11 November 1930; *Irish Times*, 11 November 1930.
11. Barrington, *Health, Medicine and Politics*, 108–9.
12. *Report on Manchester Sweepstakes*, 1931, NAI, DT, S3237/9.
13. Commission of Inquiry into Health Insurance and Medical Services file, McGilligan Papers, P35b/13.
14. DD 8, 364–7, 3 July 1924.
15. DD 17, 327, 30 November 1926.
16. *Department of Local Government and Public Health Reports, 1922–25*, 76, 143; *Irish Times*, 2 July 1928, 17 September 1929.
17. J.J. Lee, *Ireland, 1912–85: Politics and Society* (Cambridge, 1989), 124–5.

18. Michelle Norris, 'Housing', Mark Callanan and Justin F. Keoghan (eds), *Local Government in Ireland Inside Out* (Dublin, 2003), 169–72.

Chapter 15
1. Sean Farren, *The Politics of Irish Education, 1920–65* (Belfast, 1995), 111.
2. *Irish Times*, 14, 22 August 1930.
3. *Irish Times*, 23 August, 1928.
4. DD 1, 2549–83, 1 December 1922.
5. *Department of Education Report*, 1924–5, 31.
6. Donald H. Akenson, *A Mirror to Kathleen's Face: Education in Independent Ireland, 1922–60* (Montreal, 1975), 8.
7. John Coolahan, *Irish Education: Its History and Structure* (Dublin, 1981), 45–6; *Department of Education Report, 1930–31*, 8.
8. *Report of the Council of Education*, 1960, 76–100.
9. *Ibid.*, 226.
10. John Logan, 'All the children: the vocational school and educational reform, 1930–1990', John Logan (ed.), *Teachers' Union: The TUI and Its Forerunners in Irish Education, 1899–1994* (Dublin, 1999), 277.
11. *Department of Education Report*, 1930–31, 38.
12. DD 1, 2569, 1 December 1922.
13. DD 14, 691, 11 February 1926.
14. *Reports of the Council of Education*, 1954, 254.
15. Mary Raftery and Eoin O'Sullivan, *Suffer the Little Children: The Inside Story of Ireland's Industrial Schools* (Dublin, 1999), 69.
16. *Irish Independent*, 23 September 1925.
17. Evidence of F. O'Duffy to the Public Accounts Committee, 13 May 1931.
18. Raftery and O'Sullivan, *Suffer the Little Children*, 11–19, 21–7, 55, 60–75, 79–96, 124, 160–63, 204, 227, 236, 252, 331–9.
19. Diarmaid Ferriter, *What If?: Alternative Views of Twentieth-Century Ireland* (Dublin, 2006), 174–9.
20. ASTI memorandum to TDs, Mulcahy Papers, P7/C70.
21. Coolahan, *Irish Education*, 96–101.
22. *Department of Education Report*, 1930–31, 47–9.
23. DD 4, 1425–7, 25 July 1923.
24. Archbishop Byrne to Kennedy, 14 May 1928, Kennedy Papers, P4/1236.
25. Adrian Kelly, *Compulsory Irish Language and Education in Ireland, 1870s–1970s* (Dublin, 2002), 65–76.

26. Coolahan, *Irish Education*, 109; Logan, 'All the children', 291–4.
27. Pádraic Ó Brolcháin to Public Accounts Committee, 26 June 1929.
28. *Department of Education Report*, 1924–25, 20.
29. Coolahan, *Irish Education*, 49–55.
30. DD, 1, 2578–87, 1 December 1922.
31. ASTI memorandum to TDs, Mulcahy Papers, P7/C70.
32. León Ó Broin, *Just Like Yesterday* (Dublin, 1985), 69.
33. J.H. Whyte, *Church and State in Modern Ireland, 1923–70* (Dublin, 1971), 24–33.
34. *Irish Independent*, 15 September 1925.
35. Kelly, *Compulsory Irish*, 49–50, 133.
36. Correspondence re Michael Corrigan's title, Kennedy Papers, P4/1001; *Irish Independent*, 31 January 1931.
37. Terence Brown, *Ireland: A Social and Cultural History, 1922–2002* (London, 2004), 40.
38. Personnel files, NAI, DE, 19863, 20052.
39. O'Duffy to Public Accounts Committee, 13 May 1931.
40. *Report of the Council of Education*, 1960, 132–62.
41. DOE Special Report, 1931, NAI, DT, S2223.
42. Kelly, *Compulsory Irish*, 18–39.
43. Farren, *The Politics of Irish Education*, 111.

Chapter 16

1.   Richard Pine, *2RN and the Origins of Irish Radio* (Dublin, 2002), 56.
2.   DD 23, 1226, 10 May 1928.
3.   León Ó Broin, 'The organisation of the Post Office', Frederick C. King (ed.), *Public Administration in Ireland*, vol. 2 (Dublin, undated), 128.
4.   Hugh D. Butler, *The Irish Free State: An Economic Survey* (Washington, 1928), 77.
5.   Note on meeting, 10 February 1922, NAI, DT, S1908.
6.   *Freeman's Journal* (May–September 1922); *Irish Times* (May–August 1922); *Irish Independent* (May–August 1922).
7.   DD 1, 257, 14 September 1922.
8.   *Freeman's Journal*, 26 July 1922, 11 August 1922.
9.   Correspondence with Secretary's office re rule books, NAI, DPT, 13717/23, Douglas Commission file, 2246/23.
10. *An Díon*, August 1928 and January 1930.

11. Review of work of Department of Posts and Telegraphs during the lifetime of the fourth Dáil, NAI, DT, S5360/4; DPT Special Report 1931, NAI, DT, S2221.

12. Brief for Desmond FitzGerald re visit to US, 1929, NAI, DPT, H10269/53.

13. *Irish Postal and Telegraph Guardian*, March 1922.

14. DD 1, 113, 11 September 1922; *Evening Telegraph*, 11 September 1922.

15. *Irish Postal and Telegraph Guardian*, August 1922.

16. DD 1, 116–18, 11 September 1922.

17. J.J. Walsh, *Recollections of a Rebel* (Tralee, 1944), 61–3; *Irish Postal and Telegraph Guardian*, October 1922.

18. Memorandum from Walsh dated 30 January 1923, NAI, DT, RA3021, S1932a.

19. Postal inquiry commission file, NAI, DT, S890a; *An Díon*, September 1923.

20. DD 3, 164–6, 17 April 1923.

21. DD 23, 1201–4, 10 May 1928.

22. DD 23, 1230, 1257, 10 May 1928.

23. DPT Special Report 1931, NAI, DT, S2221.

24. Brief for Desmond FitzGerald re visit to US, 1929, NAI, DPT, H10269/53.

25. *An Díon*, October 1925.

26. DD, 7, 395, 7 May 1924.

27. *Irish Independent*, 5 May 1927; *An Díon*, June 1927; Dublin Postal District Report, NAI, DPT, H14500/26.

28. DD 19, 2141–6, 4 May 1927; *Irish Times*, 5 and 19 May 1927.

29. *An Díon*, June 1927; DPD Annual Report, 1925, NAI, DPT, 14500/26.

30. *An Díon*, November 1927.

31. DD, 27, 969, 29 November 1928.

32. DD, 23, 1366–7, 16 May 1928.

33. Evidence of P.S. O'Hegarty to the Public Accounts Committee, 3 May 1928.

34. DD 3, 2264, 2250, 21 June 1923.

35. Eamonn G. Hall, *The Electronic Age: Telecommunications in Ireland* (Dublin, 1993), 385.

36. *Report of the Posts and Telegraphs Review Group*, 1978–9, 17.

37. DD, 23, 1185–93, 10 May 1928.

38. Hall, *The Electronic Age*, 59.

39. DD, 11, 2073–5, 21 May 1925.

40. *Irish Times*, 29 April 1927.

41. DD, 7, 397, 7 May 1924.

42. Memoranda, 13 March 1922, 9 November 1923, Kennedy Papers, P4/271, 803.

43. *Irish Times*, 21 January, 13 February 1924; John Horgan, *The Irish Media: A Critical History since 1922* (London, 2001), 15. The BBC was later taken into public ownership and renamed the British Broadcasting Corporation.

44. Pine, *2RN*, 56–8, 89–92.

45. *Irish Independent*, 5 May 1927; *An Díon*, June 1927; DPD report, NAI, DPT, H14500/26; Pine, *2RN*, 189.

46. Maurice Gorham, *Forty Years of Irish Broadcasting* (Dublin, 1967), 10–12.

47. Pine, *2RN*, 133; *Irish Times*, 3 February 1927.

48. Donal Ó Drisceoil, *Censorship in Ireland, 1939–45: Neutrality, Politics and Society* (Cork, 1996), 10.

49. Pine, *2RN*, 23.

50. Gorham, *Forty Years of Irish Broadcasting*, 221.

51. Iarfhlaith Watson, *Broadcasting in Irish* (Dublin, 2003), 19.

52. Desmond Fisher, *Broadcasting in Ireland* (London, 1978), 20–21.

53. Gorham, *Forty Years of Irish Broadcasting*, 63.

54. Susan O'Shea, 'Cultural Politics and the Building of the Irish State, 1923–39' (MPhil, UCC, 1996), 45–53.

55. Watson, *Broadcasting in Irish*, 2–4, 19.

56. Pine, *2RN*, 161–8.

57. Peter Martin, *Censorship in the Two Irelands, 1922–1939* (Dublin, 2006), 105.

58. Asa Briggs, *The Birth of British Broadcasting, vol. 1* (London, 1961), 305–6.

59. *Irish Times*, 22 March 1927.

60. *Irish Independent*, 1 January 1926.

61. *Irish Independent*, 16 January 1928; Gorham, *Forty Years of Irish Broadcasting*, 36.

62. Mike Cronin, 'Projecting the nation through sport and culture: Ireland, Aonach Tailteann and the Irish Free State, 1924–32', *Journal of Contemporary History*, vol. 38 (3), 2003, 397–402.

63. *Evening Telegraph*, 2 August 1924; *Sunday Independent*, 3 August 1924; *Freeman's Journal*, 5 and 7 August 1924.

Chapter 17

1. Nicholas Mansergh, *The Irish Free State: Its Government and Politics* (London, 1934), 261.

SELECT BIBLIOGRAPHY

ARCHIVES
Cork City and County Archives Institute (CAI)
Irish Labour History Museum and Archives (ILHMA)
Irish Military Archives (IMA)
National Archives of Ireland (NAI)
University College Cork Special Collections
University College Dublin Archives (UCDA)
United Kingdom National Archives (UKNA)

THESES
Coleman, Kieran, 'The 1925 Cork Campaign to Abolish Income Tax', MA, UCC, 2004.
Larmour, Sandra, 'Aspects of the State and Female Sexuality in the Irish Free State, 1922–1949', PhD, UCC, 1998.
McCarthy, Andrew, 'Financial Thought and Policy in Ireland, 1918–45', PhD, UCC, 1996.
Maguire, Martin, 'The Civil Service, the State and the Irish Revolution, 1886–1938', PhD, TCD, 2005 (see also *The Civil Service and the Revolution in Ireland, 1918–1938: Shaking the Bloodstained Hand of Mr Collins*, Manchester University Press, Manchester, 2008).
O'Shea, Susan, 'Cultural Politics and the Building of the Irish State, 1923–39', MPhil, UCC, 1996.
Ryan, Raymond, 'Farmers, Agriculture and Politics in the Free State Area, 1919–1936', PhD, UCC, 2005.
Torsney, Gerard Francis, 'The Monarchy in the Irish Free State, 1922–32', MA, UCD, 1980.

BOOKS
Adams, Michael, *Censorship: The Irish Experience*, University of Alabama Press, Tuscaloosa, 1968.
Akenson, Donald H., *A Mirror to Kathleen's Face: Education in Independent Ireland, 1922–60*, McGill-Queens University Press, Montreal, 1975.
Allen, Gregory, *The Garda Síochána*, Gill & Macmillan, Dublin, 1999.
Augusteijn, Joost (ed.), *The Irish Revolution*, Palgrave, Basingstoke, 2002.

Barrington, Ruth, *Health, Medicine and Politics in Ireland, 1900–1970*, Institute of Public Administration, Dublin, 1987.

Barrington, T.J., *From Big Government to Local Government,* Institute of Public Administration, Dublin, 1975.

—— *The Irish Administrative System*, Institute of Public Administration, Dublin, 1980.

Béaslaí, Piaras, *Michael Collins and the Making of Modern Ireland,* vol. 2, Harper, New York, 1926.

Bielenberg, Andy (ed.), *The Shannon Scheme and the Electrification of the Irish Free State*, Lilliput Press, Dublin, 2002.

Bolger, Patrick, *The Irish Co-operative Movement: Its History and Development,* Institute of Public Administration, Dublin, 1977.

Boyce, D. George, *Nationalism in Ireland*, Croom Helm, London, 1982.

—— *The Irish Question and British Politics, 1868–1996,* Macmillan, London, 1996.

Boyle, Richard, Joanna O'Riordan and Orla O'Donnell, *Promoting Longer Term Policy Thinking*, Institute of Public Administration, Dublin, 2002.

Boyle, Richard and Tony McNamara (eds), *Governance and Accountability, Power and Responsibility in the Public Service*, Institute of Public Administration, Dublin, 1998.

Brady, Conor, *Guardians of the Peace: Policing Independent Ireland,* Gill & Macmillan, Dublin, 1974.

Brown, Terence, *Ireland: A Social and Cultural History, 1922–2002,* Harper Perennial, London, 2004.

Butler, Hugh D., *The Irish Free State: An Economic Survey*, Government Printing Office, Washington, 1928.

Cadogan, Tim and Jeremiah Falvey, *A Biographical Dictionary of Cork*, Four Courts Press, Dublin, 2006.

Callanan, Frank, *T.M. Healy*, Cork University Press, Cork, 1996.

Callanan, Mark, and Justin F. Keoghan (eds), *Local Government in Ireland Inside Out*, Institute of Public Administration, Dublin, 2003.

Canning, Paul, *British Policy Towards Ireland, 1921–41*, Clarendon Press, Oxford, 1985.

Casey, James, *Constitutional Law in Ireland*, Sweet & Maxwell, London, 1992.

Chubb, Basil, *Cabinet Government in Ireland*, Institute of Public Administration, Dublin, 1974.

—— *The Government and Politics of Ireland*, Longman, London, 1982.

Collins, Neil, *Local Government Managers at Work*, Institute of Public Administration, Dublin, 1987.

Consitution Committee, *Select Constitutions of the World*, Stationery Office, Dublin, 1922.

Coogan, Tim Pat, *A Memoir*, Weidenfeld & Nicholson, London, 2008.

Coolahan, John, *Irish Education: Its History and Structure*, Institute of Public Administration, Dublin, 1981.

Costello, Francis, *The Irish Revolution and its Aftermath, 1916–23*, Irish Academic Press, Dublin, 2003.

Cousins, Mel, *The Birth of Social Welfare in Ireland, 1922–52*, Four Courts Press, Dublin, 2003.

Crotty, Raymond, *Irish Agricultural Production: Its Volume and Structure*, Cork University Press, Cork, 1966.

Cruise O'Brien, Conor (ed.), *The Shaping of Modern Ireland*, Routledge & Kegan Paul, London, 1970.

Cullen, L.M., *An Economic History of Ireland since 1660*, B.T. Batsford, London, 1987.

Cullen, L.M. (ed.), *The Formation of the Irish Economy*, Mercier Press, Cork, 1979.

Daly, Mary E., *Industrial Development and Irish National Identity*, Syracuse University Press, Syracuse, 1992.

———— *The Buffer State: The Historical Roots of the Department of Local Government*, Institute of Public Administration, Dublin, 1997.

———— *The First Department: A History of the Department of Agriculture*, Institute of Public Administration, Dublin, 2002.

Davis, Richard P., *Arthur Griffith and Non-Violent Sinn Féin*, Anvil, Dublin, 1974.

De Blácam, Aodh, *Towards the Republic*, Thomas Kiersey, Dublin, 1919.

———— *What Sinn Féin Stands For*, Mellifont Press, Dublin, 1921.

De Courcy Ireland, John, *Ireland's Sea Fisheries: A History*, Glendale Press, Dublin, 1981.

Delany, V.T.H., *The Administration of Justice in Ireland*, 4th edition, Charles Lysaght (ed.), Institute of Public Administration, Dublin, 1975.

Dooley, Terence, *"The Land for the People": The Land Question in Independent Ireland*, UCD Press, Dublin, 2004.

Dowling, P.J., *A History of Irish Education*, Mercier Press, Cork, 1971.

Drudy, P.J. (ed.), *Ireland: Land, Politics and People*, Cambridge University Press, Cambridge, 1982.

Dudley Edwards, Ruth, with Bridget Hourican, *An Atlas of Irish History*, Routledge, London, 2005.

Duggan, John P., *A History of the Irish Army*, Gill & Macmillan, Dublin, 1991.

Dungan, Myles (ed.), *Speaking Ill of the Dead*, New Island, Dublin, 2007.

Dunphy, Richard, *The Making of Fianna Fáil Power in Ireland, 1923–1948*, Clarendon Press, Oxford, 1995.

Earner-Byrne, Lindsey, *Mother and Child: Maternity and Child Welfare in Dublin, 1922–60*, Manchester University Press, Manchester, 2007.

Fanning, Ronan, *The Irish Department of Finance, 1922–58*, Institute of Public Administration, Dublin, 1978.

———— *Independent Ireland*, Helicon, Dublin, 1983.

Fanning, Ronan, Michael Kennedy, Dermot Keogh and Eunan O'Halpin (eds), *Documents on Irish Foreign Policy, Volumes I, 1919–1922* (1998), *II, 1923–1926* (2000) and *III, 1927–1932* (2002), Royal Irish Academy, Dublin.

Farrell, Brian, *The Founding of Dáil Éireann: Parliament and Nation Building*, Gill & Macmillan, Dublin, 1971.

———— *Chairman or Chief*, Gill & Macmillan, Dublin, 1971.

Farrell, Brian (ed.), *The Creation of the Dáil*, Blackwater Press, Dublin, 1994.

Farren, Sean, *The Politics of Irish Education, 1920–65*, The Queen's University of Belfast Institute of Irish Studies, Belfast, 1995.

Ferriter, Diarmaid, *The Transformation of Ireland, 1900–2000*, Overlook Press, Woodstock, 2004.

———— *What If?: Alternative Views of Twentieth-Century Ireland*, Gill & Macmillan, Dublin, 2006.

———— *Occasions of Sin: Sex and Society in Modern Ireland*, Profile Books, London, 2009.

Fisher, Desmond, *Broadcasting in Ireland*, Routledge & Kegan Paul, London, 1978.

FitzGerald, Garret, *Reflections on the Irish State*, Irish Academic Press, Dublin, 2003.

———— *Ireland in the World, Further Reflections*, Liberties Press, Dublin, 2005.

Fitzpatrick, David, *The Two Irelands*, Oxford University Press, Oxford, 1998.

Flynn, William J., *The Oireachtas Companion and Saorstát Guide for 1929*, Hely, Dublin, undated.

Garvin, Tom, *1922: The Birth of Irish Democracy*, Gill & Macmillan, Dublin, 1996.

———— *Preventing the Future: Why Was Ireland So Poor for So Long?* Gill & Macmillan, Dublin, 2004.

Girvin, Brian, *Between Two Worlds: Politics and Economy in Independent Ireland*, Gill & Macmillan, Dublin, 1989.

Gorham, Maurice, *Forty Years of Irish Broadcasting*, Talbot Press, Dublin, 1967.

Gormley, Michael, *Ireland's Community Health Services*, Tower Books, Trim, 1988.

Hall, Eamonn G., *The Electronic Age: Telecommunications in Ireland*, Oak Tree Press, Dublin, 1993.

Hancock, W.K., *Survey of British Commonwealth Affairs: Problems of Nationality*, Oxford University Press, Oxford, 1937.

Hart, Peter, *Mick: The Real Michael Collins*, Pan Macmillan, London, 2005.

Henry, Maurice (ed.), *Fruits of a Century*, IAOS, Dublin, 1994.

Hensey, Brendan, *The Health Services in Ireland*, Institute of Public Administration, Dublin, 1979.

Herlihy, Jim, *The Royal Irish Constabulary*, Four Courts Press, Dublin, 1997.

Hoctor, D., *The Department's Story: A History of the Department of Agriculture*, Institute of Public Administration, Dublin 1971.

Hopkinson, Michael, *Green Against Green*, Gill & Macmillan, Dublin, 1988.

Jordan, Anthony J., *William Thomas Cosgrave, 1880–1965, Founder of Modern Ireland*, Westport Books, Dublin, 2006.

Keatinge, Patrick, *The Formulation of Irish Foreign Policy*, Institute of Public Administration, Dublin, 1973.

Keith, Arthur Berridale, *The Sovereignty of the British Dominions*, Macmillan, London, 1929.

Kelly, Adrian, *Compulsory Irish Language and Education in Ireland, 1870s–1970s*, Irish Academic Press, Dublin, 2002.

Kennedy, Dennis, *The Widening Gulf: Northern Attitudes to the Independent Irish State, 1919–49*, Blackstaff Press, Belfast, 1988.

Kennedy, Kieran A., Thomas Giblin and Deirdre McHugh, *The Economic Development of Ireland in the Twentieth Century*, Routledge, London, 1988.

Kennedy, Michael, *Ireland and the League of Nations, 1919–1946: International Relations, Diplomacy and Politics*, Irish Academic Press, Dublin 1996.

——— *Division and Consensus: The Politics of Cross-Border Relations in Ireland*, Institute of Public Administration, Dublin, 2000.

Keogh, Dermot, *The Vatican, the Bishops and Irish Politics, 1919–39*, Cambridge University Press, Cambridge, 1986.

——— *Ireland and Europe, 1919–1948*, Gill & Macmillan, Dublin, 1988.

——— *Twentieth-Century Ireland: Nation and State*, Gill & Macmillan, Dublin 1994.

King, Frederick C. (ed.), *Public Administration in Ireland*, vols. 1 & 2, Parkside Press, Dublin, undated.

Kissane, Bill, *The Politics of the Irish Civil War*, Oxford University Press, Oxford, 2005.

Kohn, Leo, *The Constitution of the Irish Free State*, George Allen & Unwin, London, 1932.

Kotsonouris, Mary, *Retreat from Revolution: The Dáil Courts, 1920–24*, Irish Academic Press, Dublin, 1994.

Laffan, Michael, *The Resurrection of Ireland: The Sinn Féin Party, 1916–1923*, Cambridge University Press, Cambridge, 2005.

Lee, J.J., *Ireland, 1912–85: Politics and Society*, Cambridge University Press, Cambridge, 1989.

Litton, Helen, *The Irish Civil War: An Illustrated History*, Wolfhound Press, Dublin, 2006.

Logan, John (ed.), *Teachers' Union: The TUI and Its Forerunners in Irish Education, 1899–1994*, A. & A. Farmar, Dublin, 1999.

Lyons, F.S.L., *Ireland since the Famine*, Collins Fontana, London, 1979.

MacCarthaigh, Muiris, *Accountability in Irish Parliamentary Politics*, Institute of Public Administration, Dublin, 2005.

McCarthy, John P., *Kevin O'Higgins: Builder of the Irish State*, Irish Academic Press, Dublin, 2006.

McGarry, Fearghal, *Eoin O'Duffy: A Self-Made Hero*, Oxford University Press, Oxford, 2005.

McGuire, James, and James Quinn (eds), *Dictionary of Irish Biography*, Royal Irish Academy, Dublin, 2009.

McMahon, Deirdre, *Republicans and Imperialists: Anglo-Irish Relations in the 1930s*, Yale University Press, New Haven, 1984.

McManus, Francis (ed.), *The Years of the Great Test*, Mercier Press, Cork, 1967.

McMillan, Gretchen, *State, Society and Authority in Ireland: The Foundations of the Modern State*, Gill & Macmillan, Dublin, 1993.

McNiffe, Liam, *A History of the Garda Síochána*, Wolfhound Press, Dublin, 1997.

Maguire, Martin, *Servants to the Public: A History of the Local Government and Public Services Union, 1901–1990*, Institute of Public Administration, Dublin, 1998.

Maher, D.J., *The Tortuous Path: The Course of Ireland's Entry into the EEC, 1948–73*, Institute of Public Administration, Dublin, 1986.

Mansergh, Nicholas, *The Irish Free State: Its Government and Politics*, George Allen & Unwin, London, 1934.

——— *Britain and Ireland*, Longman Green, London, 1942.

Martin, F.X. (ed.), *Leaders and Men of the Easter Rising: Dublin 1916*, Methuen, London, 1967.

Martin, Peter, *Censorship in the Two Irelands, 1922–1939*, Irish Academic Press, Dublin, 2006.

Matthews, Kevin, *Fatal Influence: The Impact of Ireland on British Politics, 1920–1925*, UCD Press, Dublin, 2004.

Maume, Patrick, *The Long Gestation: Irish Nationalist Life, 1891–1918*, Gill & Macmillan, Dublin, 1999.

Meenan, James, *The Irish Economy since 1922*, Liverpool University Press, Liverpool, 1971.

Mitchell, Arthur, *Revolutionary Government in Ireland: Dáil Éireann, 1919–22*, Gill & Macmillan, Dublin, 1995.

Molloy, John, *The Irish Mackerel Fishery and the Making of an Industry*, Killybegs Fishermen's Association and the Marine Institute, Killybegs, 2004.

——— *The Herring Fisheries of Ireland, 1900–2005*, Marine Institute, Dublin, 2006.

Moss, Warner, *Political Parties in the Irish Free State*, Columbia University Press, New York, 1933.

Moynihan, Maurice, *Currency and Central Banking in Ireland, 1922–1960*, Gill & Macmillan, Dublin, 1975.

Mulcahy, Risteard, *Richard Mulcahy (1886–1971): A Family Memoir*, Aurelian Press, Dublin, 1999.

Munck, Ronnie, *The Irish Economy*, Pluto Press, London, 1993.

Murphy, John A., *The College*, Cork University Press, Cork, 1995.

Nolan, Aengus, *Joseph Walshe: Irish Foreign Policy, 1922–1946*, Mercier Press, Cork, 2008.

Nowlan, Kevin B. (ed.), *Travel and Transport in Ireland*, Gill & Macmillan, Dublin, 1973.

Ó Briain, Barra, *The Irish Constitution*, Talbot Press, Dublin, 1929.

O'Brien, Mark, *De Valera, Fianna Fáil and the 'Irish Press'*, Irish Academic Press, Dublin, 2001.

Ó Broin, León, *No Man's Man*, Institute of Public Administration, Dublin, 1982.

———— *Just Like Yesterday*, Gill & Macmillan, Dublin, 1985.

O'Connell, J.B., *The Financial Administration of Ireland*, Mount Salus Press, Dublin, 1960.

O'Connor, Emmet, *A Labour History of Ireland*, Gill & Macmillan, Dublin, 1992.

Ó Corráin, Donnchadh (ed.), *James Hogan: Revolutionary, Historian and Political Scientist*, Four Courts Press, Dublin, 2001.

O'Donnell, Ian, Eoin O'Sullivan and Deirdre Healy (eds.), *Crime and Punishment in Ireland, 1922 to 2003*, Institute of Public Administration, Dublin, 2005.

O'Donnell, Peadar, *There Will Be Another Day*, Dolmen Press, Dublin, 1963.

Ó Drisceoil, Donal, *Censorship in Ireland, 1939–45: Neutrality, Politics and Society*, Cork University Press, Cork, 1996.

———— *Peadar O'Donnell*, Cork University Press, 2001.

Ó Gráda, Cormac, *Ireland: A New Economic History, 1780–1939*, Clarendon Press, Oxford, 1994.

O'Halloran, Clare, *Partition and the Limits of Irish Nationalism*, Gill & Macmillan, Dublin, 1987.

O'Halpin, Eunan, *Defending Ireland*, Oxford University Press, Oxford, 2000.

O'Hegarty, P.S., *Sinn Féin, An Illumination*, Maunsell, Dublin, 1919.

Ó Longaigh, Seosamh, *Emergency Law in Independent Ireland, 1922–1948*, Four Courts Press, Dublin, 2006.

O'Sullivan, Donal, *The Irish Free State and Its Senate*, Faber & Faber, London, 1940.

O'Sullivan, Harold, *A History of Local Government in the County of Louth*, Institute of Public Administration, Dublin, 2000.

Patterson, Henry, *Ireland since 1939: The Persistence of Conflict*, Penguin Ireland, Dublin, 2006.

Pender, Capt. Austin (ed.), *Irish Defence Forces Handbook*, An Cosantóir, Dublin, 1988.

Pine, Richard, *2RN and the Origins of Irish Radio*, Four Courts Press, Dublin, 2002.

Puirséil, Niamh, *The Irish Labour Party*, UCD Press, Dublin, 2007.

Pyne, Peter, *The Irish Bureaucracy*, The New University of Ulster Institute of Continuing Education, Londonderry, undated.

Quinlivan, Aodh, *Philip Monahan: A Man Apart*, Institute of Public Administration, Dublin, 2006.

Raftery, Mary, and Eoin O'Sullivan, *Suffer the Little Children: The Inside Story of Ireland's Industrial Schools*, New Island, Dublin, 1999.

Réamonn, Seán, *History of the Revenue Commissioners*, Institute of Public Administration, Dublin, 1981.

Regan, John M., *The Irish Counter-Revolution, 1921–36*, Gill & Macmillan, Dublin, 1999.

Reynolds, Brian A., *William T. Cosgrave and the Foundation of the Irish Free State, 1922–25*, Kilkenny People, Kilkenny, 1998.

Riordan, E.J., *Modern Irish Trade and Industry*, Methuen, London, 1920.

Robins, Joseph, *The Lost Children*, Institute of Public Administration, Dublin, 1980.

Roche, Desmond, *Local Government in Ireland*, Institute of Public Administration, Dublin, 1982.

Sheehan, William, *British Voices from the War of Independence, 1918–21*, Collins Press, Cork, 2005.

Sheil, Michael J., *The Quiet Revolution: The Electrification of Rural Ireland, 1946–76*, O'Brien Press, Dublin, 1984.

Smith, James M., *Ireland's Magdalen Laundries and the Nation's Architecture of Containment*, University of Notre Dame Press, Notre Dame (Ind.), 2007.

Steiner, Zara, *The Lights That Failed: European International History, 1919–1933*, Oxford University Press, Oxford, 2005.

Tierney, Michael, *Education in a Free Ireland*, Martin Lester, Dublin, undated.

Townshend, Charles, *Ireland: The 20th Century*, Ranold, London, 1999.

Valiulis, Maryann Gianella, *Portrait of a Revolutionary: General Richard Mulcahy and the Founding of the Irish Free State*, Irish Academic Press, Dublin, 1992.

Walsh, J.J., *Recollections of a Rebel*, Kerryman, Tralee, 1944.

Walsh, Pat, *The Curious Case of the Mayo Librarian*, Mercier Press, Cork, 2009.

Watson, Iarfhlaith, *Broadcasting in Irish*, Four Courts Press, Dublin, 2003.

Whitaker, T.K., *Protection or Free Trade: The Final Battle*, Institute of Public Administration, Dublin, 2006.

INDEX